C000265379

Melissa Hogenboom is an awar
filmmaker and editor at the BBC
films and writes articles, as wel
for television and radio on a ran
evolution, psychology and neuroscience. Her journalism
has been recognised by multiple awards, including the
Webbys, the Drum Awards, Kavli AAAS Science Awards,
the Telly Awards and the British Association of Science
Journalism Awards. She is also a New America Learning
Science Exchange (LSX) fellow. *The Motherhood Complex* is
her first book.

Praise for The Motherhood Complex

'*The Motherhood Complex* does for mothers in particular
what *Invisible Women* did for women as a whole: exposes
the myriad ways in which the system is stacked against us,
while celebrating the strengths and successes we achieve
in spite of it all. A meticulously researched investigation,
and a movingly intimate memoir' Leah Hazard, author of
Hard Pushed

'A wonderful, compassionate, honest and scientific book.
A must-read for mothers – and fathers too' Professor
Alice Roberts

'An upbeat, authoritative tirade on the contradiction between
what we think motherhood is supposed to be like and what
it is really like ... Hogenboom unfurls a proper anatomy
of motherhood, delving into the physical and emotional
changes ... This book is reassuring, warm and subtly
challenging' Viv Groskop, *Observer*

THE MOTHERHOOD COMPLEX

The Story of Our Changing Selves

Melissa Hogenboom

PIATKUS

PIATKUS

First published in Great Britain in 2021 by Piatkus
This paperback edition first published in 2022

1 3 5 7 9 10 8 6 4 2

A CIP catalogue record for this book
is available from the British Library.

ISBN: 978-0-34942-657-0

Typeset in Palatino by M Rules
Printed and bound in Great Britain by Clays Ltd, Elcograf S.p.A.

Papers used by Piatkus are from well-managed forests
and other responsible sources.

MIX
Paper from
responsible sources
FSC® C104740

Piatkus
An imprint of
Little, Brown Book Group
Carmelite House
50 Victoria Embankment
London EC4Y 0DZ

An Hachette UK Company
www.hachette.co.uk

www.littlebrown.co.uk

For Sanne & Arjen – I would go through an infinitude of identity changes for you – and for all mothers everywhere, especially my own.

CONTENTS

INTRODUCTION

My introduction to the anatomy of sex started earlier than it should have for the mid-1990s, when I was about ten. A boy in my class, in the centre of the drab and grey 'Granite City', Aberdeen, had found some pages from an old-fashioned porn magazine, which I can recall images from even now, over two decades later – they were pretty graphic. Of course, none of us had any real idea of what sex was then or what these images meant, we just knew they were naughty, alien-like and therefore a little confusing. I also don't recall knowing how babies were made, but I do remember that we all pretended to know far more than we did. 'So, does the guy just put his thing in and out really quickly?' I asked my childhood friend. 'No, he wiggles it about a bit as well,' she said convincingly. I remember wondering if he also peed inside, or how he would stop himself doing this. Unsurprisingly, our very naive lunchtime accidental porn exploration was leaked to one of the parents and I imagine an urgent memo was passed round to the rest. We were, after all, still children and sex education was not taught as early then as it is now.

A few days later, my mum beckoned my brother and me to the sofa and handed us a book called *Let's Talk About Sex*. It was full of annotations of our growing bodies and a detailed guide to what happens during puberty and beyond. That's the benefit of having a GP for a mum, I suppose.

I remember feeling empowered by this very adult knowledge and telling all my friends, secretly proud to be so in the know. Looking back, this went some way to marking the end of childhood and the start of adolescence, albeit earlier than my mother expected. It was also the most clearly defining moment when the differences between grown men and women were firmly cemented in my mind. An early insight into how much we change physically but also how socially acceptable, or not, these changes are deemed to be.

The book was welcomed at the time. However, a few years later, after I got my first period, it was not quite as welcomed when my mum explained the ins and outs of cervical mucus. My family are Dutch, and we are known for our Dutch directness for good reason. Nothing about the body is out of bounds, it's just biology.

'Have you noticed that your discharge "down there" changes throughout the month?' my mother asked me, probably over breakfast or on the way to school. I don't recall if I pretended not to know, or if I really had no idea, but, ever since, I have noticed that throughout the month, there's a small window of time when our cervical mucus does indeed become thicker, and is of clear egg white consistency. To the uninitiated, this is our fertile window and it occurs about 14 days after our period begins, or 14 days before the next one starts. This depends on the length of your cycle, of course, which is why the mucus itself can be a better indicator of our 'fertile window' than checking the calendar alone. This, I told my husband romantically when we tried for our first baby many years later, is when we would need to have sex.

I've been surprised by how few of my friends knew about this fertile window. I've since told many who are thinking of starting families – and most of them had no idea. Although this is an unscientific sample of just over a dozen, I now know there's another reason why so few are aware of this window: the prevalence of the pill, which has other, hidden effects on our physical bodies and our mental sense of self, not just preventing pregnancy alone.

The truth is that we are influenced by our monthly cycle as soon as we get our first periods. It is a stark reminder of our biological identity, one which we don't have to fulfil but society often expects us to (it's improving, but, for the most part, dolls are marketed to girls, not boys, almost from birth). Aside from these very real social pressures, this cycle manifests in physical symptoms, hormonal changes and even how attractive we appear to the opposite sex differs during our fertile versus non-fertile stages. Heterosexual women also feel most attracted to men around the time of ovulation.

In the chapters ahead I will reveal how, long before we even contemplate having children, biology and society are already pushing us to shape our identity as a prospective mother, whether we go through with it or not. And, secondly, I will explore the conflict between these two identities – as a mother and how we were before children – and the importance of understanding these changes for our physical and emotional health.

Along the way, I will share how my experience teams with the evidence and research on motherhood, to make the science more relatable as well as get to the heart of our new maternal identity and what it means for us all. Understanding the science certainly helped me see motherhood from new perspectives, which I hope will help other mothers too.

Ultimately, I will show how we need not have what I

call a 'motherhood complex', but in many ways our society has made it inevitable because of the culture we inhabit and the expected pressures we face during the change to motherhood.

This book will therefore address several questions, namely why motherhood brings with it such a dramatic identity shift that affects so many areas of our lives, from the misconceptions about our 'pregnancy brain' (Chapter 1) to how labour impacts our sense of self (Chapter 2) to how our body changes (Chapter 3), going on to consider how motherhood affects our relationships and careers (Chapters 4–6). For better or worse, humanity has always been tribal, we identify with many in-groups, from the teams we support, to our sex, race, culture and now, for me, as a mother. But I'm a journalist too, a psychology graduate, a runner, a karate black belt (a long time ago), a daughter, a friend. However, the reality is that motherhood can be all-consuming, there can be little time left for our previous passions. Even our careers can take a back seat when there is so much pressure on mothers to be perfect. There simply is not enough time, meaning we have little choice but to lose aspects of our previous lives. In some ways this is expected, but it doesn't make it easy. These are important topics to address precisely because they will allow us to better understand ourselves during a time when abrupt change becomes an everyday reality. I will also uncover why some of the changes we feel are a consequence of a world striving towards greater gender equality – and how we are defined by our gender even from birth (Chapter 7).

To appreciate why motherhood brings with it such an immediate identity change, it might help to explain the basics behind social identity theory. Our social identity is a powerful force that both defines how others see us and how we see ourselves. Our identities relate to what groups we belong to, including our individual attributes and our personal value judgements or beliefs. Some we are born with, such as our nationality and sex, and some we acquire, like our hobbies or our faith. These are extremely potent; many studies have shown that we will instinctively align with those from our own groups over others. It's why many large companies now ask their staff to take part in implicit bias training to avoid picking candidates who are most like them.

When we become mothers, most of us have already built up many identities to align with, and in some cases we freely 'choose' how we identify, such as our fashion choices or political beliefs (though even within these free choices, there are subtle forces at play moulding our preferences or decisions). Although we may choose motherhood, it is a sudden change and, as we will see, the reality can be quite far from the perception of it, which is one of the reasons why it can feel so challenging. Additionally, although motherhood could be categorised as a new personal identity, the fact that society has many expectations of what this means can make it quickly leak into a societal identity as well, which brings with it its own problems, namely a mismatch between how we are perceived as mothers and the reality of the day to day.

Many struggle with this change along the way. The writer Rachel Cusk poetically described this in her memoir *A Life's Work*:

> 'I appear to have soldered together my past and present, to be both myself and a mother.'

Shortly after, when her baby started to howl uncontrollably, she realised that this was only a momentary vision, and wrote:

> 'The fact is that I know neither what it is to be myself nor to be a mother ... I am surprised to discover how easily I have split in two. I worry; I console. Like a divided stream, the person and the mother pay each other no heed, although moments earlier they were indistinguishable ...'

Her prior perception of motherhood was a far cry from her own reality or how she was before, leaving her to question 'what a mother, in fact, is'. This same question has been at the forefront of my mind too. The facts of life, as we learn them when we are young, seem so simple: an egg, a sperm and, hey presto, a baby. The reality is not that straightforward; motherhood is messy, mutable and still so understudied precisely because our experiences are so dependent upon cultural pressures and expectations.

That there are many different ways to define motherhood shows how confusing our new identity can be. For instance, 'stay at home mothers' or 'working mothers', as if we must define the sort of mothers we plan to be from the outset, each with their own expectations and stereotypes. The assumption generally is that 'motherhood is intrinsic to adult female identity', as one psychoanalyst called Mardy Ireland wrote in 1993, with the idea that there is a glaring 'absence' even if a woman chooses not to become a mother. Childlessness, whether voluntary or involuntary, carries many subtle and overt stigmas. It is 'only when the assumption that all girls must become mothers to fulfil female adulthood is challenged will a woman's destiny truly be her own', writes Ireland.

In the chapters ahead I will argue that our society – and its gendered perceptions of mothers – is the major reason why the shift to motherhood so heavily impacts our sense of self. This comes during a time of significant biological and mental change and has the potential to make us 'fail' – both in the workplace and in the pursuit of perfect parenting (Chapter 8) and how guilty it makes us feel if we don't reach these unrealistic ideals (Chapter 9). In fact, understanding the science behind why and, in turn, embracing these changes, may even be key to our own happiness – which I will look at by identifying why some countries score so high on happiness indexes (Chapter 10). I will consider these cultural differences to happiness and self-identity through the lens of motherhood to explain why happier children could make for happier parents and vice versa and how technology could impede this (Chapter 11).

Finally, in the last chapter I will examine that the idea of a 'good mother' who does the majority of childcare without much outside help can be largely attributed as a societal, Western construct. Although this idea appears dated, its influence is still felt and the many ways we think about motherhood stem from our somewhat individualistic 'Weird' culture, that is, we are western, educated, industrialised, rich and democratic.

In fact, the pursuit of equality in many ways disguises the fact that gendered norms persist below the surface, even in households that aim for it. And if this is a challenge for middle-class mothers, remember that the most marginalised groups, especially those who face race and class biases, have even more challenges, making equality even harder to reach.

*

It's why at work we might talk about our children less, while fathers do so more with little consequence, or we purposely fail to mention that we are parents in job interviews – even being recently married is often viewed as a 'warning signal' of impending motherhood, with the documented discrimination that goes along with it. For similar reasons, the age women become mothers is shifting, we are delaying it – especially so among higher-educated women, while at the same time reproductive issues are on the rise. Why? Because women can feel they have no choice but to put their careers on hold, especially if they are to provide adequate resources, a stable home, or, worse, pursue the illusion of being 'a perfect mother'. We feel pressured to have it all when having it all is not within our control.

I felt conflicted at the very idea of becoming a mother because on some level I worried that I would be taken less seriously in my career. Though this hasn't unfolded (and I'm not just writing this because some colleagues may read this), in many workplaces this happens – numerous studies show there is pervasive, implicit and explicit discrimination against pregnant women and mothers.

The resulting discomfort goes so deep that, when I was first pregnant, I initially secretly hoped I would have a boy because I didn't want my daughter to have to deal with the long list of biases that women have to face. This was out of love. I wanted to protect her from the inevitable forms of the micro-sexism and biological hassle all women I know have experienced – the wolfwhistles, periods, childbirth. However, I'm now so thrilled to have brought a girl into a world where change is becoming possible and where we can continue to challenge the status quo, to help make vital change a reality.

First, these issues need to be brought into the open.

Society in general *is still* on the wrong side. This has created a paradox where general attitudes are shifting in the right direction, but gendered norms are still holding women back, as the prevailing gender pay gap exemplifies. I will argue that this both needs to *and* can change. We live in a world built by men yet most of these men have been mothered by women. As Jane Austen's character Anne Elliot famously put it: 'Men have had every advantage of us in telling their own story. Education has been theirs in so much higher a degree; the pen has been in their hands.'

To change one, we have to target both. This brings me to the main reasons I decided to write this book: the reality of our experience as parents is far from simple, weighs heaviest on mothers and, at the same time, the parenting and baby book market tends to focus predominantly on many of the day-to-day decisions we make for our babies, covering various methods from sleep tricks to colic to potty training. What I rarely see is how to consider the intense changes to all aspects of our emotional selves that come with motherhood. That's why in the rest of this book I will continue to share with you the science behind why our time as new mothers can feel like such a momentous, but also joyful, struggle.

This book is for mothers but about humanity, about how our species has divided our sex into a gendered and unequal lens. Our hunter–gatherer ancestors would perhaps be perplexed by the gendered divisions we have today. To discount women, albeit subtly, is to ignore or lose out on the talented, complex minds of half the world's population. This book will explain why, and how understanding this can empower us to move forward.

1

A MOTHER'S BRAIN

The subtle identity changes that pregnancy brings

My father was one of 11 children, which sounds unimaginably chaotic. This wasn't unusual where he grew up – he had a friend who was one of 15. The pressure to have large families was high in this small Catholic village and in many other parts of the Netherlands. If my grandmother wasn't visibly pregnant when the priest came knocking about once a year, he would ask her if her marriage was OK. This intense interest from the local priest sounds well meant, but that was not always the case.

In the early 1950s, in another small Dutch town in Reusel, near the Belgian border, a doctor called Bert Lemstra had an intimate knowledge of his patients, as doctors from small towns often did. One of his patients, Sandra, already had 11 children but had experienced difficulty with her last few births. It was touch and go with number 11, so Lemstra stipulated to her that she must not get pregnant again with a 12th, at risk of her own life. This was in the times before contraception was commonly used, or allowed by devout Catholic followers. After asking his patient detailed dates of her most recent menstruation patterns, Lemstra marked an X on the days on her calendar where she would most likely be fertile and should abstain from sex. If Sandra had followed his instructions closely, this should have dramatically reduced her chances of getting pregnant. Somehow the local priest got wind of the advice she had been given and, on his next visit to Sandra, told this hapless woman that the doctor was mistaken and it was actually the other way around – where the crosses were marked was actually a safe time for her and her husband's night-time frolics. This was a time when the local priest was more highly regarded than the doctor and, unfortunately, Sandra soon became pregnant again. Nine months later, her 12th child was born but, just as the doctor had predicted, she unfortunately did not survive childbirth. Her husband, a poor farmer, was widowed with 12 mouths to feed and the doctor and the priest never saw eye to eye again. Had Sandra known another way to avoid pregnancy, she may have lived longer.

Now, information about our monthly cycle is readily available, childbirth is far safer and fewer women in the West have so many children. This fertile window that Lemstra was already aware of so many years ago was precisely what helped me to make a relatively well-informed guess at when I would be most and least fertile. For my husband and me, this quest to embrace this window rather than avoid it started soon after we got married, in the middle of July 2016. We hadn't discussed it at length, but we both knew that shortly after our wedding, we would start trying for a baby. I knew this could negatively affect my career – it might mean fewer trips abroad for stories, no late nights to finish deadlines and half a year or more out of the office. It might even mean lower lifetime earnings. But the desire to have a baby wasn't a rational choice, it felt like a deeply ingrained biological need that started to feel ever more pressing as I entered my late 20s.

I didn't want our first baby's conception to be scientific, but as a science journalist and someone who has always been fully aware of the changes my body was going through month on month, I couldn't help myself tracking each and every fertile cycle gleefully and slightly jokingly telling my husband that if we tried now we could make a baby.

Two weeks after our wedding, I woke to the familiar feeling of egg white cervical mucus and knew this was the moment that an egg was ripe and ready. It perhaps wasn't the most romantic or spontaneous of beginnings, but I couldn't undo years of scientific awareness about the process my body was going through. After this came the infamous 'two-week wait' – an agonising stretch of time before a test will reveal whether you are pregnant or not, though some tests manage to detect pregnancy slightly earlier. These days were consumed with noticing every tiny biological change I felt, real or imagined. Were my breasts more tender? Did I feel slightly nauseous? (It was way too early for that . . .) I even took a test many days before I knew it would be able to give a positive result. I looked up each change that I felt, often ending up on terrible internet forums with misinformed advice. I craved facts before there were facts to be had, knowing that it could take several attempts to get pregnant.

A clinical knowledge of baby-making can leave little time for romance (sorry, husband) and so, fortunately for us, it was first-time lucky. When a pregnancy test showed the faintest positive purple line that my husband said he couldn't even see on 10 DPO – an abbreviation I learnt from afore-mentioned terrible internet forums that means 'days past ovulation' – I didn't quite believe it, even though I knew that false positives are extremely rare. I took a test each day for the following week or two and lined them up next to each other so that I could see the gradual darkening of that purple line as my pregnancy hormones got stronger and became easier to detect. Only then did I accept it. Despite considering myself a rational person, I wasn't behaving in an entirely rational manner. I couldn't help but wonder if this was the start of the so-called 'mum brain', where from here on my memory and decision-making would be slightly impaired.

You may have experienced it and, if not, you have no doubt heard of it. Mum brain, pregnancy brain, mummy brain – whatever way it is phrased, it refers to a reported cognitive deficit that starts during pregnancy and ends ... some years later, perhaps never? For ease I will refer to it as 'mum brain' and show you that it is not what it is often reported to be.

It turns out the 'mum brain' is real: our brains change during pregnancy, but not in the way you might expect. Being pregnant does not make us stupider. In fact, during pregnancy the brain is already optimising itself in a way that will have lasting beneficial consequences. With all that was running through my head during pregnancy, it's no surprise that all sorts of changes were taking place in my brain; irreversible tweaks that could benefit me for the rest of my life. A 2017 study found that the volume of grey matter in the brain declines among pregnant women in various regions. The team, led by Elseline Hoekzema of Leiden University, discovered this by performing and analysing brain scans of women before and after pregnancy as well as two years later.

At first glance, less grey matter in the brain doesn't exactly sound like a good thing. But when you look at the details it starts to make more sense. The grey matter is reduced in areas known to be active when we are involved in social interactions, including empathy. The researchers could even identify whether a woman had been pregnant or not from brain scans alone and found that the changes were still present two years later. The effects could last even longer, possibly an entire lifespan, but studies of that length are costly and time-consuming and have yet to be done. To check this was unique to pregnancy, the researchers also looked at the brains of men and non-pregnant women over a comparable time and did not find a reduction of grey matter. The results suggest that it could be due to the surge of the sex hormones progesterone and oestrogen that change the brain during pregnancy. It was the first time scientists showed that pregnancy resulted in long-lasting changes in the brain.

We see a similar surge in sex hormones during adolescence. And teenagers' brains also go through changes, including a reduction of grey matter. In both the pregnant and the teenage brain something referred to as synaptic pruning is thought to be taking place, which simply means that any useless synapses (brain connections) are eliminated so that only the most useful ones are reorganised and are made stronger.

This 2017 study shows just how much our brain changes during pregnancy, and that it may do so in ways that help a mother bond with her baby. These structural changes predicted how attached a mother felt to her child, and those with the greatest grey matter reduction scored highest on a scale used to determine mother–infant attachment. The areas of the brain with reduced grey matter were also the areas which showed a strong response when a mother sees her baby – that is, in the parts of the brain we know are important for bonding. This pruning could therefore be hugely beneficial because the grey matter is condensing in a way to make the brain more efficient, especially for theory-of-mind tasks, where we infer what others are thinking. It is therefore fitting that our brain adapts to facilitate this.

In 2020, the same lab found that an area of the brain known to be active when a mother responds to her baby's smiles – the nucleus accumbens – was reduced in both pregnant women and mothers. The bigger the reduction of this brain area, the more active it was. It was already known that this is part of a network of the brain that responds when a mother looks at or hears her infant. We feel pleasure when we look at our babies and it seems that the area of the brain involved has adapted to become even more efficient when we do so.

The structure of a mother's brain also changes after her baby is born. A 2010 study that looked at mothers' brains at one and then four months post-partum, found that grey matter increases in numerous areas. The most growth was found in places known to be important for social behaviours like empathy, emotional regulation and sensory information. This could be occurring because neurons increase in the very areas of the brain that are vital for mothering, once again showing just how plastic the brain not only is during pregnancy but also after birth.

Despite the emerging evidence revealing that changes in the brain during pregnancy are beneficial, a large body of studies report cognitive deficits during pregnancy, widely stated as confirming this idea of 'mum brain'. In light of the studies above, this sounds contradictory. In research published in 2018, for instance, a team looked at how women perform cognitive tasks during pregnancy and noted many shortfalls, especially prevalent in the third trimester. This was a meta-analysis, where researchers looked at the combined results from many papers studying the topic. It involved insights into over 700 pregnant women and 500 non-pregnant women. At first, the results appear to be backing up the forgetful pregnancy brain stereotype (and indeed it was reported this way in subsequent headlines), but the findings do not show that pregnancy is necessarily causing the cognitive decline, it could simply be the tiredness associated with many pregnancies. The pregnant women who experienced small cognitive impairments were still performing in what was considered a normal range, and the impairments were only slight memory lapses, not ones that would noticeably affect demanding tasks at work.

Studies in this area remain scarce and the differences the team found were small. In part this area is understudied because even the direction of research is influenced by our culture. If there is so little still known about how the brain changes during a defining moment for our species – one that is key for the next generation to be born – then what else are we still missing about the physiology of motherhood? Fortunately, the many neuroscientists I have spoken to for this book say it's now an area of active interest.

The way 'cognitive impairment' is measured has the potential to be misleading. That is, if the brain is becoming optimised in ways that are beneficial when caring for a baby, but cognitive functioning is measured by memorising words and numbers, then the tests may be asking the wrong questions. In studies of rats for instance, spatial memory increases during pregnancy. That ability is further enhanced when rat mothers have multiple pregnancies, perhaps reflecting the heightened survival need for a mother to remember where to find food when she has babies that depend on her.

This means that mum brain is not entirely a myth, but it is not quite the detrimental decline it is commonly painted to be. I suffered from insomnia during each of my pregnancies and would often lie awake for hours, only to fall back into a deep sleep right before it was time to get up. This sleep deprivation felt extremely cruel as pregnancy should be a last chance to rest before the chaos of a new baby. Given how badly my sleep was affected, it's no wonder that on some days my brain felt so foggy.

The fact that the myth persists could also be due to societal expectations and stereotypes. Research has shown that men and women rated pregnant women's abilities as inferior because of their expectations that they would perform worse, rather than actual cognitive decline. It is already well understood that expectations of our behaviour have a powerful impact on how we act or feel, even if that doesn't reflect reality. Along similar lines, another study found a self-reported cognitive decline among pregnant women in the last trimester, as well as three months postpartum. These differences didn't actually exist but were only in how competent these women *felt*. And despite some studies showing slight declines during pregnancy, the brain changes we now understand more about show that the mum brain could actually be an extremely useful adaptation that helps women prepare for motherhood.

Though we may lose some functioning in certain aspects of our cognition, like memory, we also seem to become superior in the areas important for attending and responding socially to our babies. This certainly makes sense as it helps babies to have mothers with a heightened ability to understand facial expressions and social information, even if it comes at a cost of some memory impairments.

Mothers' brains also look younger. In a 2019 analysis of over 12,000 mothers' brains, for instance, they showed reduced signs of ageing compared to non-mothers' brains and the differences are larger the more children a woman has. It is not yet clear why this occurs but we know from other research that when the brain is engaged in something new for many weeks, it ages less too.

In short, the grey-matter shrinkage finding explored earlier, coupled with the results of minor cognitive decline, may both be a consequence of beneficial structural changes that are taking place, optimising our superior mum brains. Pregnancy affects many of our major organs, so the brain changes that occur during pregnancy should be expected too. Perhaps the surprise lies in the fact that many of the changes are positive and long-lasting.

We've seen the powerful biological link between mother and child, how hormones can shape behaviour towards her baby and how the brain changes. It might therefore appear that women are hardwired to be carers, but this is not the case. Biologically speaking, we are the ones who grow and birth our babies but, intriguingly, pregnancy is not the only trigger for brain changes to occur for new parents, biological or otherwise.

A 2014 Israeli study on male same-sex couples who had parented their infants from birth showed that the male primary caregivers had similar levels of oxytocin in their brains as mothers have. Just as mothers do, these men also showed activation in an area of the brain called the amygdala, a pair of almond-shaped structures important for our emotions. This was not observed in fathers whose female partners were the primary caregivers. Pregnancy, and all the hormonal changes that go with it, definitely help prime the brain to be sensitive to a new baby, but this study revealed that postpartum brain changes also occur simply by being a present parent, regardless of our sex. This reveals that women are not biologically destined to be the primary parent. Men clearly can and should play an important role, but in many (though not all) societies, women still do the lion's share of caregiving in heterosexual couples. A stronger amygdala response would not be primed to occur in the brain of a less-present partner. Nor would they benefit from as big an oxytocin surge, which could affect how much they bond with their baby in the earliest days. The study supports the idea that it is time spent and the intensity of the emotional bonds that helps strengthen optimal brain responses to our babies.

Just as a mother's brain changes postpartum due to experience, so can a father's – but only if he is around more to do hands-on parenting. We therefore all have the necessary brain power to nurture a close attachment. If time spent and the subsequent bond is equally strong for both parents, not only will it literally make more love go around, with the beneficial hormones that go along with it, but it could provide a subtle biological incentive for the father to continue to be more hands-on. It would then take pressure off the mother and thereby potentially cause a less-dramatic motherhood complex for her – if the onus and expectation of parenting is not so heavily her domain.

It's not only during pregnancy that the brain is modified in ways we may not anticipate. Those preventing pregnancy are also undergoing unintended brain changes. I'm talking specifically about women on the pill. The contraceptive pill contains hormones, so perhaps this should be expected.

Let me preface this next section by saying that the benefits of the pill have been huge for women. They have freed us from the burden or risk of pregnancy, liberated women to control their fertility and helped countless others with debilitating monthly period pains. Given these benefits it seems unforgiving to now focus on side effects, but the long-term impacts of being on the pill are still not fully understood. Emerging insights of how the pill can change us warrant a closer look.

At the same time, trials testing the male pill have been withdrawn precisely because of the potential side effects, and while research into new types of male contraceptives is ongoing, progress is slow for the same reason. Women on the other hand have endured side effects since the pill was developed, including depression, skin disorders and mood swings. We can't fully pinpoint why the burden of hormonal contraception must fall largely on women, but we are already expected to bear the pain of childbirth, the biological stress of pregnancy and the hormonal changes that go with it, so hormonal contraception being in our domain feels unfortunately fitting.

Side effects are so common that several types of the pill can be offered until one is a right fit. Many are expected, but lesser known is the emerging evidence that the pill can change both the structure and function of the brain. This leaves us with a bit of a conundrum. Teenagers, whose brains are not yet fully developed, can be on the pill for many years and yet while the physiological effects are understood, less is known about the neurological ones.

Science is slowly catching up on these biological effects. In 2015 one team found that two parts of the brain were thinner among pill users in areas involved with decision-making and emotional regulation. Many pill users also report emotional changes such as mood swings.

Other research has found strong links between the pill and depression, looking at over one million women in Denmark. One study looking at over 1,200 women showed that pill use in the teenage years could even impact mental health years later. Those who had indicated they were on the pill as teenagers were more prone to be clinically depressed as adults. Women who started using the pill as adults did not have this link. Though the science can't yet tell us for sure, the fact that the brain changes on the pill could go some way into explaining some of the effects found so far.

For instance, emotional memory has been found to be influenced by sex hormones. A study showed that during the second half of their cycle, when progesterone is at its highest, women were better able to recall the details of an emotional story rather than the overall gist. As the pill alters a woman's sex hormones, researchers questioned whether the pill might change this. It did; the team found that on the pill, the pattern reversed. On the pill, women were better at recalling the gist of an emotional story, rather than specific details. Both groups performed similarly for a non-emotional 'neutral' story. In a follow-up study, brain scans revealed that the amygdala was less active for women on the pill when they were presented with unpleasant pictures. In short, the pill caused the amygdala to be somewhat blunted to emotional stimuli. We now know that the pill changes several aspects of brain function and memory, but there isn't yet enough evidence to tell us exactly what this means for our overall health.

Aside from brain changes, there could be other subtle effects too. One 2016 study showed that children had different health outcomes if their parents met while their mothers were on the pill, compared to those who met off pill. In line with their prediction, the study found that children born in the first scenario were more prone to allergies, needed more medical care and were ill more often compared with children of parents who met when the mothers were not on the pill, implying that 'mate choice' is altered while on the pill. This study was correlational, so the authors cannot say that choosing a partner while on the pill played a role. Despite these uncertainties, as pill use is so widespread, it would be worth investigating this further, to see if partner choice while on the pill has lasting consequences. Other research points to the idea that it does. A 2019 study by the same team found that when women stopped using the pill, it changed who they were attracted to. When I discovered some of the early findings in this area in my psychology undergraduate degree at the University of Edinburgh, it left such an impression on me that I stayed off the pill during my entire relationship with my now-husband. Had I been on the pill it may have changed who I ended up with in the first place.

We've looked at the brain during pregnancy and the brain on the pill, but what about the other changes that we feel in the first few weeks of pregnancy? Those of us who plan it will find out roughly two weeks after conceiving – that's when a test can give a reliable result.*

If positive, by this point you would be four weeks pregnant. This seems confusing. Why two bonus weeks? It's because doctors calculate the number of weeks of pregnancy from the first day of your last period, meaning that for two

---

* This is assuming a 28-day cycle, but the length of a woman's cycle differs significantly – mine is usually about 33 days.

of these four weeks you are not actually physically pregnant, but the body is already preparing to release the egg (or eggs) that will eventually get fertilised. For the next eight weeks many women don't widely share the news. This is for a number of reasons: first and foremost, the risk of miscarriage is highest in the first trimester.

The first 12 weeks can be very daunting. Until I saw blurry outlines of my babies on a screen, it was hard not to let my mind question whether there really was a living human inside me. These weeks are also when the physical side effects, including nausea, can be worst. This invariably means that there is an incredible life-changing secret growing inside of us, which can make us fatigued, nauseous, sick and go off our food. Yet we have to appear as if everything is OK, and that we are the same versions of ourselves we were before we were pregnant.

Keeping a secret like this has several potentially devastating effects: as many as 25 per cent of pregnancies end in miscarriage, though the longer the pregnancy continues the risk drops. Emerging evidence points to rates as high as 50 per cent in some age groups. It is precisely because a miscarriage most often occurs before anyone knows about the pregnancy that many people do not realise how common they are. The difficult thing is, if pregnancy was announced earlier, those who miscarry would then have to share this painful event with anyone who knew about the pregnancy. This means suffering in secret or sharing the news retrospectively.

All these options are challenging, but more emotional support could be available if awareness of the prevalence of a miscarriage was higher. Out of dozens of my friends and acquaintances who now have babies, many have had miscarriages, four of whom had repeat miscarriages and three of those were past the 12-week 'safety' point. Whoever we decide to tell, of miscarriage, pregnancy or both, it need not be a secret at all. It's common to feel unwell, but not common to tell anyone the news in the early months. This is a real contradiction because it is in those first weeks that we would most benefit from more rest. It's easy to see why we keep things quiet in the initial weeks. It's a personal choice and there is no right answer, especially because when we finally decide to tell our news, we will start to be treated differently.

That we rarely share news of pregnancy widely before 12 weeks can make this time extremely difficult. If we feel sick or tired, we can't openly say why. With my second pregnancy it certainly felt taxing. I was launching a new video platform, managing a new team and overseeing the production of dozens of short films. The same week I found out I was pregnant, I flew to Mexico to present at a science journalism conference. It was a testing time mentally already, perhaps not an ideal time to add pregnancy into the mix, if there ever is an ideal time.

It didn't matter that I was exhausted constantly, if not from early mornings with my toddler, then from the added mental load of a new role, but I had to continue performing as if I wasn't nurturing a growing foetus. This wasn't exactly a healthy attitude to take. A bit of rest could have been more beneficial for my productivity, health and stress levels. At the same time, I didn't want my colleagues to know precisely because I didn't want to be treated differently, or for anyone to expect me to perform below my usual capacity. Not that they would have, but it was an internal conflict that, I was later to learn, was valid. We are judged differently as soon as we are pregnant, as much of Chapter 4 will outline.

Remaining as stress-free as possible is important because

studies have shown that high levels of stress can have a dramatic impact on the health of an unborn child. Infants born to extremely stressed mothers have increased mental health problems and worse tempers. There are even longer-term effects, such as behavioural problems, anxiety and depression. One 2019 study found that extreme stress also leads to increases in child and adult personality disorders. Stress is a normal part of life so we shouldn't be overly alarmed at this, as for the most part these studies looked at severe or prolonged stress. However, as pregnancy can be a stressful time anyway, it can be beneficial to take things more slowly if we need to – advice I would have given myself if I could go back in time. That doesn't mean we need to slow down completely, but to optimise our environment in subtle ways to benefit our own health. This could be as simple a change as working from home more if the role allows it, or commuting after rush hour, which in London is considerably more bearable. Never again do I wish to enter a packed hot tube worrying about who might unknowingly nudge my growing bump or having to make a split-second analysis of which person I should ask to give up their seat for me, which felt like a daily intrusion into their space and mine. This small act instantly announced my pregnant identity to complete strangers.

Fortunately, despite feeling extremely nauseous if I didn't eat every two hours, the distraction of keeping busy actually helped me, and it was only when I got home from work each day that I felt completely drained of all energy. I was lucky that my nausea largely subsided after 12 weeks. I know of others who had it much worse. A friend felt so nauseous every single day of her pregnancy that it had a terrible effect on her mental wellbeing. She is now considering another baby, but is doubting whether she wants it enough to have to go through pregnancy again. Nine months can feel like an eternity if you feel sick almost every day. Another friend experienced constant dizziness and was signed off work for six months. This is one of the reasons she is definitely stopping at two, despite previously considering more. The biological side effects can be so severe that some women are extremely unwell for several months, especially those who suffer from hyperemesis gravidarum (HG), which can result in severe nausea and vomiting, weight loss and dehydration.

We spend our whole adult life getting used to the body we have and then, in only nine months, everything changes; a time when others routinely make personal, unsolicited recommendations.

When I first told my colleagues, I was already 18 weeks pregnant. I was easily able to hide it as I looked a bit bloated-from-a-big-meal; nobody would have noticed unless they knew me well. I also told them the news on one of the most memorable days of my career, a live interview with Sir David Attenborough in his own home – this was as nerve-wracking as it sounds. I may have waited even longer, but the amount of mysterious appointments I was attending would soon have given me away.

On the day itself, a colleague, perhaps making small talk, told Sir David my news. This came after he complimented me on my interviewing style, to which my colleague responded: 'But she's off to have a baby soon.' Sir David replied, 'Well don't lose her because she's good.' Both were compliments of sorts and the experience was a career highlight, that or he was being polite because I looked so nervous.

I had waited a fairly long time to share the news precisely

because I wanted to avoid my pregnancy overshadowing, well, anything else. I didn't want people to think of me differently, even if it was well intended. I wanted to remain 'myself' for as long as I could possibly get away with. I didn't want special treatment. I didn't want to appear vulnerable, even though the truth is, I was.

That's also perhaps why I didn't take a single sickness day in either pregnancy, even though I had an extremely supportive team. I felt I couldn't give in to the fact that I wasn't feeling as energetic as usual. During my first pregnancy I still went running two or more times per week and relished the fact that I could sustain a level of fitness, perhaps as a way of maintaining control of my body that would soon see a dramatic transformation. For me running helped me feel as though I could mitigate the changes. It also kept the nausea at bay.

The truth is, I was different. I was going to be a mother, and when my bump was more visible this became obvious. So why was I so hesitant to be identified as pregnant? With hindsight, I now see why. My newly emerging identity as a mother-to-be started to jar with my personal identity in a way I couldn't quite put my finger on at first. I didn't want pregnancy to be my only identity, and yet it still consumed every part of me. It was a constant physical presence, especially in the later months when the baby started to kick and turn more. There's evidence that some women adopt a more masculine identity at work in order to succeed in their careers, and if these women become pregnant, they try to hide it at first to maintain this persona.

It's also why pregnant women have been referred to as 'public property', because pregnancy is embodied and therefore so visible. It's a constant physical presence that attracts attention, advice and even judgement. It means we cannot leave something extremely personal, our pregnant 'identities', hidden at home – because it infiltrates our physical being. People open doors for longer, offer their seats on public transport or there are innocent comments from supermarket staff. The parody of strangers touching pregnant bellies is, after all, based on reality. I didn't like my bump signposting my obvious fragility. It's also why I chose not to wear a 'baby on board' badge, something offered to pregnant women in London. I found the whole experience awkward especially because during pregnancy there's little time to be invisible, even if the last thing we want is any attention.

The physical change is so public and, for me, pregnancy was also a constant mental presence; it played around in my mind at any time of rest, commuting or even walking past strangers. *'I'm pregnant, I'm pregnant, I'm pregnant ... Do they realise I'm pregnant?'* I don't usually pay attention to what others might think of me, but, for some reason, this played on a loop, albeit a quiet one, and fortunately it faded into the background when I was busiest. The reason this might be is that pregnancy disrupts our 'illusion of control' and defines us more obviously as insubordinate to the standard and dominant sex – which is male. During pregnancy we are an 'antithesis of the male standard' as one team put it.

The idea of pregnant women being public property is only one element of the physical takeover. As soon as pregnancy begins, our body is no longer truly our own. Aside from the public comments, the reality is that a growing infant really is sucking up all our excess resources. They will continue to take from the mother even if there is nothing left for her, a reason why iron deficiency is so common in pregnancy. On one antenatal visit, when I informed a stern, elderly midwife how tired I was, she warned me: 'Don't you know that you now have a parasite growing inside you ... it will suck everything it can from you', and tried to encourage me to take supplements to help ease my tiredness.*

Pregnant mums are also frequently asked what food or drinks they miss and some even consider whether the food they eat during pregnancy will affect their child's preferences later on – we know that flavours transcend into the amniotic fluid. This type of commentary does not stop after giving birth; those who breastfeed can be advised to watch how much alcohol or coffee they consume. Someone once even told me I should give up broccoli as it might upset my baby's stomach.

Having been through it twice now, I realise it's somewhat obvious that pregnancy would bring so many changes. For one, the physical effects we feel are constant: sickness, food aversions, a growing stomach, a sharper sense of smell. On my morning commute my nose was so sensitive to the stench of alcohol that I could smell it on anyone who had been drinking the night before, and it was nauseating. Then there's the constant reminders from external events, the midwife or doctor's appointments, the smiles from strangers, the knowing nods from friends. All these nudges are welcoming at times, not so much at others. This brings me back to the idea of 'mum brain'. Our brain is physically changing in a way that will optimise social bonds between mother and child. A heightened awareness of pregnancy could naturally be a consequence of that.

But could there be other reasons why it consumed me so completely? Was it an evolutionary trick keeping my mind on my unborn child and their safety? Or was it part

---

* Aside from folic acid and vitamin D, the latest research suggests there is no need to take pregnancy supplements when eating a balanced diet.

of the brain changes we explored earlier? It's not an easy question to answer, but studies do show that myriad things occur. To start with the physical, even though pregnancy is a time when weight gain is expected, the fact that an 'ideal' pregnant body is still perpetuated by society pressurises women to feel as though these changes should be within their control.

A 2014 paper investigating the impact of pregnancy on body image looked at numerous studies over a 20-year period and found that how women felt about their body depended on the 'socially constructed ideal'. That is, weight gain when associated with pregnancy was acceptable; anything outside the 'ideal' such as excessive weight gain, acne or stretch marks, was not. Overwhelmingly women felt that bodily change was not within their control and that they were therefore 'transgressing' the ideal. One woman stated that: 'It was as if suddenly the whole world had access to my body ...'

While a bump and weight gain is expected and accepted, gaining fat is not. The review also showed that pregnant women felt one of two ways, as if they were sharing their body with their unborn child or were being invaded by it: 'a bit like the invasion of the body snatchers'. These latter unwelcome thoughts were what the researchers said could indicate an unhealthy relationship with their postpartum bodies and even infant bonding.

How well women responded to their changing bodies during pregnancy depended upon protecting themselves against social norms of female beauty. While a larger body and bump was seen as a confirmation of being pregnant, after the baby was born women felt they then had to conform to a socially constructed ideal of beauty.

The pressure was on to return to their pre-pregnancy

bodies. Women who experienced this most also found it more distressing if their bodies were different. The authors concluded that we should not underestimate the physical changes that women undergo during and after pregnancy, as they are key to how well they adjust to their new role and identity as a mother. Women who feel bad about their pregnant bodies are more likely to be depressed and less likely to breastfeed or do so for a shorter time, while better body satisfaction is linked to higher-quality relationships, and a higher bodily interoception (self-awareness).

One thing is certain, bodily change during pregnancy is something that occupies many women's minds. Given how prevalent postnatal mental health issues are, questions about bodily identity could and should be better monitored as part of routine antenatal appointments. It would be easy to implement early on and allows interventions for those at greater risk of postnatal distress. This could then help women feel more like themselves and therefore in control, ultimately helping them form stronger bonds with their infants.

The change from pregnancy to motherhood is profound. After nine months of anticipation and of physical growth, there is a brand-new human to look after. Anthropologists have called the birth of a new mother 'matrescence', a phrase now made more prominent by the reproductive psychiatrist Alexandra Sacks. She writes that the birth of a mother identity is just as demanding as giving birth itself. Motherhood is a time much like our teenage years, when we are full of hormonal changes that affect us physically and mentally. To parent better, we need to understand this identity change.

The transition is immediate. We go from thinking of the

'baby' as an abstract concept to the world completely revolving around him or her. Throw in months of sleep deprivation and little time to ourselves, and naturally this can cause stress. This stress should not be confused with postpartum depression, which Sacks found that many of her patients mistakenly believed. If we acknowledge and reframe our mindset, discuss this time more openly, then it will be easier to differentiate between what is a normal level of stress, and when it is necessary to ask for help.

In these earliest sleep-deprived days, my husband was the one listening to most of my moments of stress related to juggling two children as I tried not to burden others with how tired I was. In hindsight, having one baby seemed blissful compared to the chaos that came with the second. Looking after a newborn and toddler by myself brought a new level of stress. I was brutally honest to anyone who asked how it was going. For instance, a friend asked how I was and this was my reply:

> Mostly great, except I was woken up eight times last night, my toddler has also peed on the floor six times today (while potty training) and my nine kilogram four-month-old won't let me put him down without crying, so I wasn't able to eat lunch today.

I reserved these kinds of comments for friends with children, mainly because there is an intense pressure from society to feel happy and grateful for these beautiful new humans, and not to be mourning past freedoms, especially as it was our choice to have them in the first place. Of course, on the whole I usually am, and many did warn us it would be challenging. That doesn't mean we can't feel both love and miss our previous freedom, we just have to find time to reconcile these conflicting emotions and understand that it is normal to find this clash uncomfortable.

The highs are high – I can almost feel the oxytocin rush to my brain when I look at my baby's face or look at photos of my toddler once she's asleep, but the lows were unexpected and, for me, were tied to losing control of my own time. With careful planning I was able to go out on occasion, but it required fitting in pumping so that my baby had enough milk. With my first, bottle-feeding was not even an option between months three and five, as she refused to accept one. Meanwhile, I found pumping so harrowing the first time round, I barely tried to teach my second to drink from a bottle, so any evening plans could only begin once I had put him to bed after his last feed, which was also a time of peak exhaustion. I remember cancelling on a friend's birthday once because after factoring in travel, by the time I got there, I would almost have to leave again to be in bed at a decent hour. Knowing I would be woken every hour or two, I couldn't risk staying up late. I agonised over how to cancel: an early bedtime might seem an absurd excuse for anyone who is blissfully unaware of the harrowing effects of a sleep-regressing baby.

Each plan that deviated from my normal routine required careful planning with my husband, making a swift spontaneous after-work drink impossible – which comes with consequences. And when I did go out, it was rarely with my husband; one of us would invariably stay home. Babysitters were no use during clingy phases when only a parent or grandparent would settle a half-asleep toddler. That and London prices for babysitters when already on a reduced salary made the idea even more off-putting.

Overall, there is a rift between the changes we expect

when we become mothers – a loss of time, freedom and sleep – and those that come as a more unwelcome surprise – the judgement, the pressure, the guilt. On the whole, we must remember that this is a spectrum and though each individual experience can be different, all are equally valid and 'normal' within the constraints of what our new normality means. The birth of a baby signals the birth of a new mother, and key to our changing sense of self is accepting ourselves in this new light. It is never easy, but understanding why will help resolve our motherhood complex.

2

BIRTH

Labour, birth and all the messy
bits in-between

Traumatic birth events can be devastating, for the mothers, babies and even partners. I had a scarring experience, but, aside from the unpleasant memories, I came out the other end relatively unscathed. In this chapter, I aim to understand why and consider how easily it can go the other way, and can result in lasting mental ill health.

Four days after my daughter was born by emergency C-section, my guts spilled out of me, all 20 or so feet of them, dangling from a gaping hole in my stomach, which my husband later said reminded him of the scene from the classic horror movie *Alien*; fondly referred to by its fans as the 'chestburster'. I haven't seen this film – nor do I ever intend to – but you get the idea. The medic who arrived by motorbike had never seen anything like it, nor, it seems, had any of the countless medical professionals I would see over the following days.

Fortunately for me – and for you, readers – my husband told me not to look so I didn't see the full extent of the damage, only a slightly protruding mess of red and white seeping out of my opening wound. Initially, before I called for him, I had assumed it was only pus, but when I felt my scar begin to tear further, I knew something was very wrong. Calling out to my husband increased the pressure and the rip continued to open up from one side to the other like a broken zip. All I could do was cry out in a small, quiet voice:

'Stephen, I need help.'

He later told me he knew it was serious because he'd never heard me speak with an urgency like that before. He was by my side in seconds. He didn't say anything before he grabbed his phone and called an ambulance. I started to realise how bad it was when, prompted by the medic on the phone to describe what he could see, he left the bathroom to spare me the reality of what was happening.

'I think her intestines have fallen out,' he whispered, hoping I couldn't hear him. Of course, I heard the whole conversation and the shock of this absurd reality made me shake so badly that I'm surprised I managed to remain standing. He also very sensibly asked what he should do with me as 'gravity was, you know, happening'. I was standing, fully naked in the shower – and as luck would have it, it happened before I started to wash my hair, otherwise I would have had a full head of shampoo for the foreseeable future. Funny what occurs to you in moments of trauma.

It only took seven minutes for a paramedic on a motorbike to show up. We know this because the operator stayed on the line until help arrived. A motorbike paramedic is often sent ahead of the ambulance in serious situations, but it also happened to be a Friday night – a notoriously busy time. It was another agonising 20 or so minutes until an ambulance arrived. The first paramedic managed to coax me out of the shower, a difficult task as it meant stepping out of the bath first. He then held me together in gauze lubricated with saline solution and wrapped me with towels while I sat on a chair shaking and repeatedly asking after my baby. I remember repeating, 'she's only four days old'.

I was reassured that my baby would be fine and could come with me in the ambulance. My milk had only just come in and she had never been given a bottle. At this moment I was her only source of food, which was all I could focus on.

After a three-hour wait with my insides on my outside, still wrapped in saline solution and with minimal pain relief (I refused morphine in case it got into my breast milk ... skewed priorities perhaps), the out-of-hours surgery finally became available. During this wait I had attempted to breastfeed my baby (tricky when lying flat on a bed), pump milk from my ballooning boobs – also tricky for similar reasons – and signed a form saying I consented to surgery that might, the consultant warned me, leave me with permanent bowel damage.

There was even a vague suggestion that if any issues were found I might need a stoma, and I was quizzed on whether I understood what that meant. An anaesthetist asked me all sorts of questions about any potential allergies and a kind nurse put in a catheter and a drip to administer antibiotics and pain relief, which, after two hours, I finally consented to (although it did nothing for the worsening cramps I was by then experiencing). It felt like the longest three hours of my life and, more than anything else, I recall wanting to be fully anaesthetised so that this nightmare might be behind me more quickly. I knew it was serious when even my husband couldn't tell me everything would be OK, his face the ashen shade of someone not quite sure how to gauge the severity of a situation. All the while he nervously cradled our baby, with no idea where to take her when I was whisked away to surgery. He didn't want to detract attention from me by asking where he might go or how he would feed our soon-to-be hungry infant.

When I was finally wheeled into surgery after midnight and asked to count down from ten, I only managed three seconds. A specialist bowel surgeon was called in together with an obstetric consultant and they performed an 'exploratory laparotomy', which consisted of checking every inch of my small intestine for tears or damage, before putting me back together. I woke up two hours later in what I probably mis-remember was a long, dark and rectangular room in which I was the only patient, and I woke up hysterically happy, still high from the medication. I was merrily informed by two grinning nurses that everything went well and that my hus-band and baby were on their way. I giggled with drug-fuelled delight as the recovery team told me funny stories about the bathroom habits of post-op bowel patients – at least this is how I remember it. Then a doctor came with an industrial-grade pump to allow me to relieve the pressure from my milk-filled breasts, as she had heard how keen I was to pump.

My baby was asleep by then. In those hours I was in surgery, my husband had managed to find the maternity ward where a confused junior doctor gave him some for-mula for our howling baby girl. Nobody understood why he was in the hospital with a hungry newborn without her mother in the middle of the night. 'Your wife is where? What happened? Who sent you?' Maternity wards are under-standably wary of anyone who is not a patient, even more so out of hours.

Recovery was painful, but everyone remarked how happy and surprised they were that I was OK. I was offered leaflets on where to get counselling and, over the days in hospital, I saw many obstetricians trying to get to the bottom of what exactly went wrong during my original surgery. It was a 'non-event' they unhelpfully said; one that shouldn't have happened. We still don't know the cause, but I'll never forget how many times I was congratulated for managing to pass wind. It was a sure sign my bowels were working again.

Despite the trauma, medication and healing my body was put through, I managed to continue breastfeeding with my oblivious baby well looked after by a brilliant team of midwives – perhaps the only upside to my extended hospital stay. With their help, I didn't have to worry about how much she was eating, sleeping or whether she was gaining weight.

Whatever the reason, and it's really best not to dwell, I recovered fully with no lasting side effects. The event was traumatic: at one point I didn't think I would survive. I realised that there were two main reasons I have no lasting psychological impacts, aside from a few flashbacks and the occasional bad dream. One: I recovered fully and had an amazing support network around me, and two: my baby was fine throughout the whole ordeal.

Psychiatrists are well aware that a feeling of safety and security in an otherwise chaotic time can help buffer against the onset of a mental health issue or trauma. Although I was initially upset and angry at the probable medical error that caused it, I felt safe in the hands of the medics who fixed me and was supported by an incredible team of consultants and midwives who did their utmost to find clarity.

It could easily have gone the other way. For many, traumatic birth events have lasting psychological effects, and can send new mothers into a deep depression. It need not be a medically rare event like mine either that causes trauma.

Our identity changes instantly when we become mothers

and there is perhaps nothing as stark as a mental breakdown, where a woman's previous sense of identity is not only lost, it is confused, murky, painful and potentially long-lasting. The mind can be affected in many ways after childbirth and there are several conditions that women are at risk of: post-natal or postpartum depression (PND), postnatal anxiety and, to a lesser extent, post-traumatic stress disorder (PTSD) and postpartum psychosis. Even after being 'cured', these can have an enduring impact on a woman's sense of self.

During labour and birth women are already vulnerable, which means that if things go wrong and that feeling of security and trust from the clinical staff is absent, it can contribute to lasting trauma. This means that even if women experience life-threatening situations, the perceived support can make a huge difference to staying well and preventing PTSD. The key aspect of this is a woman's own perception of the event. Even if a birth intervention such as a C-section is considered fairly routine, it is a woman's subjective experience of that event that needs to be taken into consideration and that can contribute to a lasting ordeal. It is one of the strongest predictors for a mental health issue after birth: studies have shown that 'poor satisfaction with health professionals' is linked to chronic and delayed PTSD.

It is clear that mental health issues following the birth of a child are no longer as rare as once assumed, especially as more people now openly discuss their trauma. Postnatal depression experienced after childbirth is characterised by feeling low, hopeless, tearful, irritable, angry, and, for some, having suicidal thoughts as well as difficulty feeding and bonding with their baby. It is believed to affect about 10–15 per cent of women after childbirth, amounting to about 400,000 new mothers in the US each year.

It's hard to get at the true figure because it is under-reported, and there is a huge difference in the severity of the condition. Women in Europe and Australia have also shown lower incidences of PND than those in the US, though it is unclear why. Anyone can be affected, but several factors increase the risk, including poverty, domestic or sexual violence and mothers with little family or social help. It's not entirely clear how exactly postpartum depression differs to depression in other times of life, but we know the two are linked – mothers with previous episodes of depression are at increased risk of PND. Mothers who work more than 40 hours a week also have higher instances. For milder cases, talk therapy can help and, in the most severe, it is often treated with antidepressants. If it is left untreated it can last for many months or, in some cases, years.

If a mother is unable to bond with her child, the consequences can be devastating for the whole family. The effects can start before birth. When a mother is depressed during pregnancy, a baby's amygdala has been shown to be altered in ways that could affect their emotional control later on. This is in line with other findings that depressed mothers are more likely to have depressed children.

Postpartum depression is perhaps the most widely known and cited mental health condition that can occur after pregnancy (though it often starts during), but a rarer mental health issue is postpartum PTSD. There is overlap between depression and PTSD, meaning the conditions can be hard to distinguish at first. PTSD is where trauma is relived, often through flashbacks and nightmares, and can cause severe anxiety and depression. Patients often report a fear that they or their baby were going to die. First referred to as 'shellshock' and thought to only affect soldiers who had been traumatised by the battlefield, PTSD is now better understood. It can occur following any traumatic event, which is why it can manifest after a traumatic birth. An additional risk factor of developing PTSD is poor sleep, which, after childbirth, is almost a given. The prevalence is reported to vary between about 1.5 and 6 per cent. In the UK this amounts to about 30,000 women a year, according to the Birth Trauma Association. It could be many more, as there are indications that one in six women who miscarry show symptoms of PTSD, according to a 2020 study analysing 737 women who experienced miscarriage or ectopic pregnancy. Of these, 29 per cent showed PTSD symptoms after one month. Nine months later, this dropped slightly but was still at 18 per cent, while 17 per cent experienced anxiety and 6 per cent depression. Given its prevalence, the authors believe that many women may be suffering silently.

To illustrate the debilitating effects of a condition like PND, I spoke with two mothers about how the condition affected their experience of early motherhood and their changing selves.

ALICE

My life has been completely redirected since my diagnosis of PND.

It helped me to assess my priorities and redirect my attention so that it reflects my values. At first I felt like a victim, and then I was almost possessed with the mission of fixing myself. And now I feel like both an underdog and a people's champion, set on making the world a better, kinder place for mothers. But there's still a sense that the wound that opened up will now forever need extra self-care.

Throughout all of this, my sense of identity as a woman [was in flux]; my gender and its place in the power structure. I had never experienced my gender to such a degree as after having a baby. There's a lot of pressure on mothers – idealised mothering that populates social media.

So many mothers are pathologised and then still left largely unsupported. 'Take some pills and on you go!' They don't realise it's not an individual problem, it's more like a social issue.

My husband was very angry with the diagnosis and it changed our relationship. He refused to accept it and forbade me to talk about it with my friends. I had to give up my support; he made it hard for me to even see the physio. 'You keep forgetting, you are a mother first and foremost,' he would say.

I was so independent and carefree pre-motherhood. I was also so naive to what it meant to be a mother, and how hard it would be to hold other identities simultaneously to mother. Alice the mother has more strength, patience and empathy than I could have ever imagined. I am grounded and motivated in a way I wasn't before. I have purpose, and boundless love. And now that I have seen through the looking glass, I feel much more free to push boundaries and care for myself in a world that expects me to perpetually sacrifice (which I used to do to such an extent it would make your toes curl, and it breaks my heart to think about).

JANE

When my child was three and a half months old, I was diagnosed with postnatal depression and admitted to a private mother and baby unit in Melbourne, Australia for five weeks. The three-day wait between diagnosis and admission was agonising – I counted the hours until I could get professional help. The experience of being a mental health patient in an inpatient ward was both one of the worst and best experiences of my life. I was in a crisis when I was admitted – I caught sight of myself in the mirror and didn't recognise myself. The midwife searched my belongings for string and medications and I remember thinking 'this can't be happening to me'.

Normally a very organised thinker, I had thought that I had failed to make the transition to motherhood and that my child would be better off adopted out, while at the same time not being able to leave my baby for a second. None of the self-soothe techniques worked and I became obsessive about the amount of milk my child was getting and when my baby didn't settle at the times of the various baby books I had been reading, I thought I was a failure.

I thought I had a personality that would lend itself easily to motherhood – highly organised, well read, independent and high-functioning. In retrospect, these personality traits worked against me in the first year. The loss of control that is completely normal with a newborn had me spinning out of control and I thought I would never recover. Instead of writing a list of things I wanted to achieve with my baby each day, just like I had done each day at work, I should have thrown out those lists and focused on building connection, learning about my baby and self-care when I could.

But I did recover, with professional help (the mother and baby unit, a perinatal psychologist and medication), and the love and support of family and friends. I more than recovered; over time, I began to thrive and redefine my sense of self.

Motherhood isn't something that you add onto your existing identity, motherhood is a completely new stage in your life.

I took what I needed from my old life and left what I didn't. Everything changes – not just materially and physically but psychologically and emotionally – and the scale and abruptness of the change shouldn't be underestimated. The identity that I have now is more multi-dimensional and complex and much richer. Motherhood feels so right that I find it hard to remember pre-motherhood Jane. I enjoyed that stage of my life as well, but motherhood has given my life purpose.

PTSD is similarly debilitating and can influence a woman's life and mind for many years. Take Gill, who shared her experience with me. She had severe PTSD following the birth of her first daughter. She was an ambitious, highly motivated early 30s professional working in the oil industry, used to making huge financial deals and presenting to hundreds of people. Her birth experience left her altered in a way that she will never return from, and she believes that it was one key moment, among many, that caused her PTSD.

Out of the countless things that could have gone wrong for Gill, many did. She wanted a vaginal birth with no drugs, but due to back problems and as her baby measured large, her labour was induced. Her contractions lasted several days, but then unexpectedly slowed down. It was only later that she realised her labour wasn't progressing due to an error from a trainee midwife who had failed to insert an oxytocin drip correctly, a hormone used to help kick-start labour. When her labour was finally coming to an end, a series of events meant she was brought to surgery for a forceps delivery with an episiotomy (a vaginal cut). After her baby was out, she had a haemorrhage and lost a lot of blood, which left her unconscious. Her baby needed antibiotics and was taken to neonatal care.

When Gill woke up, she was alone. She was convinced her baby was dead. She recalls the exact moment that led to these visceral fears. It was after countless interventions, delirious with sleep deprivation and on her third day of labour, when a new midwife asked her to move herself so that her bed sheets could be changed. She said she didn't want new bed sheets, but the midwife didn't listen. She was then told that moving herself would make the whole process quicker. When she resisted, the midwife told her she had to move quickly or else it might harm her baby. At this, Gill began to move herself with great difficulty because of her back pain. It was excruciating. The fear that her baby might be harmed, that she was the cause, became the catalyst that would see her suffer from mental health issues and changed her sense of self in ways she could not have anticipated.

She was in a recovery ward with several other new mums and their babies. 'I was convinced my baby was dead, and they didn't tell me because I was too poorly to hear the news.' When her baby was brought to her, she did not believe she was hers.

At home, it was after a disagreement with her husband that she realised that something would have to change:

He got in between me and my baby. It wasn't an active thing ... He just took a step between me and my baby. The rage that overcame me was indescribable. I say it half-jokingly now, but it was true. Had I had a weapon I would have killed him. This feeling that he was taking my baby away ... I would have done something had I had the means. I wanted to die, I wished I had died on the operating table when they saved my life. I wanted to be dead. I didn't want her to know the reality, that I was cold, and distant, was in so much pain, didn't want to leave the house.

That her mum was not a good mum. I didn't want her to grow up knowing that. I couldn't bring myself to kill myself, so I wanted to find a way to disappear.

Now with more clarity, Gill is able to pinpoint how fractured she became from the moment labour started:

I felt these people didn't care about me. They wanted this baby out healthy and that's all they cared about. I was an inconvenience to that process ... I was made to feel like a naughty child. It's such a shift from grown-up adult life to being infantilised in hospital.

Gill's sense of who she is remains forever altered. Once a confident professional, now her voice quivers with uncertainty, which she attributes to a constant flow of excess adrenaline. Even walking down the street, holding her daughter's hand, she feels as if people only see her as a mother, not Gill, an individual. 'I am not as strong as I was. I don't have another armour to put on that's not mum.'

Perhaps there lies the issue. While most of us have several identities, Gill's most prominent identity became one of a mum with mental health issues, but that was not how she wanted to identify herself, which left her feeling stuck and unable to go back to the type of work that was once second nature to her.

She now volunteers with the Birth Trauma Association in the UK and often discusses how the experience affected her at the time and many years later. Although it can be uncomfortable for her to relive, she does so in the hope it will help others and to raise awareness of the triggers that caused her PTSD.

Alice, Jane and Gill's stories show that even those without a previous history of a mental illness can easily be affected. Then there are still many thousands who are traumatised by childbirth on some level, but not enough for a diagnosis. The Birth Trauma Association suggests one-third of all births results in mental trauma. Many of these are not deemed serious enough to be given a diagnosis, or for it to have any continued effect on day-to-day activities. That said, a traumatic experience lingers on in the mind, perhaps for ever.

I too had occasional 'what-if' thoughts for several months afterwards. The first few days of new motherhood had been quite peaceful, with my baby sleeping most of the time. My husband had even planned to play football, when all was still well. Although he was there to help me, I couldn't help but dwell on the fact he had planned to be away: *What if he hadn't been there that night / what if he wasn't in earshot of the shower / what if I had passed out from the pain or blood, for hours, or worse? All the while my baby was helpless without me.*

These thoughts were heightened in the weeks following the incident but, fortunately, they faded away. It is when thoughts like this become intrusive, as they did in Gill's case, that it can result in an extremely fraught time. PTSD results in feelings of being emotionally overwhelmed and out of control, as if in a permanent fight-or-flight mode. That's why a moment of panic can be triggered so easily. It can be caused by something as simple as a clip on TV about birth.

Never once during my birth complication was my baby's life at risk, nor did I believe it to be at risk, which is another aspect that helped me overcome my experience. This was not the case for Gill. Identifying these distinctions is therefore clearly important for anyone in the 'at risk' category.

Although mental health issues after pregnancy are routinely screened for, many are missed precisely because there is so much pressure to be a 'perfect mother', to give everything to your newborn even at the expense of your own happiness. This can start even before labour and birth, so mothers may not even realise that they are affected for some time.

Mental health issues during pregnancy and afterwards can be difficult to treat, but understanding the hormonal and brain changes women experience could help. With PND, a small study in 2010 found that areas of the brain important for emotions were less active, explaining why, in some cases, mothers with depression find it difficult to connect with their baby. In this study, both depressed and non-depressed mothers were asked to look at angry and scared faces, to see how their brain responded to these pictures. The mothers who were most depressed showed lower brain activity when shown the faces with negative emotions. This could explain why mothers with PND show less empathy. It could be one reason why depressed mothers are less responsive to an infant's cries than non-depressed mothers. Depressed mothers also show reduced brain activity when their baby cries.

Along these lines, in 2017 one study found depressed mothers' brains responded differently to happy faces in areas of the brain important for identifying positive emotions and understanding the thoughts and feelings of others. The areas may therefore not be working optimally to help the mothers understand their child's emotions or needs. The brain areas crucial for bonding and learning new information, the amygdala and hippocampus, are also affected by depression.

We know that hormones are a key part of the maternal brain during pregnancy and when our babies are born. For instance, the hormones cortisol and oxytocin play an important role in how mothers focus on and bond with their babies, but the balance is crucial. If there's too much, or not enough, it is linked to depression. In the first few days, post-partum cortisol is important for heightened attention to an infant, but, several months later, a high level of cortisol has negative effects on how a mother interacts with her child.

Studies have shown that a mother can recognise her own baby's smell and sounds due to the hormone cortisol. While cortisol is a stress hormone, it also enhances attention and alertness. Too much cortisol can cause chronic stress, but an optimum level helps a mother zone into her child's needs.

New mothers have been found to be more sympathetic and alert to an infant's cries compared to non-mothers, primed again by cortisol released shortly after birth. The more sympathetic mothers also had a heightened heart rate, which sped up when they heard their baby cry. Mothers were also better at differentiating between a pain or a hunger cry compared to non-mothers. Those with increased cortisol reacted more positively to their baby's smell, were more affectionate and showed more caregiving behaviours.

This goes to show that when a child is born, hormones really do increase the intensity of our nurturing feelings and help prime us to react a certain way, creating physical responses that can be measured. Then exposure kicks in – simply spending time with those we love also releases important hormones for bonding, explaining why non-biological parents also show hormonal responses to their infants.

With regards to PTSD, the reason birth traumas can revisit those with the condition for so long afterwards has to do with how the brain processes fear. Disorders like PTSD can occur when a situation is coupled with a fearful event – as Gill's case shows, the event (childbirth) occurred at the same time she experienced an immediate and lingering fear that her baby would die. This can lead the person to later associate other memories from that time to the fearful event, from the place it happened or sounds they heard or what they smelt. It's why hospitals or any medicalised areas can bring back the clinical feel of childbirth and trigger those with a birth trauma.

Pinpointing the brain processes is complex, especially as PTSD involves many parts of the brain. It taps into so many of our senses: sound, smell, touch – these can all trigger different experiences, which, in turn, are represented by various areas in the brain.

Usually when a fearful event takes place, it is beneficial for us to associate it with the place where it occurred. This would mean that if we found ourselves in a similar environment, we would quickly understand it to be dangerous which could prompt us to change our behaviour. For instance, toddlers easily learn when something causes pain, and will subsequently avoid putting themselves in similar situations. My toddler knows not to touch lightbulbs as she learnt the hard way when reaching for our bedside lamp.

The problem is that many fearful events are unexpected or the first of their kind, which can lead to the brain's fear processing area to go into overdrive. Research shows that during a frightening or stressful situation that causes PTSD, the memory is heightened in a way that can make the event appear much more vivid than a normal memory. Fear alters the way the brain stores these memories. Even mundane everyday facts are more clearly recalled when they occur close to a fearful memory, thought to be amplified by adrenaline. I remember exactly what I was doing before I got in the shower where my scar opened, and how I discussed looking forward to seeing the midwife the next day to check on it as it felt a bit tight and lumpy. I remember that Sanne was sleeping, and how quickly my husband had to repack the hospital bag – and which hat he put on our baby. My husband even remembers what song he was listening to at the time of the event.

To understand how this happens, neuroscientists analyse specific pathways in the brain that travel between the place a fear is learnt and the eventual expression of that fear. So far, they have done so in mice. In 2014 a team was able to deactivate brain cells crucial for transmitting fearful memories from one part of the brain to another. This highlighted that there was a separate area of the brain responsible for experiencing an event, and another part corresponding to the context or location. The fearful learning seems to take place in the amygdala, which we know is important for emotions – including fear. Naturally a fearful memory triggers our emotional centre but it is another part of the brain, the hippocampus, that forms the associated 'place' fear. The two areas can easily communicate, neurons travel between them to transmit information, which is how the hippocampus can 'tell' the amygdala where this fearful event took place. If a set of these neurons is deactivated, then a mouse is prevented from associating a fearful event with the place it was first experienced. The place where they became scared could no longer trigger their fear. That's why neuroscientists want to understand how fear associations are formed. This would be a critical start to better understand how to tune down overpowering fearful memories.

Another team that same year got one step closer to doing so, also in mice. They managed to change fearful memories into 'pleasant' ones. The researchers did this by artificially activating the neurons associated with a bad memory while the mice were in a happy situation – in this case with a female companion. Just as the mice were enjoying themselves, they 'switched on' the fearful neurons. This essentially reprogrammed these neurons to their new, happier environment, making them less afraid when they returned to the previously fearful place.

Think of it this way: if you were attacked on a beach you might later associate any beach with a memory of the attack. Imagine we could measure the exact brain cells related to this fear. Later, if we could activate these fearful neurons in a more relaxing, preferred environment, say with a favourite person, it could change them from negative to positive. You could then go back to the beach and feel no fear, flipping these neurons back to how they were before the fearful memory took place. Following on from this, a year later, the same lab showed that they were able to activate happy memories when mice felt stressed. They knew which neurons were associated with the positive memories, so when the mice were in a stressful situation, they stimulated these neurons, which helped them out of their depressive state.

While studies like this are providing groundbreaking insights into the brain areas involved in responding to fear, applications to humans are a long way off, not least because an intrusive method of brain modification is involved.

Another issue is that even though scientists can manipulate memories in mice, it is unclear what impact this would have on other memories. We have fearful memories to keep us safe, so getting rid of them completely could be a problem.

These studies are important because understanding the processes in the brain that occur during PTSD and depression will be key for finding treatments that work, or medication that is more specific.

For now, other methods are more suited for living with postpartum mental health issues at a time when normality is already flipped on its head. For Alice, she was helped by a combination of things: therapy, reading and shared experiences with friends. She also felt that time for 'self-care' was crucial, and gave herself permission not to be perfect, to rest and to prioritise time with her children over other obligations.

Jane also made more time for herself, especially for sleep, making it a priority at the expense of other, less important things like housework. Medication and counselling were important too, but most of all it took time for her to 'settle into' motherhood. Reading about how others transitioned was also valuable. As for Gill, counselling, therapy and sharing her story with others helped. Gill is adamant that a more supportive environment would have stopped her developing PTSD. Research backs this up: perceived control from compassionate hospital staff has been shown to dramatically reduce anxiety in the first place. These experiences show that each woman is affected in a slightly different way. What is clear though is that a traumatic birth or postpartum experience can result in irreversible change that can worm its way into our identity.

I too will now forever be someone who has experienced a

trauma, which comes to my mind every time I hear someone else's birth story. I went from avoiding any negative birth stories to sharing a fairly gruesome one. It is not uncommon for our mothers to continue to share their birth stories even many decades afterwards, memories that can be recalled in vivid detail.

It surprised me how many people shared their own 'horror' stories with me while I was pregnant, including recounts of miscarriage. I see now that it's precisely because motherhood and the accompanying experiences creep into so many aspects of a mother's identity, so that when you join the club, these stories, feelings and emotions will naturally be thrust upon you. To share is to be social and to be social is an important part of what makes us human, but if these shared experiences become a fixation, that's when it can become detrimental and all-consuming.

This is a slight paradox, given that it has only recently become more normalised and even encouraged to open up about a traumatic birth experience. In the 1960s my grandmother had a stillborn baby girl. She was her second daughter and sixth child. The baby was quickly whisked away and my grandmother was sent home, with no mention from the hospital staff that the experience might have a profound emotional impact. It was only later that my grandmother talked about her, saying that she thought about her every day, about how perfectly formed she was, with her beautiful head of thick black hair. It affected my grandfather deeply too, but this was only apparent on his deathbed when he asked for his stillborn daughter to be recognised by marking a small cross on his gravestone. It was a different era, clearly, and as my mother remarked, there was an unsaid assumption that bereaved families should move on quickly. That they would be better off focusing on the present, than on what was lost for ever, a stillborn offering a glimpse of life but immediately and tragically united with death.

These lonely tragedies clearly linger; another close friend's grandmother had a similar story. She didn't even get to hold or see her child. The very words we use to describe stillbirth hint at our desire to shield ourselves from the truth. Born still, not born dead. Now that we understand the importance and impact of the surge of hormones that flow through new mothers, key for attachment, it is only natural that a loss can create a lifelong trauma. Ignoring this loss will undoubtedly intensify the ordeal.

Considering the impact birth can have on a mother's sense of self, it's no wonder we want to tell others about our experience, the good and the bad. This comes with its own downsides. Nobody outside of the bubble of motherhood usually asks for much detail. And yet, there is still a dominant emphasis on 'natural', positive births, leading some women to feel disappointed when a birth does not go as planned.

The best piece of advice I was given was not to worry about a birth plan at all, as they are rarely followed. I still wrote one, but surgery immediately discounted most of my plans for a vaginal, medication-free birth. The one thing I did ask for was for my husband to tell me the sex of our daughter, which the midwife carefully reminded everyone in the theatre. When my baby was presented to me not long after, the obstetrician was accidentally holding her in a way that obscured her genitals, so my husband couldn't even see what sex she was. It was the obstetrician who then informed us kindly that my daughter was, in fact, a girl. By that point

I didn't much care about my birth plan, but the point stands that even minor birth wishes are out of our control.

I went into my first labour convinced that I would be the exception and not require any intervention. In hindsight this confidence was naive, but I knowingly chose to think positively because I realised that the calmer we are, the better our hormones help labour progress, while stress releases hormones that can put a brake on labour. This is a clever evolutionary adaptation. If one of our early ancestors was giving birth and a dangerous animal appeared, it would certainly help if her stress hormones delayed labour until she found a safer place.

Home births are encouraged in the Netherlands, with about 20 per cent of women having them compared to 2.3 per cent in England and Wales. The idea is that there is a lower risk for interventions (for low-risk pregnancies) in the calm, non-medicalised environment of home. There are also fewer C-sections compared with the UK, about 17 per cent.

Naturally, an unplanned C-section is also out of our control. That I needed one seemed implausible to me at the time. I was convinced someone had made a mistake; I even told the midwife that my baby couldn't possibly be breech (when a baby is head up instead of head down), not realising how common this actually is.

My waters broke at about 4 a.m. six days before my due date, and, as advised, I went into the hospital to be monitored. I knew I would be sent home again as I had not started contractions. I was told that if they did not start within 18 hours, I would be induced. After your waters have broken, I was told that midwives will rarely do internal investigations, as in, check how far the cervix has dilated with their fingers, until they really need to, due to an infection risk. After a quick feel of my stomach to check that my baby's head was where we thought it was (spoiler, she wasn't), I was sent home. Contractions started a few hours later, and I was adamant I would stay in the comfort of my home for as long as possible, worrying that labour would slow down as soon as I entered hospital, as my hypnobirthing book had advised it might. I even made time for a nice big breakfast and a shower. At about midday my industrial maternity pad looked as if it had a tiny drop of green on it, which could have been a sign of meconium (aka a baby's first poo). Babies don't normally poop in the womb but when they do, it can be a sign of distress. I called the labour ward again and was told to come in immediately. I shoved another towel inside my trousers and sat uncomfortably in the taxi, careful to hide the fact that I was both in actual labour by this time, and still leaking water. Waters don't break the way they do in the movies: it continues to drip out for many hours afterwards. Labour can also start very slowly, so, with some careful breathing, I was able to act fairly composed from the outside, but, in reality, each contraction felt as if there were needles inside me.

The midwife performed a cervical sweep to see whether there was indeed any trace of meconium. This is where they insert a couple of fingers inside you to 'sweep' the membrane to try and help stimulate labour, or in my case it was done to check my amniotic fluid and to see how far I was dilated.

There was no meconium. Relieved at this news, I thought I would be sent home again, as I was only three centimetres dilated, not quite enough to be admitted, I thought. The midwife then swiftly remarked, 'That's not a head there. That's a bum.' I asked if she was sure. I had been told for weeks that my baby's head was down. 'I'm pretty sure I know what a bum feels like ... ' By the time it was confirmed, it was just after 1 p.m., only half an hour after I had arrived. I was asked whether I understood what would happen next. 'Yes, a C-section,' I whispered, and a tiny, guilty part of me felt relieved that the decision was final, but another part was disappointed that I would not have the birth experience I had been so convinced I would have.

The consultant read out some complicated stats to me about how much more risky breech deliveries are, compared to when a baby's head is down. All the while I was having contractions. My husband and I were put into scrubs and the consultant spoke urgently to her deputy: 'This woman is in active labour, the baby needs to come out.' I view this memory through the distorted lens of it happening to some-one else, in a melodramatic TV show with serious facial expressions and theatrical music, myself a character with no speaking role with a shocked look on my face. It was urgent but not an emergency, so, all in all, I felt surprisingly calm.

Being in labour, I didn't have time to process what was happening, but I trusted the experts. Only 30 minutes after my baby was confirmed in a breech position, I found myself holding my breath mid-contraction while a huge needle was inserted into my back to numb my lower body. Soon after, my baby was out, crying healthily, making me cry too. We attempted skin on skin, but it was impossible with all the equipment around me. She was quickly whisked away to a warmer recovery room and placed skin on skin on my husband for over 20 minutes while my incision was closed (not well enough, it turned out). Nobody told me I would be left alone, but I didn't know otherwise, and assumed it was best for my baby to be in a warmer room. Almost exactly two years later when my son was born, I didn't let him out of my sight and he was wrapped up warmly until the doctors fixed me up. Only then did all three of us go to the recovery ward.

I found out later that misdiagnosed breech occurs in about 30 per cent of all breech babies, and a breech position itself occurs in about 3–4 per cent of all pregnancies. Perhaps unhelpfully, I also looked up all I could find about delivering breech babies in the scientific literature and found a comprehensive review that stated that breech deliveries should not always be carried out via C-section, but that it should be decided on a case-by-case basis. I looked this up because I wanted to understand just how much this decision, and the resulting complications afterwards, were out of my control, or whether I would have had a choice. When I read that breech deliveries are known to be riskier for infants, with a slightly higher fatality risk, I quickly realised it was no choice at all.

However we choose to deliver, or whether the choice is taken away, it's clear that our birth stories can affect us for a long time. Women experience a positive birth when their main expectations are met, one small study found, and, as we know, expectations are rarely met when intervention is needed. Women who had a second baby tended to have more positive experiences as they had changed their expectations from the first time to prevent disappointment. A feeling of being in control was found to be important for a positive birth.

My first experience meant that my second was born via planned C-section, as advised by the lead consultant. It was reassuring to know that despite this intervention and subsequent painful recovery, I knew what to expect this time around.

However, there remains a deeply curious part of me that will always wonder what a vaginal childbirth feels like (aside from painful) and how I would have coped with it. Especially as birth is often seen as an ultimate defining moment of motherhood, as if the pain we go through is some kind of virtuous rite of passage.

This is very unhelpful, considering that about 25 per cent of women in the UK give birth via C-section, 15 per cent of which are emergency. In the US over 30 per cent have C-sections, while in Cyprus the figure reaches 52 per cent. The narrative that a 'natural birth' is what the female body was made for is harmful for those who require intervention. We are not all destined to have a positive birth experience. Birth, in all its messy beauty, is a time when we can lose all control, even more so if any medical intervention is required – and if the idea that 'natural is best' is too heavily emphasised, then women who have assisted deliveries or emergency C-sections sometimes wrongly believe that their own body has let them down, and worse, that it was somehow their fault.

Consider that over 82 per cent of women who experienced vaginal deliveries reported feeling 'extremely' or 'quite a bit' proud of themselves, this dropped to 64.5 per cent for C-sections. Those with unplanned C-sections also felt more disappointed, upset, sad and angry. Over 15 per cent stated they 'felt like a failure', compared to 3 per cent who had vaginal deliveries. In all, those who had unexpected C-sections felt the least positive about their birth.

Though irrational, I felt as though I had somehow cheated my way to an easy birth, even though that was certainly not the case. The frankly ridiculous 'too posh to push' stereotype lingered in my mind. Having a repeat C-section also meant I wasn't able to lift or carry my toddler for six weeks. This only increased her feelings of jealousy for her new baby brother, who was constantly in my arms where she once lay – though this jealousy may have happened anyway.

We've considered how hormonal and brain changes can result in lasting mental health issues. From speaking with psychologists and neuroscientists, it's clear that there are many factors at play, from biological changes to the social support we receive. Perhaps it is precisely because birth is so messy and unpredictable, and that women go into it with a huge range of life experiences, that it can affect our ability to cope. What is clear is that communication, support and compassion are all crucial components for us to process and adapt to one of the most profound experiences new mothers go through, birthing our babies, with all the physically expected, as well as unwelcome, bodily change that comes with it. This, in turn, represents the birth of a mother, our 'matrescence'.

BODILY CHANGE

Will my body ever feel the same again?

It started with my breasts. They were the first pregnancy symptom I felt. They became extremely sensitive and painful when I touched them. They gradually grew bigger, but the sensitivity didn't go away for the full nine months. This happens for many women during pregnancy and, towards the end, your breasts may even start to produce small amounts of milk.

However, the pregnancy boob change is nothing compared to what happens shortly after a baby is born. For the first two to three days after birth, breasts don't produce breast milk yet, but a thick yellow, nutrient-rich substance called colostrum. It's roughly around day three that the 'milk comes in', and you may begin to hear your baby gulping down large mouthfuls of liquid.

For those who are able or choose to breastfeed, your breasts will slowly learn to self-regulate how much your baby needs. It's often a game of supply and demand, but, in the first few weeks or so, breasts don't tend to get it quite right. For some this can mean they don't produce enough, while for others it goes in the opposite direction, as mine did.

I had too much. They became hard, like two round balloons, and looked how I imagined they would if I'd had breast-enlargement surgery. Even my unwieldy breastfeeding bras didn't fit comfortably. If you think this sounds a bit sexy, believe me, it wasn't.

At the same time, the very act of breastfeeding was caus-ing my uterus to contract back to its pre-pregnancy size. When nipples are stimulated by our suckling infants, the hormone oxytocin helps this process along. These painful post-baby contractions, sometimes called afterbirth pains, were yet another change I hadn't anticipated, exacerbated by the pain of surgery recovery. The cramps lasted less than a week, but it takes about six weeks for the uterus to shrink back into size, after expanding slowly for nine months. After my first, I couldn't tell what pain belonged to what process, as I also experienced severe cramps from my intestine returning to its rightful place after its unexpected adventure. This, coupled with C-section recovery, postpartum contrac-tions, and cracked nipples, was an abrupt and painful start to motherhood.

My breasts were so tight and filled with milk that as soon as I even thought about whether or not my baby was hungry, they would start spurting liquid all over the place. The brain–body link was so strong that my baby's cries would also stimulate lactation. The only way I know how to describe this feeling is of a churning sensation, as if a tap had been turned on but water had not quite reached the end of the pipes yet. It was as if my breasts instinctively knew when my baby might be hungry. The same tingling sensa-tion would occur after a few hours had passed and it was time for a feed, or even if I thought about babies or the act of breastfeeding. In those first few weeks my nipples had to get used to constant, hard sucking, which led to painful blisters and bleeding nipples. The initial few seconds after my baby latched were the most painful. I would bite my tongue and bear it, but it slowly became less sore and, eventually, felt natural. The start of motherhood is marked by a colliding world of love and pain, intricately linked.

It became quickly apparent how physically tied I was to my baby when, away for a rare moment on a Saturday morning group run, another runner asked me how motherhood was going, and, before responding, I started to leak. I learnt that in order to prevent this, I should either pump before running (possible, time permitting) or stop thinking about my baby (not easy). Either way, breast pads became a new necessity. In the blur of new motherhood, they were often the last thing on my mind when leaving the house.

Feeding became as intuitive as it was constant. In the dark depths of night-time, when most people were asleep, her cries would wake me and she would easily find my nipple, smelling my milk glands to enable her to take hold. For her it was intuitive, innate, as it should be. A baby's latch is so strong, it is sometimes only possible to remove your infant, mid flow, by inserting your finger into their tiny mouth, so that they release their clasp on you. Otherwise it's literally too painful to separate. Perhaps by design, she was a part of me as her lips clamped firmly around my nipples, until I physically removed her. We were entwined together, day in, day out, a link that clearly provides a baby great comfort. It wasn't unusual for her to fall asleep still attached, and I would struggle to remain awake in those early days. My own self was buried many layers beneath the needs of my baby. A process that started all over again when baby number two arrived.

*

We know our body will change during pregnancy and childbirth – it is as obvious as it is natural. I expected some of these changes and yet our somewhat preachy antenatal classes couldn't quite prepare me for the reality. The advice seemed more of a surreal, worst-scenario type affair than something that would happen to me. For instance, a breast-feeding consultant warned 11 eager mothers-to-be about the possibility of breasts becoming engorged: 'They'll be like a slippery balloon for your baby and your baby won't be able to latch properly.'

If motherhood doesn't feel visceral and prominent enough already, hand-pumping milk to relieve pressure is as reas-suringly grounding as it is surreal. This requires gently massaging the breasts from the outside in until there is a 'let down' and the milk starts to flow. I would need to do this each time my baby had missed a feed from me, which was any time I wanted to organise a few hours away – never quite free of the physical needs of my baby, for good reason. This can become a vicious cycle: the more we pump, the more milk our body produces. One memorable day, two months after Sanne was born, I went to a friend's hen do brunch. I timed it so that I left after a feed and I had pumped enough for the next two feeds that I would be absent for – estimating that I would be back early evening. In order to prevent becoming engorged, I brought my breast pump. Bars don't provide quiet places for pumping or breastfeeding and so I had to excuse myself to the bathroom for 20 minutes to pump milk that I would later have to discard.

The convenience of being a portable meal was worth the effort it took to maintain supply, though this strong bio-logical link to my baby was yet another reminder that my body was serving someone else before myself; a change that occurs immediately after conception. That it can be so painful, difficult and time-consuming means that not everyone chooses to or is able to breastfeed. This is another factor that new mothers are often made to feel guilty about, as if new motherhood isn't already all-consuming enough. In one 2019 survey, half of the 1,162 participants reported feeling guilty about struggling to breastfeed, with one reporting she felt as though feeding formula was like 'giving poison'. The intense pressure to breastfeed is not at all helpful for new mothers, it can make an already hormone-filled, exhausting time even more stressful when things don't go as planned.

The rapid changes during pregnancy and shortly after can have psychological impacts too. In the early weeks or months after a baby is born, many women do not want their breasts to be touched in a sexual way. In fact, the constant closeness with their infants can leave them feeling 'touched out' with little desire to be touched by their partners, mainly because they are so rarely alone. As soon as the baby is asleep, it is time for much-needed personal space. I felt this too; that I was always on, catering to their every single need for over 12 hours a day. When they were finally asleep, sometimes all I wanted was to be alone.

In a qualitative study, women overwhelmingly reported feeling less interested in sex after their baby was born. They reported their breasts changing from sexual to functional. One respondent said: 'They don't add to you being a woman any more, they're just practical ... I suppose they've lost – lost something sexually maybe.' Another stated: 'You feel like someone's mum and not a woman.'

At the same time, the surge in oestrogen experienced during pregnancy drops soon after a baby is born to help stimulate breastmilk, as oestrogen prevents lactation. A drop in this sex hormone can mean that sexual activity often declines too; it can decrease sexual desire and result in vaginal dryness. Breastfeeding women reported a greater reduction in sexual desire compared to non-breastfeeding women, according to a 1996 study looking at 570 women and almost as many of their partners. On average, the participants started to have sex again at about seven weeks after childbirth. The authors noted that 'couples can expect a decline in sexual satisfaction at childbirth and slow recovery during the following year'.

Aside from hormonal changes, it's a time when a woman hardly feels her best, with the sleep deprivation, physically recovering from childbirth and round-the-clock breastfeeding for some. Reduced desire is therefore extremely normal for the first six to seven weeks and, sometimes, months. The reasons are somewhat obvious: tender stiches, tiredness, limited time and just not feeling like it, while some worry they might get pregnant again.

When sexual desire is consistently reduced or non-existent, a woman is said to have female sexual dysfunction (FSD) and some researchers suggest it is extremely common. One 2010 review paper puts the figures as follows:

- 70.6 per cent have postpartum FSD in the first three months after delivery.
- 55.6 per cent during the fourth–sixth month.
- 34.2 per cent at the sixth month.
- 7.17 per cent will never reach pre-pregnancy levels.

Put like this, these figures are exasperating. The term 'female sexual dysfunction' is not at all helpful given the reasons why it occurs – especially so if coupled with unpleasant physical changes such as vaginal damage from severe tearing, haemorrhoids and reduced body satisfaction.

Of course, if a lower sex drive results in limited physical contact for prolonged periods of time, that might adversely affect a relationship, but this is rare. For the rest of us, another label for mothers during this time is not only unhelpful, it is damaging. Pregnancy and childbirth are already highly medicalised. Being given a medical term for a reduced libido is yet another outside authority telling a woman how she is supposed to be, or how far she is from 'normal', backed up with serious-sounding statistics.

If knowledge about the fact there is no one way to be 'normal' post birth was shared between partners more widely, then perhaps not as many women would be considered to have a dysfunctional sex life, rather than being compared to a perceived norm. Every other aspect of life changes after childbirth, meaning relationships are bound to change once a little person enters the scene. Each experience of birth and the aftermath is valid and unique.

A lot of these changes will feel difficult, but that does not automatically mean they should be defined as bad.

When Susan Walzer, a professor of sociology at Skidmore College, interviewed 50 new parents, she at first intended not to ask her participants about sex, feeling there was often too much emphasis on it. That was until many of the mothers voluntarily mentioned their sex lives. Or rather, they spoke of not having sex; how they didn't feel like it and that this made them feel guilty. After this, Walzer routinely asked about it as she realised it was something new parents were fretting over. She noticed that women took the responsibility for the decline, especially as some felt obligated to 'accommodate their husbands sexually'. The reasons women didn't want to have sex were varied and tally with other research: they mentioned tiredness, lower desire and wanting to do other things, like read. One woman stated that as her baby 'needs her all day', all she wanted come evening was some time to herself. 'There's a lot of times I just don't have the desire. And it's not that I don't love him . . . ' she says.

Even though they didn't want to have sex, many women still often thought about the fact that they weren't having it, or that they were somehow neglecting their husbands, a reflection of just how sexualised the female body is. The expectation of what they should have been doing to please their partners weighed heavily on them, and some therefore reported an 'obligation to buck up'.

Growing a human for nine months takes its toll in other ways. Take your pelvic floor. To the uninitiated, these are the group of muscles you use to control your bladder. We are constantly reminded to squeeze them throughout pregnancy to keep them strong. We are told that this could prevent incontinence and even make our sex lives better after childbirth. A growing baby rests there, so, throughout pregnancy, the pelvic floor can weaken. Push a baby out and it can become weaker still, sometimes leading to lasting issues. There's good reason to be wary. In the US, a large study in 2008 involving almost 2,000 women, found that 23.7 per cent had at least one pelvic floor disorder, and 15.7 per cent experienced urinary incontinence.

Almost 3 per cent will suffer from prolapse, where pelvic organs drop down into the vagina, and women can see or feel a bulge. After two vaginal births, women are more likely to need surgery for prolapse compared to women who have never had a vaginal delivery. A 2018 study from Ethiopia of over 3,000 women also found that about one in five experienced at least one pelvic floor issue and one in ten reported prolapse. The figures could be higher, as milder cases often go unreported and therefore untreated.

One acquaintance of mine told me that she cannot hold in her pee for more than a few minutes, meaning she needs to be hyper aware of where the nearest toilet is. Her children are now ten and eight. Others report no longer being able to jump or sneeze without leaking. Even running can be problematic if your bladder is not completely empty before. Though it's extremely common, there is still stigma surrounding pelvic floor disorder, meaning the issue is not addressed as frequently as it could be and many women suffer in silence.

The female body is amazing. Unfortunately, it is all too common to hear women lament about losing their pre-pregnancy bodies, of looser skin, more prominent veins and smaller or misshapen boobs after breastfeeding. These changes are largely perceived as negative.

Women go through nine months of pregnancy and, afterwards, are still held up to the same standards of beauty that our Western, perfection-obsessed society has put on us our whole lives. This has meant that women have unrealistic expectations of how their body will look after childbirth.

In terms of the physical changes during nine months of pregnancy, for many it is the most rapid, alien extension of ourselves. For nine months we are literally a living, breathing vessel, carrying precious cargo whose health is entirely in our hands. It felt alien to hold an ever-growing bump, to feel something kicking, moving, gurgling and rolling inside me. From the outset, many will wonder if this marks the point at which our old body will be lost for ever.

I was obsessed about maintaining my pre-pregnancy

fitness and continued to run and cycle almost throughout my first pregnancy. I competed at a high standard of sports for most of my life. It has therefore always been important to stay and feel physically fit and to push myself to achieve this. At university, some weeks I spent more time in sports clubs than I did studying, obsessively training for a black belt in karate in four years. The worry that pregnancy would 'ruin' my body felt like a looming threat. The idea of controlling that element, of staying 'me', was a way to cling onto the only body I have ever known. Physically I seemed almost the same and though this was in many ways an illusion, it felt comforting to know that exercise could help me feel like myself inside my own skin.

A huge upside of this was that continuing to be active during pregnancy helped me recover from my birth complication and return quickly to my pre-pregnancy size. I watched my body revert with a new sense of awe, as if it hid all that I had been through. I felt a bit guilty that I didn't do much to achieve this afterwards either, attributing it largely to pre-pregnancy fitness, 'good genes' and an unexpected stint in hospital on antibiotics.

But with some distance now, I realise focusing on my old body wasn't a healthy attitude to take. While it was important for me to feel like my 'old self', I was irrevocably changed in ways I am now only beginning to understand. It was a personal goal, yet it was still an aspect of postpartum recovery open to public scrutiny. Comments about how a postpartum body looks, even when they are complimentary, belie an expectation of somehow overcoming the odds. The words 'you look well' take on another meaning. These remarks are largely innocently meant, but they emphasise that the female body is open for judgement. Besides, an element of this is down to pure genetic luck. My mother had a similar experience of 'bouncing back' after all three of her children. It would be untruthful to say I didn't enjoy these compliments (who doesn't?) and they were a confirmation that I was still 'me', but I am aware of how damaging that expectation is in general.

If our bodies become public property during pregnancy, this continues postpartum, too. There is the expectation that pregnancy can change a woman's body, yet at the same time women are congratulated when they have bucked this trend, affirming just how much we are judged for something we have relatively little control over. The latter can be damaging. In a survey of over 2,000 women in the UK, 77 per cent reported being shocked at physical changes after pregnancy and childbirth. Dramatic weight loss by celebrities exacerbated the expectation mothers felt of how their bodies should look. And when that ideal didn't match up to reality, they felt a loss. It's worth keeping in mind that our bodies are all bound to change, but not every body will change in the same way.

Aside from bodily change, I didn't want to live up to any other ideals. Making an effort, putting on make-up or real clothes felt unnecessary at the best of times, especially on the most sleep-deprived days. This meant that beyond obsessively starting to run again, I didn't much care about my appearance – I enjoyed washing my hair less regularly (which is better for it in the long run anyway) and excelled at only getting dressed after lunch time, if wearing leggings and hoodies counts as getting dressed at all.

And that's fine. During pregnancy and the first few months after birth, whether we like it or not, biologically speaking we are there for one main purpose, to nurture a new and totally helpless human being. Beyond unhealthy weight gain, it shouldn't matter if our bodies look a bit different than they did before. Once we are more liberated from the physical bond of pregnancy and breastfeeding, that's when for me it was vital to step back and reconsider that I didn't exist solely for my children. It was the wish of continuing to be there for myself that prompted me to consider the numerous aspects of identity change that I am exploring here. Of course, a crucial bond remains and will do so for life; children will always need an abundance of attention and my mother heart swells when I see their faces, but it was after nine months of breastfeeding that I came to the end of the most energy-consuming physical link.

How a woman's body changes during and after pregnancy is driven by myriad processes. It may be genetic, how physically well they were during pregnancy, any existing health issues, their diet or a blend of all of these. Gaining weight is normal and expected, but only up to a point. In many parts of the world it's a more serious issue – in the US, for instance, about 48 per cent gain too much weight during pregnancy and, as we know, as soon as there is excess weight, it's harder to lose later. This can have adverse effects on children too, such as a high birth weight and increased risk of obesity later in life, simply because they were born to obese mothers. The worry of weight gain is yet another concern for many women at a time when they already have so much to consider mentally and physically.

Although it is far from easy, maintaining healthy habits may be key to holding onto one aspect of our 'pre-pregnancy' selves in a manageable way. There will undoubtedly be bodily change, but if this causes severe weight gain, which impacts upon physical and mental health, then the associated negative adjustment to a woman's identity could endure if the self that is reflected in the mirror is beyond recognition.

Aside from the physical and visible changes, a remarkable emerging finding is that inside this new version of me, other physical shifts were taking place completely hidden from view. My breasts, after breastfeeding two babies for nine months each, are now better protected against breast cancer. We don't yet fully understand why breast cancer is lower for mothers who have breastfed their infants, but countless studies have shown this link. I am also better protected from ovarian cancer.

While the effects of hormones on our behaviour have been studied for several decades, we now know there are other hidden changes too, which we are only beginning to understand. Cells from my children exist inside many of my vital organs as well as my brain. This was shown by the detection of foetal male DNA in mothers. These cells could be key to the protective benefits against some types of cancer. They could also provide clues to why we feel so 'other' at times during motherhood, or why pregnancy is such a psychologically intense time. We literally harbour our children's cells inside of us, running through blood, heart and brain, for life.

That mothers carry their offspring's cells was first hinted at several decades ago, when male foetal cells were found in the mother's blood. Given that only male cells have a Y sex chromosome, while female cells carry two Xs, for simplicity, testing was done for male cells or male DNA. Following this work in 1996, another team showed just how long-lasting they were. Not only were male foetal cells found in women currently pregnant, but also in a woman who had been pregnant 27 years earlier.

When Lee Nelson, a rheumatologist at the Fred Hutchinson Cancer Research Center in Seattle saw this work, she knew she had to investigate further. She phoned the senior author of the paper and suggested they look into the role these cells play in autoimmune diseases, which is where the immune system begins to target some of its own cells. These include rheumatoid arthritis, multiple sclerosis and the lesser-known scleroderma. This was more than just a hunch, she told me 'it was like a light went off'. We know that pregnancy can affect a woman's risk of developing an autoimmune disease or change her experience of it during pregnancy. For instance, rheumatoid arthritis and multiple sclerosis usually improve during pregnancy but flare up again afterwards. Nelson's work suggests that changes like these could be due to our baby's cells that live on in us. Intriguingly, she has also shown a link between scarcity of foetal cells and breast cancer. Looking at 85 women, of which 35 had breast cancer, a study revealed that male foetal DNA was found in higher numbers in the healthy participants than in women with cancer.

This phenomenon has been called 'male microchimerism', and these chimeras carry foreign DNA. The word comes from ancient Greek mythology – a chimera was a monstrous fire-breathing creature described by Homer as a hybrid 'of immortal make, not human, lion-fronted and snake behind, a goat in the middle and snorting out the breath of the terrible flame of bright fire'. Fire-breathing creatures with part goat, part lion bodies may be the stuff of legend, but microchimerism has shown that an abundance of foreign cells live on inside us.

That this occurs in humans remains relatively little understood, but Nelson has since been looking at the significance of these foetal cells. She has written papers with titles such as *The changing maternal self, Your cells are my cells* and *The otherness of self,* and in reading her research it quickly becomes apparent that we are all a collage, or, as she says, we need to shift from thinking of the 'self-versus-other' to understanding that the normal self, as we know it now, is inherently chimeric.

An intriguing discovery by her team was that male DNA was abundantly found in the female brain. It showed that male foetal DNA is able to cross the blood-brain barrier, a barrier that is not absolute and may be more permeable during pregnancy. They studied the brains of 59 women, about half of whom had Alzheimer's disease. Out of this total, 37 of them had male DNA inside their brain tissues, presumably from being pregnant at some point with a male infant.*

This DNA wasn't located in only one area either, but in many parts of the brain.

The male DNA (evidence of male cells) was more prevalent in the disease-free brains, hinting that these cells could protect us against disease. The cells must initially arrive via the placenta before entering into the mother's circulation and then travel to her other tissues. As the 1996 study had suggested, it's a long-lasting change too. One of the eldest women with male DNA was 94 years old.

We cannot definitively conclude what benefits this extra DNA has, but the researchers are sure it must have

---

* All mothers are likely to have both male and female foetal DNA, but it is only the male chromosomes that can be detected as males have a Y and an X chromosome.

'evolutionary significance'. That is, traits which are beneficial have helped our species to survive, and therefore continue. It is telling that those who had this excess DNA were less likely to have Alzheimer's.

But there is something perhaps even more compelling about microchimerism that hints further at its importance in our evolution. It's bidirectional. Just as mothers acquire cells from their children, babies also get cells from their mothers when in the womb. I'm not talking about the normal inherited part of DNA – we all get half our genetic material from our mother and the other half from our father. With microchimerism, we also get a mini dose of the half of our mother's genes that we did not inherit. We now know that women retain these additional cells more effectively than men do. Nelson believes this is no accident, evolution has acted in a way that protects women from autoimmune diseases precisely because when we become mothers, we go on to accept other 'foreign' DNA from our own children. Further, not only do the cells travel from the foetus to the mother and back, but the mother could then potentially transmit her first baby's cells to her second baby, and so on, though this is believed to be rare. We are all, it seems, a mix of many organisms, and some of these could be changing our behaviour and ourselves in subtle ways.

A pregnancy does not need to be carried to term for this invasion to occur, either. Male DNA can be detected in those who have had an abortion or a miscarriage. A 2015 study again concluded that pregnancy was the cause of this foetal DNA. Here the team had a very rare set of subjects: they obtained tissue samples from 26 women who had died during or shortly after pregnancy and found male cells not only in the brain, but numerous organs, including the heart, lungs and kidneys.

Microchimerism shows that the very essence of our children creeps into areas that make us who we are – our brain. Genetically we are not only a product of our mothers and fathers, but of our children too. Although microchimerism could play a role providing protection from breast cancer, there are many unknowns and so the picture remains complicated. Foetal DNA could increase the risk of other cancers, like colon cancer, and foetal cells have also been found in two types of brain tumours, though it is unclear why.

Emerging evidence points to the idea that these cells help the female immune system adapt to tolerating a half foreign organism – a baby. Foetal cells may also promote wound healing – an abundance are found in C-section scars and in breasts and breast milk – so they could help us feed our babies. That these invaders show both positive and negative links is still somewhat mysterious.

Given they are found in breast milk, foetal cells could help the baby get resources it needs even after birth, as a clever trick for the baby to remain 'part' of the mother even when he or she is out. There is even the suggestion that these cells could impact our hormonal and psychological health, working as a sort of insurance policy. That's because when a baby is inside its mother's womb, the baby has some ability to direct resources to itself. But when the baby is out, this immediate control quickly lessens. What better way to maintain an element of this control, than by leaving little parts of itself behind? This could then help the baby hijack some of the maternal hormone pathways to make sure the right chemicals continue to be produced, ones which are important for bonding and lactation. That these foetal cells have persisted throughout our long evolutionary journey means they must be useful; we just don't know the full extent yet.

However we put it, after a child we are forever altered from the inside out, so, naturally, the shift to motherhood feels dramatic. The most obvious physical changes are only a small part of that. Inside of us, mothers are altering and transmitting genetic information to and from their children in lasting ways. As our environment changes our genes too, we are physically no longer ourselves at all. We are a mixture of foreign genes, microbes and viruses, which respond in unexpected ways during the transition to motherhood.

PREGNANT THEN SCREWED

How pregnancy starts to define us

In 1971 in Cleveland USA, a teacher in her early 20s, Jo Carol LaFleur (now Jo Carol Nesset-Sale) was expecting her first child. When she informed the principal, he told her she would need to stop teaching by the time she was four months pregnant, as was the rule for most public school teachers at the time. She was matter-of-factly informed that a pregnant body may embarrass or disgust her young students. Pregnancy was seen as something to be hidden away from the rest of society and a prevailing view at schools like hers was that mothers should be at home to 'take tender care of the babies'.

The head teacher even told her explicitly that had her baby been a tumour growing in her stomach, she would have been able to stay. Promptly, she refused to tell him her actual due date and managed to stay on until she was five months pregnant, only leaving when, finally, the principal deemed her too pregnant and physically barred her from entering her classroom.

Restrictive maternity policies in US schools were the norm. Despite the sexual revolution in the 1960s, Jo Carol's pregnancy was at a time when most rules around the workplace were made by men, often with men in mind. Jo Carol was told to go on unpaid leave and could not return until the term that started three months after the birth of her baby, with no guarantee of the same position. She saw this as needlessly disrupting her students' education. This type of treatment was routine, but she knew it was unreasonable, so she took the school to court while still pregnant. She wanted to set an example to her students to take a stand against discrimination, and that's why she let her 'lone uterus become a battle ground'.

Unfortunately, her case came before a 73-year-old chauvinistic judge, James Connel, described as a crusty and conservative man, who, like many others in the era, held the view that a woman's place was in the home. Judge Connel ruled in the school's favour. One reason cited was that pregnancy was a distraction for the children. Pregnant teachers, he said, 'suffered many indignities as a result of pregnancy, which consisted of children pointing, giggling, laughing and making snide remarks causing interruption and interference with the classroom program of study'. Teaching was also deemed a health risk for the mother and child. The active lifestyle of our hunter-gatherer ancestors, roaming from place to place, outrunning competition, seemed to have been conveniently forgotten.[*]

The reason the judge considered it unsafe for pregnant women to be present at school was reported incidences of violence, overlooking the fact that teachers were not usually targets. He also thought it acceptable to note that 'frequency of urination increases', and that a woman's agility is impaired in the final three months of pregnancy. Jo Carol's

---

[*] Research, in fact, shows that exercise during pregnancy is beneficial for both mother and baby.

legal opposition painted an extremely bleak picture of pregnant women, as if they were weak, subhuman beings who would struggle to walk erect while carrying their books. 'He portrayed us as enormously fragile and incapable of managing a career,' Jo Carol said.

Her lawyer appealed and the case was taken to the Supreme court in 1974 (Cleveland Board of Education v. LaFleur). She won. The court stated that her treatment violated the 14th Amendment to the United States Constitution. Shortly afterwards, all public schools dropped the requirements for women to leave teaching positions while pregnant.

Her legal battle was compounded by her meagre teacher's salary, and court proceedings were only possible after she found a lawyer who would take her case pro bono. 'You needed money to go against power,' she told me. Although women made up the majority of teachers, the head teachers were largely male, as were most of the legal professionals involved in her case.

It made what should have been a wonderful and happy time into an uncomfortable conflict for her.

'But I did not want to go easy into that dark night, and I wasn't going to just lie down and let them treat me without a fight in this cruel manner. And my poor students who were going to lose a teacher. Their education was being disrupted needlessly.'

As pregnancy is such a normal part of life, Jo Carol had not expected this pushback. Most surprising was the view that pregnant women should not work outside the home. It wasn't only men who thought this either. During her case, a mother of six wrote her a provocative letter, stressing that pregnancy should be a time of confinement.

Jo Carol felt victimised by society – mistreated while pregnant and again during court proceedings. While family values were reportedly held in high regard, pregnancy was not. This experience was to have a lasting influence on her. It motivated her to become a lawyer. Now aged 74, she is still practising and continues to represent pro bono women and children who cannot afford legal fees.

While her experience took place several decades ago, some of these outdated views still persist in a way that permeates the policies and attitudes towards pregnancy and motherhood, especially in the US. Decades on, Jo Carol believes that this will not change until we see women in greater positions of power. It should be in society's interest to consider mothers in all areas of policy, given that we are the ones who grow the next generation to term and shoulder the burden of care.

In the UK, a case nearly 30 years after Cleveland Board of Education v. LaFleur, reveals a similar neglect of pregnant women at work. In 1990, Mary Brown worked at the company Rentokil delivering and replacing sanitary bins to businesses. When she became pregnant, she suffered from complications such as bleeding and backache. She obtained a doctor's note and stopped working. The company's sickness policy stated that if an employee was off for more than 26 weeks their contract would be terminated. Long-term illness due to pregnancy was not an exception.

As she did not return to work, Mary lost her job in February 1991, while still pregnant. Her baby was born the following month. As she had been with the company for less than two years, she was not entitled to any maternity benefits. This led her to bring the matter to court several years later as 'sex discrimination' because her condition was linked directly to pregnancy, which had not been taken into account during her dismissal.

Her case was rejected at the time because illness due to

pregnancy was not included in statutory maternity rights. Mary then brought her case to the attention of the House of Lords. It was passed onto the European Court of Justice, which ruled in her favour in 1998 – it was indeed discriminatory on the grounds of sex to dismiss an employee for a pregnancy-related illness, even if their absence from work exceeded a company's sickness policy. Men, after all, cannot get ill from being pregnant, so penalising a female-specific issue was found to be unlawful. The consequences of this case were far-reaching. It set the precedent for similar sex discrimination cases for unfair dismissal during pregnancy. That it took Mary seven years to hear this decision demonstrates how arduous it was to push for a basic human right to be recognised by law.

The difficult victories of Mary Brown and Jo Carol Nesset-Sale might lead us to believe that times have moved on in the decades since then, but sobering cases and statistics continue to come to light. Overt discrimination may be illegal, but evidence suggests it remains common. The title of this chapter exemplifies the problem. Pregnant Then Screwed is, fittingly, also the name of a UK organisation that represents women who have faced discrimination.

In January 2020, Pregnant Then Screwed helped one woman, Helen Larkin, win a legal battle against her previous employer, a beauty company – after she was made redundant at eight months pregnant and was not interviewed for comparable roles. She represented herself and was awarded £17,303 in damages, not a huge sum to account for losing her job, but she didn't do it for the money. 'I only ever asked for what I had lost.' She went through 18 months of stress to make a stand against this kind of discrimination.

The company had actually offered her double the amount

to settle out of court, but the offer came too late and she explained to me that she 'couldn't agree to be silent ... I had seen them treat other people so badly and didn't want them to keep getting away with it.' Helen said that the case cast a 'massive shadow' on her maternity leave, but she was fighting for women everywhere, given the scale of the issue. She had no choice to delay the legal action, as any claim for pregnancy discrimination must be filed within three months, a time limit that disproportionally disadvantages new mothers when they are otherwise occupied with a newborn.

Research by the Equality and Human Rights Commission (EHRC) also brings to light just how often pregnancy discrimination occurs. In their 2018 research findings, the UK-based equality body, whose aim is to 'make Britain fairer', interviewed over 3,000 pregnant women and 3,000 employers to find that:

- About 11 per cent of women faced dismissal or compulsory redundancy while pregnant. Some felt they were mistreated and forced out of their role. The EHRC extrapolate this to say there are about 54,000 cases of discrimination per year.
- One in five experienced harassment or derogatory comments about their pregnancy or working patterns.
- 10 per cent felt unsupported to attend antenatal appointments, even though allowing paid time off for these is a legal requirement.

The EHRC also found that 35 per cent of private employers thought it was reasonable to ask women about their reproductive plans while recruiting, and 59 per cent thought a woman should tell their prospective employer if she was pregnant during recruitment.

Again, this is illegal but it does regularly occur. Of course, the levels of discrimination could be higher than we will ever have true data for, as much of it is implicit. The research from the EHRC is eye-opening, but perhaps not surprising given the many subtle examples I have come across. A friend of mine, who worked for a small health start-up, says she was promised a promotion, but that was revoked when she told her boss that she was pregnant. Though this was overt discrimination, she didn't have the mental energy to take it up with HR and could not face the idea of having to work in such an unsupportive environment. She quit with no maternity rights at all. She felt it was better for her health and that of her baby, not to let the situation become more stressful than it already was. As we know, severe stress during pregnancy can have lasting negative consequences.

Another friend felt forced out of her hands-on client-facing role in a marketing agency when she was denied the ability to work flexibly, despite the company being amenable to the idea of flexible working before she went on leave. She could not pinpoint that her case was discriminatory and yet if a company does not offer parents any flexibility at a time they need it most, it hinders career progression. Meanwhile, Pregnant Then Screwed cites dozens of overt cases of discrimination. Of being sidelined and almost made redundant, one woman wrote that 'the stress and long hours it put me through left me in pieces – I didn't feel I was in a position to challenge anything further ...' Another wrote of a promotion she felt she was due, 'I was patronisingly told my priorities would change and that once I had my baby I wouldn't want the job ... [He] said he discussed the interview with his wife (she doesn't have anything to do with the local authority) and they had agreed my priorities would change.'

Given examples like these, even revealing a pregnancy can

feel challenging, but at the same time, a shifting workplace identity is already in progress, from the emotional to the physical. That is, fatigue, excitement or fear about the upcoming changes, and, professionally, the worry of who may be covering our position. This could in turn lead us to question how our absence may affect our role when we return. All these processes at play have competing demands on our attention and have the potential to cause undue stress. Pregnancy at work is legally protected, but it hasn't been for long, and the legal protection is not enough to prevent discrimination and fewer opportunities to progress.

In the US today, sadly the story is unsurprisingly similar. In the summer of 2019, a pregnant employee at Google wrote a memo about discrimination that was widely shared. It was titled: 'I'm Not Returning to Google After Maternity Leave, and Here is Why'. In it, she details negative comments about her health, how she felt unsupported and that she was not guaranteed a manager-level position upon her return, which would effectively be a demotion. This was despite the fact that Google is one of many tech companies that prides itself on its family-friendly benefits, but, as we have seen, this type of discrimination is pervasive. Often it is subtle, but sometimes it is blatant.

An in-depth investigation in the *New York Times* highlighted that discrimination during pregnancy is 'rampant' inside America's biggest companies. It starts with pregnancy but continues upon returning to work. Getting pregnant is often 'the moment [women] are knocked off the professional ladder'. The authors found that 'many pregnant women have been systematically side-lined in the workplace. They're passed over for promotions and raises. They're fired when they complain.' This inequality often continues during motherhood, as we will explore later.

This kind of environment is damaging. One 2016 study found that highly educated, career-driven women felt their pregnant and work identities were incompatible, especially so in careers with minimal female role models. This mindset led them to conceal their pregnancy for as long as possible and made them feel they 'had to choose between their work and their family'. This self-identity conflict also led to greater stress. The study found that those in careers with other female role models found the identity switch easier to manage because they had seen pregnant colleagues cope well previously. In spaces designed for males, pregnancy is an embodied and physical invasion of the norm of this 'male territory', scholars have suggested. That's why women often feel they have to blend in with male norms in male spaces, which is obviously impossible when pregnant, while others see it as losing physical control of your own body. During this time, as one researcher succinctly noted, women are 'open, vulnerable and leaky' – literally, with regards to sickness and later on, urine and maybe even leaking breasts. This type of negative perception of pregnancy in the workplace leads to a culture of secrecy around it, especially as pregnancy is often associated with sickness, therefore unpredictability and in some cases even shame and disgust.

Pregnancy at work needs to be normalised because when it's not, or when we hesitate to share the news because we fear how it will be received, it can be the start of an enduring conflict between home life and work.

*

When to go on maternity leave is not just a question of choice, but of cultural expectations, policy and biology. In countries like the Netherlands and France, mothers are required to stop working four to six weeks before their due date, whereas in the US and UK many work until their due date. Doing so could make for an uncomfortable commute, but taking leave earlier means there is less time after the baby comes. I wanted to work right up until the last minute but, in truth, the last few weeks were physically draining; I simply pretended otherwise.

For my first maternity leave I stopped two weeks before my due date, wrongly assuming she might be late. She was a week early, so I only had one week to attempt rest while preparing for her arrival. Our second was conveniently scheduled 11 days before my due date, so I knew exactly when to expect him. Although in the end I only had three days off before he came, as I had given notice before I knew he would be early.

In the US it's policy that largely defines the 'choice' of how long to work for, given the lack of universal paid leave. In fact, one in four women go back to work ten days after their baby is born, according to the campaign PL+US. Women on low pay with little job security, often affecting more ethnic minorities, tend to have the least access to paid leave.

The amount of paid parental or maternity leave varies enormously from country to country, with far-reaching consequences for the wellbeing of mothers and their children. A 2019 report, compiled by Unicef, ranked the top 41 European and OECD countries to find that Sweden, Norway, Iceland, Estonia and Portugal had the most family-friendly policies while Switzerland, Greece, Cyprus, the UK, Ireland and the US ranked the worst, with the US coming bottom. The US was the only country featured which offered no universal paid leave for mothers or fathers. Fewer than half these countries provided six months of paid maternity leave. The average was about 18 weeks in OECD countries and 22 weeks in the EU. The aim of the report, which considered access to affordable childcare as well as parental leave, was to highlight the many benefits of family-friendly support and concluded that it makes families less stressed and society better, something apparently not yet obvious to some policymakers.

In the UK, the idea of maternity leave itself only started with some basic rights during the start of the 1900s, but most women stayed at home. It took the Second World War for the nation to realise that the workforce needed women but that working mothers required solutions for childcare. This led to over 1,000 nurseries being opened after 1941. Though women were needed at work, being pregnant at work was still deemed abnormal, making it routine for businesses to dismiss a pregnant employee. It wasn't until the 1970s that the UK introduced maternity leave similar to what it is today, gradually increasing the benefits received. We took a while to get here, though it is not yet enough. Even with legal protection, there are still plenty of discriminatory cases.

Today UK mothers are entitled to 52 weeks off. This sounds generous but only the first six weeks are paid at 90 per cent of average pay, and after that at a rate of £151.20 per week for the next 33 weeks. While many larger companies top this up to provide full pay for longer, this is not a legal obligation.

Unless notice is given to return earlier, the employer assumes a full year will be taken. It can be shared with partners and divided however they choose, though take-up among fathers is extremely low, currently hovering at the 2 per cent mark. This is due to a combination of factors, largely financial. Beyond statutory pay, fathers are not generally paid their full salary when on leave, and, on average, men are the higher earners, so the policy leaves little in the way of encouragement for actual change for who takes the most leave. For many couples, it would therefore not be afford-able for the father to take much, if any, paternity leave. The maternity benefits on offer do not help everyone either. Over a quarter of women are not eligible for any statutory pay, due to being self-employed or not employed for the required length of time.

Like the UK, the concept of maternity leave in the US has only gradually come into existence, and it is the only rich country in the world with no mandated maternity pay. As elsewhere in the world, there was no need for it over a century ago, as women rarely worked. Working patterns changed during the First World War when the government even created a marketing campaign to show the value of women in the workforce. The slogan read: 'The Greatest Mother in the World', depicting a nurse carrying a wounded soldier as if an infant. Women were needed, but even when encouraged to work, they were seen and marketed as mothers first.

Today, federal law allows women to take 12 weeks unpaid leave and return to their jobs, but those who cannot afford to live without pay have no option but to go back early or use as much sick and holiday leave as they can. This law is also only for companies with 50 or more employees.

Many larger companies do offer their staff paid leave, but this is typically in higher-income roles where women are already in a better financial situation to start with. It is those who could benefit most from maternity pay that have the least access to it, often disproportionately affecting women of colour, who are statistically more likely to be lower-income workers. It's no wonder the US comes bottom of the aforementioned Unicef list when it comes to family-friendly policies.

In my country of birth, the story differs too. I visit the Netherlands often to see family and friends. I'm the only one in my extended family of 14 aunts and uncles and over 30 cousins who lives abroad. Before I had a baby, I had no idea what the policy was for maternity leave in the Netherlands. I was surprised and slightly disappointed that a country that is regarded as progressive in many areas only has 16 weeks maternity leave. It is paid, which is a good thing, but only 10–12 of these weeks is postpartum, with four to six weeks taken before. Some will accrue holiday or request unpaid leave to lengthen the time, but it is rare to be able to take more than four months off.

Given that the majority of women in the UK take nine to twelve months, it seems a short time to spend with a small baby before going back to work. This perception is in part due to my cultural conditioning, as to US friends this seems like a luxury. When I mentioned my surprise at how 'short' this was to a family friend, she said it was ideal for her. She had three months to bond with her baby and was then able to go back to a job she loved, with minimal disruption. One of my aunts chose to only take two weeks with each of her two kids and was also glad to be back in the office. This made me wonder that perhaps the shorter maternity policy in the Netherlands is in place precisely because the country has equality built into its very nature. If women aren't out of the workforce for too long, they are less likely to have a skills gap on returning.

The support new mothers get in the Netherlands is exceptional, and usually covered by health insurance. For one week, women get what's called *'kraamhulp'* in the form of a special maternity nurse who comes to the family home for support, be that checking stitches, breastfeeding tips and looking over the baby. The nurse will do the laundry and serve any arriving guests with drinks and a very traditional treat, *'beschuit met muisjes'*, crackers spread with aniseed sprinkles. This sounds strange to the uninitiated, but it is routine when a new baby is born, and yes, these sprinkles are gendered – pink for girls, blue for boys. Receiving guests soon after the birth is normal, expected even. In some cases mere hours after the birth, made easier due to a high number of home births. Visiting a newborn even has a special name, *'kraambezoek'*, which means 'maternity visit'.

If there is a best place to be on maternity leave, many would point to the Nordic countries. Take Sweden, where parents are allocated a staggering 480 days – roughly 16 months of leave – with most of that at 80 per cent pay, though this is capped. This can be shared between parents, with three months set aside for the fathers, and three for mothers, in a use-it-or-lose-it approach.

In Sweden, paternity leave is paid. This works – within a generation it has become normal for men to take it. There have been other hidden upsides too. Parental leave is not only more socially accepted, it is expected. This has a subtle trickle-down effect where dads who take parental leave become more involved in daily tasks involving their children, and these same involved dads have been shown to do more equal amounts of childcare at other times, too, even nine months later. Similar findings have been shown in Spain, where the introduction of only two weeks of paternity leave resulted in men doing more later on too. Such policies could even make for happier marriages – in Canada, extended parental leave for men led to more equal parenting and, in turn, a lower divorce rate. Sharing the load literally helped save marriages.

Another upside has been discovered – for every month of paternity leave taken by Swedish men, women's earnings increased by 7 per cent. Like Sweden, Iceland has also seen more men taking up parental leave, where three months is set aside for fathers. It's no coincidence that Iceland also has many women in high-powered private-sector roles and is highest among the Nordic countries in the Global Gender Gap Index. In February 2020, to much fanfare, Finland joined its Nordic neighbours in upping its parental leave policies – with men granted the same amount of parental leave as women. Crucially, they also rebranded it from 'maternity' leave to parental leave, an important step away from thinking about this leave as mainly for women. This very policy was implemented under a female prime minister in a female-led coalition government.

Overall these kinds of changes can clearly inspire wider social change. It's telling that when given the statement: 'When jobs are scarce, men should have more rights to a job than women', Swedish respondents were most likely to disagree in 1995–1999 and saw a marginal decrease when asked again between 2010 and 2014 (90 per cent and 93 per cent disagreed). In other words, even in 1995 the idea of equality was already there. Japan, which scored very low for disagreement, saw minimal differences –18 and then 14 per cent disagreed in these respective timepoints, which rose to 27 per cent in the 2017–2020 survey. Worryingly, four in ten people in developing countries agreed with this statement, with research showing that when this attitude persists it reduces women's employment rates. (Today 89 per cent in Egypt agree compared to 5 per cent in the US.)

Even if generous parental leave exists for men, cultural norms can prevent them from taking it. In Japan both men and women are able to take a year of partially paid parental leave, but men rarely do, largely due to social pressures and gendered norms. It was about 3 per cent in 2015, increasing to 6 per cent in 2019. In Japan, devotion to your job is expected and valued, and the idea of men taking parental leave clashes with that.

In early 2020 when a government minister, Shinjiro Koizumi, announced he would be taking *two weeks* of paternity leave, it was applauded. It was so out of the ordinary that it was covered by the local and national press. There are reports that men who take leave have been sidelined as a consequence. It's not that men don't want to, but they feel pressured not to by perceived workplace norms, according to a study looking into the issue. As you might expect, the gender pay gap is high – at about 25.9 per cent. This is a problem, given that the birth rate is below replacement rate as women are putting off having families due to the cost of childcare, a precarious economy as well as gender inequality at work. If generous parental leave was set up to counter Japan's ageing population, it won't be successful until workplace cultures change.

We've considered different options offered in various countries, but is there an optimum amount of maternity leave that gives a mother adequate quality time for her baby but doesn't leave her feeling too disconnected from her workplace? Too long and it can increase the gender pay gap, too short and it can increase mental health problems.

It turns out Michelle Budig from the University of Massachusetts-Amherst has put a figure on it. In her research she looked at leave taken and the size of the motherhood penalty, a term sociologists have coined to describe the negative impacts on career and earnings identified as soon as women become mothers. One 2014 report highlighted that after each child a mother's hourly wage drops, while the father's increases. Budig's research, spanning over 15 years, has shown that there is a 'wage penalty' of motherhood of 4 per cent per child, which naturally continues to widen the gender pay gap. However, she found that taking just under a year of leave led to the smallest motherhood penalty, which she refers to as the 'sweet spot'.

This tallies with the finding that separation anxiety, which affects many mothers, eases at about eight months for women who are career orientated, and several months longer for those who would have preferred to stay home.

Longer leave can seem appealing at first. In parts of Germany, where three years family leave is allowed and especially in West Germany, where historically the social pressure to stay home was high, it's common for women to stay home for the first few years of their child's life. If they have more than one child in quick succession, then this can take them out of the workforce for several years. After several years away, skills can get rusty, which can effectively push women out of the competitive workforce. When they do return to work, it is invariably part time and on lower pay, and so the gender pay gap not only persists, but widens. On average, mothers only earn about 45 per cent of their pre-pregnancy pay seven years after their first baby is born. A working mother in West Germany can expect her earnings to halve.

In East Germany, before the two sides were unified over three decades ago, working after childbirth was encouraged, and female employment rate was among the highest in Europe. Housewives were dubbed parasites, *'Schmarotzer'*, and there was abundant childcare available. Policy and cultural norms made it difficult and undesirable to stay at home, whereas in West Germany it was difficult to even find suitable childcare for children under three, meaning working before then was rarely an option. Women who return to work early or, in the past, those who worked at all, have been called *'Rabenmutter'* meaning 'raven mothers' – they were literally compared to a bird leaving her nest full of hungry children.

Still today these cultural differences persist, but, interestingly, women who move from West to East adopt the shorter leave. So too do Western mothers when they are exposed to women from East Germany who move into their workplace: both are then more likely to go back to work earlier. This exposure to other working mothers was enough to influence change, and quickly, a 2020 paper found. That is, mothers from the East behave as they historically have but mothers from the West, who typically took several years out or left work altogether, are now adopting more Eastern-style working practices. The implication here is that egalitarian attitudes we are exposed to growing up are powerful, even when women move to more traditionally minded areas as in West Germany. The positive thing to note is that exposure to egalitarian attitudes can accelerate cultural change.

Aside from workplace norms, stereotypes or social expectations, the length of maternity leave has implications for mental health too. In one study of over 570 women returning to work after a baby, women who took short leave, defined as about six weeks or less, were more prone to depression and marital problems. Four months after their baby was born, women who were working full time were more likely to have higher levels of anxiety while paid leave has significant mental health benefits both at the time and much later in life. Research also shows that when family leave is mandated by law, it is more accepted and less stigmatised for women to take it.

Despite the acknowledgement of a sweet spot, simply having a child is still enough to be victim of a lasting motherhood penalty that starts in earnest after women have children.

It is clear that new mothers are faced with a complicated backdrop of policies to consider while embarking on perhaps one of the biggest life changes they will undergo. They are confronted with the prospect of reduced earnings when off and, upon returning, a large proportion of their pay will go to childcare. Time out of the workplace doesn't just impact on pay or career progression, but as one 2012 review of parental leave and pay noted, will continue to 'promote outdated stereotypes and inhibit men and women from partaking in the work and home life on equal terms'. That is, as soon as women become mothers, they begin to experience a more gendered division of family life, which I will come back to throughout this book.

The problem with seemingly progressive family leave policies is that, on the face of it, they appear to go some way to addressing gender equality, but they can actually penalise women even more when they come back to work. This has not been solved with policies like those we have in the UK, where men and women can share parental leave, because, as we saw, the take-up for men is extremely low. This further emphasises their role as breadwinners and women as primary carers.

Looking at it this way, maternity leave policies – even progressive ones – can actually perpetuate parental gender stereotypes even more. Generous paid maternity leave puts women at home for longer, when a solution could be better subsidised, high-quality childcare of the kind we see in many European countries, such as Sweden and the Netherlands. This would enable women to come back into the workforce more easily without the extra burden of debilitating childcare costs.

Parental leave is still largely taken by women, even where it can be shared. We can only hope that more countries will put the onus on men to take leave, which we know can help to improve gender equality. If both sexes are expected to have similar career gaps for childcare, hiring women would not be seen as such a liability. This will take time, as stereotypes and workplace norms are very slow to change. Unfortunately, here in the UK, unless we see a radical shift in paid paternity leave, it means we won't be seeing an influx of British dads at baby groups any time soon.

There is one important caveat. Of course many women want to take maternity leave and, physically, often need to when recovering from difficult births. While this may be true for the earliest months, there's no reason it all needs to fall to the mothers – many fathers report wanting to take more time too. If it is a choice between men or women, we expect it to be us as we nurture the babies inside us for nine months after all. But gendered expectations play a powerful role too, making it difficult to separate choice from social conditioning. Cultural norms shape our behaviour and desires. If norms and policies were changed, fathers might well take more time off than they currently do, as is the case in Sweden.

Some of us embrace maternity leave while others find it a challenging change. Most have little time to think about it too deeply given how time-consuming taking care of a baby is.

This is compounded by a societal infrastructure that means when we're off, we're completely off, and when we're at work, the children are in childcare for long days, in our case ten hours a day once you factor in commuting time. Our work and home life are like two separate worlds, two identities, rarely meeting. Whatever choice we make comes at the cost of the other. Returning to work 'early' means missing time with our children, but staying away for a long time has a knock-on impact on our careers.

While there is no simple solution, as we saw in Sweden and Iceland, the use-it-or-lose-it approach for men to take leave does have positive consequences, in that it can help change societal norms and expectations of what roles the mother and father have when it comes to parenting and the division of childcare. Unfortunately this doesn't mean it changes gendered norms completely, or quickly enough. As an article in the *Guardian* put it in 2019, Sweden's generous leave policy still ties women to the home. Even though much of parental leave on offer can be split, women take most of it, which reinforces the idea of women as main carers. A report in the *Nordic Labour Journal* states that this is due to a combination of two factors: traditional gender norms, and the expectations and pressure that businesses put on fathers to use only their allotted quota and no more.

This shows that even a renewed focus on paternity leave

does little to change that. Take Italy, where men may be expected to take some paternity leave but it is only five days and must coincide with when the woman is also on her maternity leave. In the Netherlands too, the leave for fathers has historically been absurdly low; men only got three days leave until 2019, when it was increased to five days, but had to be taken in the first four weeks (so never alone with the baby, that part is left to the mothers). This was increased in July 2020 to an additional five weeks to be taken in the first six months.

It's a start, but until men have choices with the same financial benefits, and societal expectations to match, equal parenting will be difficult to reach. Without this it will remain a constrained 'choice' within the parameters available.

5

ON MATERNITY LEAVE AND ENTERING A NEW WORLD

The wheels on the bus go round and round and round again

April, 2017 – Sanne

I try to cast my mind back to the day before and the day after becoming a mother. The truth is that the first few months passed in such a haze that I cannot pinpoint the time that I became Melissa the mother, versus Melissa a pregnant 30-year-old, versus Melissa pre-children. They all somehow fit, but equally they are all different sides of the same coin, an enchanted coin with more than two faces.

Before she was born, I recall being both surprised and intrigued by my growing belly. Physically it felt more real by the day, but mentally the idea that I would soon be a 'mum' felt huge, unreal, impossible.

As many parents have voiced before, the reality felt otherworldly at first. We left the hospital after only one night. How could they possibly let us take her home? Where was the instruction manual? Is she really ours? It was a blur of exhausted delight. We made this tiny, helpless creature. She was part of me, and now she's herself.

And just like that we are three.

The mind on maternity leave and the foggy feeling of this new world is like nothing I have experienced before, or since. Our self becomes fragmented in both subtle and overt ways.

It's when the changes of our new role as mothers feel most raw – physically and, for some, emotionally. Our bodies, lives and identities need time to recognise and shift into this new identity, both for ourselves and for the friends we surround ourselves with, new and old.

Some of us cannot quite mould our competing identities together. Of 'the break between mother and self' the author Rachel Cusk voices what I have also felt, that: 'even in my best moments, I never feel myself to have progressed beyond this division, I merely learn to legislate for two states, and to secure the border between them'. The experience differs for us all. I still find it peculiar to be labelled 'mum', but others I have spoken to are most proud of their mother identity, that it comes first, that it is a welcome and positive new self.

The first year of motherhood is when our new identity truly begins to take a firmer hold. Exactly when this happens differs between individuals, but the combination of social, physical and emotional changes that start in pregnancy are cemented during the so-called fourth trimester.

The earliest moments with our newborns are quickly forgotten, especially as the time is so intense and our memory is impaired when sleep-deprived. What's clear is that there is often a reported discrepancy between what we believe motherhood will be like, and how we experience it. We are told countless times how little sleep we'll get, but it's hard to know what this brain haze feels like day to day until it happens. It's perhaps why some new mothers who are not depressed still show many similar negative feelings also found among depressed mothers, revealing that negative thoughts are not only common, they are normal. These include feeling the need to be perfect and worrying that their baby might die. Over half the mothers surveyed believed their lives should be 'centred wholly on their infant'.

After navigating when to go on maternity leave and how long for, then coming to terms with the idea that we have no choice but to ignore the 'real world' for a while, I found that it was surprisingly simple and much needed.

It's easier to momentarily forget about work than to worry about what we are missing – focusing on what we cannot control is futile. Aside from that, caring for a small human or two without getting much sleep leaves little mental power left over to worry about the parts of our lives that temporarily fade into the distance.

May 2019 – Arjen

In hindsight, pregnancy the second time around is barely something I notice passing. The physical constraints are worse, walking and standing feel uncomfortable early on; I cannot run after 21 weeks, but managed to 35 with Sanne.

I always feel as though I need to pee, even just after I've been. Nights are torture, knowing I will be woken early, and my old foe insomnia prevents me getting the rest I need.

Time appears to speed up, given how busy life is already. Aches and pains feel worse and the sense of incongruity to be doing this a second time feels even stronger. I feel extremely vulnerable, but I simply don't have much mental energy to reflect on it this time around. It's more of an uncomfortable fuzzy ache in my body and brain.

'Again? That was quick,' is the response of an estranged friend. A two-year gap is common, but it seems very much like I have only just had a baby. That perception is clearly felt by others too. It shouldn't matter what others think, and yet those split-second assumptions that we cannot undo show the sense of how much motherhood is steeped in expectation and judgement. Reproductive decisions are fair game for scrutiny.

There's no handbook, there's no prescriptive gap or the right number of children we need to abide by. And yet society is always watching, quietly judging. Damn.

We are four.

I've discussed the various differences of maternity leave policies, but what about the day-to-day reality of what we actually do and how we change? While the length of maternity leave varies from country to country, in the UK the assumption is a year, and many take it if they can afford to. I was determined to only take six months the first time. This seemed luxurious compared to friends in the Netherlands. To those in the UK it was greeted with slight surprise that I was going back so 'soon'. For me it felt like a happy medium, capturing the best of both worlds. I worried that being away from work for an entire year would hold me back.

After recovery from surgery, the first few months of maternity leave were actually among the most social of the previous year, having the prospect of 11 local mothers to meet up with, all experiencing the strangeness of life with a newborn. The type of conversations I had with other mums were unique too. Going through childbirth leaves little time for inhibitions and this sense of openness continues.

Given the extent of the physical and emotional changes we experience, it's only natural that we feel different too. The changes are most apparent and raw during maternity leave, a time when there's little space left, physically or mentally, for ourselves.

Aspects of the changing body, worries and fears tend to be more openly discussed from the outset. Mothers who barely know each other will routinely consider intimate details of their birth stories, pains and worries, in a way that would feel like it was overstepping boundaries in any other time of life. Experiences like sharing the shock of a month of bleeding after childbirth, or that our period can stop altogether for months and months if we are breastfeeding. The body becomes functional, and so does conversation around it. Discussions in the early hours were normal, there was always someone else awake. There was always a worry, a concern, a milestone. Every day was much the same but often something *felt* new. Take, for example, anxieties:

The strangest worries occasionally pop up in my head. When my tiny month-old baby was lying on the mat before her bath, I worried I might step on her, squash her. I later dreamt we were on the highest rickety metal steps and she fell out of her buggy into the void, and in my dream I had no other option but to tumble after her, because how could I go on living if she was gone? Before she was born, I dreamt of a hole in my stomach where she popped out to say hello, and I had to push her back in.

With hindsight this sounds like a strange premonition but, in reality, it's likely that it was simply my subconscious mind playing out a strange form of a fairly expected scenario of a C-section.

Outside, my mind regularly jumps to what might be dangerous. Roads, cars, bikes, falls. It's like my evolutionary desire to protect goes into overdrive, spotting each routine obstacle as a potential for danger. My mother told me she felt the same when we were near water or stairs, always imagining the worst. I got used to it, came to expect it. It's mostly good to spot potential dangers, but it's a nuisance when the thoughts creep in during routine events.

Except of course for that first fall, that first graze, the howl. I can't protect against everything. It's a whole new world.

Friendship is vital at the best and worst of times, and it's clear that mum friends can provide a special kind of connection for open discussions. I wouldn't want to burden other friends with the unique strangeness of new motherhood – like when I had to massage milk out of my breasts to relieve the pressure, or how some days I couldn't achieve much at all, as Sanne would barely stop crying unless I was on my feet with her in my arms, and I would prepare food with her attached to me in a sling.

A 2010 study looking at the importance of friendship groups that form during mother-and-baby classes, agreed that these connections do not 'conform to the usual parameters of friendship formation', and that social support during this time is extremely important for new mothers. Friends can help us to establish our new identity in a positive manner, helping us find 'an equilibrium of who I am', in order to form a positive and secure identity, the report noted. That's because it is reassuring to hear others go through similar experiences, which, in turn, helps support mental wellbeing. Without friendships, motherhood may otherwise fail to become normalised.

The caveat is that, beyond having a baby in common, if there is little else, these friendships do not necessarily last. This was apparent at some of the mother-and-baby groups I found myself in, where the expectation seemed to be of immediate bonds with otherwise strangers, simply because we had lots of baby-related anecdotes to share. The horror of nursery rhyme singing and clapping in a circle was too much; an alter theatrical reality. I rarely returned a second time, guiltily enjoying time with just my baby. If she had lapped it up maybe it would have been a different story, but she looked as baffled by the whole affair as I was.

Many good friends of mine now also happen to be mothers, and we have formed even closer bonds since, but it was talking about babies with strangers that felt uncomfortable and was something I actively avoided. Social comparisons seemed to be heightened: *How does your baby sleep, how often does she nap, are you following a routine?* For the first few months I sought it out, but once the shock of my new reality ebbed away, it no longer felt necessary.

A womb, a uterus and a baby, we all had that in common. In other circles, having only our sex as the main basis of a friendship would be jarring. There was always plenty to discuss, but it quickly became repetitive.

The thing is, the first time around I didn't really feel like a mother yet, so the deeper I delved into that world, when all we talked about was the baby, the harder it was to claw back aspects of the pre-motherhood me that felt important. I yearned for more than conversations around sleep patterns, dirty nappies, weaning and breast milk. It felt unsatisfying, tiring and all-consuming.

This may sound selfish, but forgetting ourselves to prioritise only our infants actually has a tangible downside. Naturally our baby's most immediate needs must come first – their crying literally makes us stressed for good reason, so we do our utmost to stop it. But if we exist only for them, and by doing so create idealistic goals for ourselves, we are more likely to fail to reach these unachievable goals. We know that when new mothers have unrealistic expectations, it's harder for them to adjust to their new roles as mothers.

During my second maternity leave, the first two months passed in a blur. I must confess that I enjoyed not having to get dressed in normal clothes at any decent hour, if at all, or take the baby to classes. The pressing need to discuss every change was unique to my first time, and I actively avoided meet-ups with anyone new.

In one moment of desperation I took a pair of scissors to my ponytail and chopped three inches off, then carefully tidied the ends as best I could. I did not have time to organise a hair appointment and the length of my hair was becoming unmanageable. I reasoned that I would get it properly cut before I 're-emerged' into society.

Surprisingly, it looked quite good – that or there was the very real possibility I had lost the ability to be objective. I share this experience because it shows how far removed we can become from reality during maternity leave and how low on the priority list my physical appearance was. I even hesitated whether or not I should tell my husband, ironic perhaps as I have now written this down for all to see.

Besides, every spare, precious minute I got, I either slept or spent it writing, in part because I felt like my brain needed more stimulation. I wanted to prove, if only to myself, that my ambition remained. I knew that this was illogical – why should I need to be more, when being a mother is overwhelming enough? It was as if I needed an additional validation that I was still a writer, a journalist, a functioning member of society, albeit on the fringes and with a baby in tow.

This paradox of mothers feeling like less, and thereby doing more isn't just an isolated feeling of my own: it is reflected in research that shows that mothers who come back to work feel they are taken less seriously and that they need to re-establish themselves as good employees. Similarly, professional women find the transition to motherhood more difficult because they experience conflict between their status and expectations as a mother and their professional role.

Further, how mothers see themselves is related to their own upbringing, their career motivations and pregnancy history. In one study, women indicated that their own mothers' employment status influenced how they saw themselves as working mothers with 'multiple possible selves'.

I used to envy others who couldn't wait to leave work and go on maternity leave, who could relish the simpler (though intense) moments and not feel compelled to chase other goals. To be more present and in the moment and not be concerned with what they are missing.

Feeling lonely and isolated as a new mother is common – overwhelmingly so for those with babies born during Covid-19 lockdowns. Isolation can be devastating for mental health. It can result in depression as well as developing 'distorted standards about the self and others', a 2019 study found. The clash between expectations and the reality of a mother's identity plays a key role in this.

For many, maternity leave should be a social time, but there's truth in the parody of leaving the new 'mum friends' we made behind when we go back to work. There's a scene in the UK comedy TV show *Catastrophe*, where the lead character, played by Sharon Horgan, is on leave with her second baby in casual clothes, and walks past her 'mum bestie' dressed in smart office attire. There's a friendly though awkward conversation but it's immediately obvious they are now operating in different, incompatible worlds. That these two worlds are such stark opposites is exactly why an identity shift feels stronger.

There's a reason it can feel difficult to retain contact with the new people we meet on maternity leave. Several decades ago the British scholar Robin Dunbar suggested that there are only so many friends we can keep mental tabs on at any given time: about 15 who we might reach out to and be in regular contact with, but only five in our inner circle. This is out of a total of 150 friends in our wider social circles, who we would be happy to have a drink with if we met them in a bar. If new friends come to replace those, it can be hard to mentally maintain more friendships without losing others. I didn't want to be the type of person who lost contact with my old friends, which can easily happen given shifting time schedules and a loss of the freedom to go out in the evening, especially hard for me when breastfeeding and sleep-deprived. I reached out to my core group of friends as much as I could but changing lifestyles, the sprawling enormity of London and our busy schedules made this difficult.

Once, when a good university friend came to visit, I felt torn between how she used to know me, carefree and spontaneous, and my new child-centred world of set bed, bath and dinner times. She brought a bottle of champagne and I felt caught between wanting to celebrate with her and crawling into bed to sleep after yet another disturbed night. She would have understood, but I didn't want to let either of us down. It was as if simply by being a parent, these two sides of myself could not easily co-exist. To set the scene, here's how countless nights went.

Arjen is waking up, on average, eight times a night. I know this because my fitness tracker tells me so. The night feels like an enemy, a dark, unwelcome and unpredictable stranger. The day refreshes the slate and I remain hopelessly optimistic that the next night will be better. For two agonising months, it isn't. My existence feels blurry, like a cloudy mirror, never sure who is looking back. It's a nice feeling at times when the days pass with a natural rhythm of not doing much at all. Stephen sleeps in the baby's room. I feed Arjen several times a night, it's what gets him back to sleep quickest, a bad habit perhaps, but rationality and strategy – if such a thing exists with babies – have disappeared. Nap times become my new saviour. Sometimes the toddler is at childcare, but sometimes she's with us. I dread a day alone with the two of them, unable to enjoy the highs, while the lows, the tantrums, tired howls, feel relentless. How is that so? I am their mother. Crying is normal, so why does it bring such a rush of cortisol to my brain? And yet I am the solution, I must always serve, solve, comfort, fix.

It's cruel that we value sleep most when it's least within our control. I try not to rebut anyone else who tells me they are tired because they went to bed late. I can barely go to bed early enough as it is. Going to bed any earlier would mean forgoing eating.

It is temporary, it is a phase, we'll be out of it soon. I

remember how much I love them, I remember how much
I love sleep, I remember they need me. I exist for them, for
a moment, I am them.

In the end I stayed up with my friend and we toasted to
our respective successes and I felt much more human for
it, more like me. The lesson for me was that if a friendship
has a good foundation, it doesn't matter if either one of us
has experienced a big life change. The same rules of shared
experiences, empathy and common worries apply. They may
not entirely relate to a world that is so consumed by a new
baby, but, equally, they will understand that mine is. Time
with good friends was vital for me to feel as though I could
crawl back into my own skin.

Becoming a mother does change our lives a lot, but our
new status doesn't have to fully replace our old selves. It's
common for people to lose friendships once children enter
the equation. But connecting to our old friends, whether
they are parents or not, can allow us to re-establish parts of
ourselves that still exist somewhere, but have to be dragged
to the forefront, gently at first.

There's no easy solution, but, for me, the closest friendships
that lasted were the ones that had deep roots before, regardless of whether we had children in common. Meet-ups remain
harder, but children were not the basis or barrier of these
friendships. And, anyway, our friends care about us, so they
care about our family too. It shouldn't have to be either or.

For working mums, maternity leave is perhaps the first time
in a women's career when they have to truly 'let go' of their
former selves, which can have some unintended effects on

how they feel they fit into society. At first, the time 'off' feels like it will be endless, but on reflection it is but a passing snippet that ends abruptly. As we have explored, workplace identity can already begin to change during pregnancy, internally and from external forces, but it is only once the baby arrives that a new mother can truly begin to reflect on the experience she is living. Or, more accurately, the days can pass in a sleep-deprived haze, so it's not so much reflection, as dramatically living this change. Any routine as we knew it before is flipped on its head.

For me this meant I slept when I could, rarely got dressed into proper clothes, especially in the first few months as both babies drank so voraciously that they were often throwing some back up, usually over me. It was as if this milky overflow was their way of leaving a physical mark on me. At the time of writing, my second is now eight months old, but already I see myself as very different to the person I was only a few months ago, having now just started back at work. A few months ago, she rarely slept more than two consecutive hours, I sleep a bit more now. She didn't speak to many people during the week, I spend my whole week having adult conversations.

My life as a mother of two already seems so far away from her, two years ago, who was only a mother of one. Those days felt hard, but I now smile at her in sympathy, knowing now the added chaos with two. But equally, the first time is when the journey into motherhood feels much more abrupt. The mental energy spent worrying about each new development, red rash, fever or fall was more intense. Having two means time divided, never quite giving one child enough but of feeling like I have to give each of them everything all at once.

I'm writing this chapter as if I have several selves, because that's how it can feel. The self that went into hospital pregnant, and came out with a newborn, feels like a different person than the self today, with a baby growing almost noticeably bigger every day; as if when I don't watch him closely enough, his cells multiply faster. A transformation that appears slow at first, but the more the days bleed into each other, the more time has the illusion of speeding up. He grows while I stay the same on the outside, but I know I am changed for ever inside. Any absence from him feels like a freedom coupled with a loss: who am I without a baby attached to me? Still me, clearly, but another me. When I'm apart from him I imagine that time stands still, as if I've propped him on a shelf like a doll, and he will be there waiting for me to retrieve him. Then I well up at the thought of him being alone. He will only be small once, how can I leave him for ten hours at a time when he's this tiny, will he even notice? I read stories of mothers recalling how it felt to return to work at six weeks, then feel guiltily lucky at the luxury of having had six and eight months, yet it still felt short. It goes past fast, but the idea of so many months away initially felt like a lifetime, like time stretched before me. The days go slow, but the months go fast.

November 2019 – Berlin

A weekend away feels like I have stolen some time to myself that was not mine to take.

It's the first time I'm apart from the second baby. It feels both disconnected – like an invisible but stretchy chord has been cut – but I also feel some parts of myself again. One that is bruised from an absence, but free from a 9.8kg attachment.

The freedom is mixed with a feeling of being bereft

and I wonder if the baby feels the loss. I have a hands-free pump; I use it on the plane, in a cute Berlin beer house in the evening surrounded by the group I am with. I confide in them that I'm pumping while eating, there was no other time. We laugh, it doesn't feel quite real. I am empty, it is full. I have to empty it in the bathroom sink. Liquid gold, wasted, there's nowhere hygienic to store it, but I am obsessively determined to maintain my supply.

I miss his comforting closeness, his hand that grabs at my skin, stays there twitching, holding onto me with a solid reassurance that I am his. I feel guilty.

A full schedule means I even have to pump while walking down the street. Nobody seems to notice, though the hand-sized pump that is tucked into my bra makes me lopsided. It's intending to mimic an infant's suck – but it doesn't do it quite right. On day two one breast becomes lumpy, sore, huge. The threat of mastitis is a cruel confrontation of how being apart can be damaging. A tender reminder that being a mother is my reality; the cord still binds us. To relieve the pressure, I attempt to massage myself in the restaurant over dinner and on the plane. It must look strange, though nobody seems to notice, and – anyhow – it doesn't work. I arrive back at midnight and he is sweetly sleeping, but I risk waking him to solve this particular problem. I lift him out his cot and let him feed, which even half-asleep babies can intuitively do. Within minutes the lumps disappear, and he fixes what the pump could never mimic. I narrowly escape mastitis. It wasn't fun the first time.

I understand now that maternity leave is all about balance. The longer we are away, the harder it can be to re-enter the workplace, and return to our old lives. The less time we take

off, the more stark and abrupt the feelings of guilt, anxiety and sleep-deprived juggling. And for those who don't
return to work at all, they face perhaps the starkest, selfless
challenge of a lived reality of choosing to be present. If it's
a choice at all, mothers everywhere should be valued and
saluted, as each 'choice' involves less of something else. Less
of ourselves, or less of our children.

WORKPLACE IDENTITY

Office politics, watercooler moments and pumping at work

When Maureen Sherry started to work in an investment bank in Wall Street in the 1980s, she knew she was entering a male-dominated workplace. Sexist comments, groping, and non-disclosure agreements were far too routine to spend much mental energy on. She was thick-skinned, she reasoned, so this environment would not hold her back.

It was extreme, though. One trader reportedly passed around plasters to women on cold trading floor days so he would not get distracted by them. The message was clear: women were different, a sexual distraction.

She was in a senior role, prided herself for her resilience and, for the most part, felt respected for frequently smashing targets. Despite this, her bonuses were not on a par with her male counterparts, and when she returned to work five weeks after the birth of her first child she was confronted with a very different form of explicitly sexist expectations and subtle workplace bullying, though she didn't call it this at the time. She had returned several weeks earlier than she had intended to do, after a frenzied call that her 'replacement' seemed to be stealing her clients as well as her workspace. He had already been packing up her things into boxes.

In a male majority workplace, once Maureen became a mother she was even more overtly defined by this new identity. On her way to pump milk every day, she had to walk through the trading floor, which she referred to as a 'walk of shame'. It was not unusual for male colleagues to mutter 'moo' sounds as she walked past them. She recalls that she walked on proudly with her middle finger in the air.

Once, as a dare, a male colleague drank a shot of her breast milk from the fridge. She and others mostly kept such stories to themselves. Large cheques were routinely offered for non-disclosure agreements, so what happened on the trading floor stayed concealed.

Though her experience took place in the 1990s and the discrimination Maureen faced would now be illegal, the perception of women in the cut-throat business world remains rife with bias and sexism.

When she was on maternity leave, her replacement was rewarded for the clients she had brought in. When a male employee was off sick for a similar length of time to her leave, he received his bonus but she did not. She mentioned that this was unfair – in both cases others had to cover the absent person's clients. To this, her boss replied, 'Jerry did not decide to have a heart issue – you decided to have a baby.' In her world, the idea of having both a career and a child was seen as incompatible, which many mothers still feel today. Ideals of the perfect mother directly clash with the expectations of an ideal worker. This is also a reflection of a society that promotes individualism without any public policy to support mothers.

Most of her predominantly male colleagues had stay-at-home wives. 'I think they all felt that that was the right model, the correct way to be in the world,' she says. 'When men are the sole breadwinners, they feel very hunter-male, testosterone-fuelled, head of the castle ... That's the mentality. So that's what I went back to.' This type of attitude still occurs. Research shows that when women are primary earners, some feel worried about undermining their husbands' masculinity.

Maureen stayed at the same bank for another four years and had a second child while working there. Despite the discrimination she faced, she found it hard to leave. But something had to give; the way she was treated left her feeling insecure – habitual comments such as 'your family comes first now', meant she frequently over-compensated. It still wasn't enough, as she couldn't routinely meet clients out of hours or work as late as her male colleagues. By doing a normal work week, she was already less in their eyes. Still today, in careers where staying late and working long hours are an expectation, those with caring responsibilities tend to fare worst.

When she left, Maureen was offered a non-disclosure form with a generous cheque, but she didn't take the money as she wanted to own her story. True to her wish, she did. She has since written a fictional account of working in this toxic environment inspired by her career.

Maureen describes her experience as 'dated'. For the most extreme sexism that may be so but, since publishing her book, she has been inundated with women writing to her detailing their own discrimination.

Today, many of us still conform to stereotypical gender roles, it's just more subtle than it was for the housewives of decades past. While there are positive, more egalitarian attitude changes, this can mask the fact that inequality and sexism remain rife, making it more difficult to call out discrimination when it occurs.

Perhaps that's why in order to be on an equal footing with men, women need to act less like themselves. In one German study, female politicians in the UK and Germany could only begin to compete with men if they acted more like them, but, even then, the culture was heavily male dominated. Similarly, lower voices are seen as more authoritative, but women have naturally higher voices. That's reportedly why Margaret Thatcher took elocution lessons in order to sound more commanding. Adopting another identity is exhausting. It is also extremely difficult to change aspects of our natural self as it requires constant mental processing, but many women have been doing it for years just to get a seat at a male-dominated table.

There's a reason Sheryl Sandberg's advice was to be more like men. In her 'lean in' movement following her 2013 book, she encouraged women not to settle for less even if they were concerned that pursuing certain careers would later impact upon family life as they might foresee it as incompatible with being a mother. Many women already compromise before they have children and continue to do so after. They are less likely to go for promotions or look for other jobs when it clashes with caring responsibilities, while men are more likely than women to describe themselves as highly ambitious. Women's self-reported ambition actually declines as they get older – in part because it's harder to get ahead in the first place.

For the past few years the 'lean in' mantra has been facing a backlash. Maureen 'leaned in', but had to lean out again. It can be impossible to 'lean in' during pregnancy or shortly after, as how mothers are perceived is outside of our control – and numerous biases can hold us back.

The idea of leaning in also lends itself to the fallacy that if we 'lean in' then our career is in our own hands, especially with the bombardment of messaging that we can 'have it all'. If we don't get that pay rise or promotion despite having leaned in, we might ultimately blame ourselves. And women do, especially if raising children is pitted as a personal problem. A lack of social policy and support ingrains this type of self-blame culture, especially in the US. It shouldn't be this way, but it reflects the fact that society and the workplace can hold women back before they even try to get ahead.

Despite progress, equality in the workplace is disappointingly fragile. This was made abundantly clear during the Covid-19 pandemic and the resulting economic aftermath. With schools closed, having a child and a job became increasingly incompatible; especially for mothers. Women were disproportionately affected by job losses and faced an even higher burden of childcare, undoing years of progress for gender equality.

Leaning in is not going to change decades of gendered perceptions despite a growing awareness that they persist. A motherhood penalty exists for a reason, after all. Subtler versions of gendered pigeonholing are still prevalent in so many areas of work and home life, which can edge women out of the workforce while continuing to shape a notion called parental essentialism – that women are innately better at parenting than men. That this idea endures is precisely because our world is so gendered from the outset.

It's why I tell my daughter that bus drivers can also be women, or emphasise how it was a policewoman waiting outside in the police car, not a policeman, or why I change the gender of so many of the male-dominated animal characters in her books. I shouldn't have to assign different genders to her world so early, but it's important that I do because, if I don't, her exposure and assumption of male characters will vastly outnumber female or gender-neutral ones. I don't want her, aged six, to draw a man when she's asked to depict a scientist, as children have been shown to do. In the 1960s and 70s, 99 per cent of children drew a male when asked this question. This is changing for the better, but later studies still find an average of 72 per cent drawing male scientists.

Views around working mothers are shifting, albeit slowly. One 2015 survey found that support for women working varied enormously depending on the circumstances given. On the whole, American respondents still supported the father breadwinner model, and a large proportion – 51 per cent – supported a mother staying at home if the family did not specifically need her income, even if the mother was depicted as enjoying her job and felt satisfied with her childcare.

Those who most strongly opposed mothers working were politically conservative churchgoers. Interestingly though, and a reason the authors proposed that social attitudes are changing, is that the circumstances given could override the long-standing preferred male breadwinner model. For instance, if depicted as a single mother who needed the income, 92 per cent supported her working.

The reason some respondents don't support mothers working can be gleaned from social attitudes surveys. One 2012 report found that over a quarter of respondents disagreed with the statement 'a working mother can establish just as warm and secure a relationship with her children'. The view that mothers should be at home remains entrenched among a high percentage of the US population. In a 2009 survey 21 per cent still believed that women shouldn't work for pay when their children were young. These types of perceptions feed heavily into how a mother feels she should act and therefore continues to fuel a pervasive feeling of guilt for working mothers.

Coming back from any leave of absence can feel difficult, but this is heightened for women who return to work after having a baby. Challenges that threaten our very identity fire at us from many angles. Women report feeling 'invisible', that they are taken less seriously, or that they have to redefine their workplace identity. They are also less likely to get a pay rise or a promotion than both men and women who are not mothers. Feeling unsupported and underappreciated is a common experience for new mothers.

For instance, a friend recently voiced her frustration about how she was excluded from meetings that were scheduled for late afternoon. She had been back at work for over a year and her colleagues knew her working hours, but she still felt guilty about it. 'People don't see me arrive, they just see me leave before them every day,' she said.

Then there's the following from a 2019 *Guardian* article, where the author Stephanie Gardiner recalls how a friend of hers said: 'A work colleague joked on my first day back saying, "You're one of them now, only a half day," after I clocked an eight-hour day.' Gardiner wrote how she had wrongly believed views of working mothers were 'antiquated' until she experienced the challenges first hand. She is now, as she calls it, 'underemployed' as a homemaker. This is unsurprisingly common. A 2020 report found that one in three mothers considered scaling back or leaving work altogether due to the difficulties of combining a career and family life.

It is parents and predominantly lower-paid mothers, who

suffer most when companies habitually expect overtime. If your worth as an employee is in any way measured by staying late, it automatically puts those with care responsibilities at a disadvantage. The expectation of overtime is so common in many Western countries that there's a term for it: presenteeism, but it comes without the necessary social policies, like adequately subsidised childcare to support it.

Passive comments about putting in the hours may seem innocent, but research shows that biases and assumptions about motherhood in the workplace are etched into our cultural mentality. For starters, mothers are viewed as less committed and motivated when they first come back to work. One 2011 study found that the length of time a woman was on leave affected how others saw her future potential to advance. Looking at HR professionals in Hungary, the research found that those who took over a year were seen as less dedicated compared to those who returned earlier. This is despite the fact that many women are highly motivated when they return to work after several months away.

Another study asked 500 undergraduate students how they perceived an absence from work that was either due to an injury or caring for a child or relative. These students then assessed the employability, qualifications and responsibility of a series of potential (though fictional) applicants. They rated the men as more employable than women, and fathers were rated more highly than non-caregivers. We get burdened with a motherhood penalty whereas fathers get the opposite, which has been dubbed the 'fatherhood bonus'.

Considering that cultural ideas about womanhood and motherhood go hand in hand (a woman of a certain age is often assumed to also be a mother – and of those who aren't, it is assumed she wants to be), when a woman becomes a mother she will naturally be bombarded by this new identity, internally and from her workplace. Research shows that ambitious mothers who strive to move up the career ladder, rather than working out of financial necessity, are perceived negatively.

That's because mothers are expected to behave a certain way and anything outside these norms is put under scrutiny. Sociologists call these assumptions 'normative beliefs' around parenting, and these can have subtle, negative effects on new mothers. They are expected to prioritise family life over careers when their children are young, and so those who go back full time are judged negatively for doing so. In one study, new mothers who reduced their hours when first returning to work, but eventually went back full time, were viewed more favourably and as more committed to progressing to management positions. Those who did not reduce their hours were rated less capable and given lower ratings of potential to advance. In line with that, women are judged for being *less* family-focused when working full time, while those who work part time are seen as *less* committed and less ambitious. This shows the paradoxical judgements given for whatever choice is made.

Even seemingly positive assumptions affect how mothers are perceived. Take the following example. One friend, Jessica, a manager, came back to work after six months maternity leave. She was welcomed back with enthusiasm in a department with several other parents. Even so, over the course of her first day back she was asked, 'Wow has it already been a year? Doesn't that go by quick? (assumption one). Later, a senior leader from another team asked her whether she was back full time or part time (assumption two). On her way to pick up her baby she bumped into a neighbour who, for the first time, saw her without her child. 'Are you an emotional wreck today?' the neighbour asked (assumption three). These were well-meant comments, but consider all three together and it's easy to see how such remarks form part of a broader expectation of what a mother does. She was fortunate to have the option to take a year off, but that does not mean she would definitely take it, start back part time and be an emotional mess without her baby.

This type of experience tallies with research that shows women quickly notice that colleagues and their superiors treat them differently as mothers. When women like Jessica come back to work, studies show that some employers question their commitment to their jobs. It's no wonder that this prods at their identity both in the workplace and at home.

Even worse, as soon as a woman's commitment is challenged, even subtly, she is less likely to get a promotion. This is the type of unfortunate cycle that leads women to lower their ambition – not out of choice but because it's hard to stay motivated in the face of dwindling career recognition. When these biases and expectations exist in the workplace, even if they are implicit, questions about the length of leave taken or part-time work intentions no longer seem so innocuous after all.

Most of this chapter was written before the coronavirus pandemic disrupted our lives. It reflects just how sticky work cultures still are that it took a global pandemic to change ingrained expectations and habits. And yet, even though many people now work from home – this is only for the types of jobs that can be done remotely. Biases around working flexibly still remain difficult to change – especially with increased digital contact and the pressure to be logged on.

In an article in the *Daily Mail*, journalist and campaigner

Anna Whitehouse discussed how outdated a lack of flexibility was in the modern age. She was denied a request to have more flexible hours. While it's generally a bad idea to read newspaper comments, doing so was eye-opening. They revealed a usually otherwise hidden form of prejudice. 'Here we go again, these women with their sense of entitled (sic). They seem to want it all,' and similarly: 'Don't do the crime if you can't do the time. You chose to have kids, I didn't. You slyly leaving at 4.55pm to "pick up your kids" is unfair. I want to leave at 4.55 too.'

Another reader commented: 'I am sick of these women thinking they are special because they have had children. They get too many allowances ... If they want children, they should stay at home and bring them up, that is their job. Companies have to pay for them not working during maternity leave, children's illness ... it is not right or fair.'

These remarks reflect the individualistic views that children are a personal 'problem' when, in order for an economy to thrive, support for those who are nurturing the next generation is vital for a country's social and economic success. The extra care work mothers disproportionately do often *does* require greater workplace flexibility. When such flexibility exists, women can be penalised for even requesting it or overlooked for being less visible. It's another contradiction that contributes to a double motherhood penalty: a lack of flexibility can push them out of the workplace entirely, but too much flexibility can make them less visible, even in a culture of increased homeworking.

As the eminent legal scholar Joan C. Williams outlined, the many pressures women face are a consequence of the fact that the workplace is best suited for those 'unencumbered by family responsibilities', who are, of course, more likely to be men. Even women at senior levels who take family support are seen as less worthy of a promotion. Rigid hours do not account for the fact that most parents at some point need flexibility for the school or nursery run. A preference for the unencumbered worker therefore only intensifies inequality.

While many companies have policies that support working mothers, there are still countless examples of how these accommodations are not quite adequate. As one friend said, when the pumping room for breastmilk was a ten-minute walk away, she ended up attempting to discreetly pump at her desk in her small office, and there are reports aplenty of women pumping in the toilet.

In my case, the pumping space was also used as a sick room that was kept locked and so required me to ask a security guard to open it for every single use. 'Oh, are you unwell?' I was asked the first time. I told the truth and was never asked again. It was private, comfortable and had a fridge, but that was also locked and full of what I presumed was insulin.

I was too embarrassed to ask for access to yet another locked door, so I would wrap the milk bottle in a paper towel and store it in the main fridge, hidden from view. I didn't think much of it at the time and did not want to draw attention to myself. I now realise that's because overtly signalling motherhood this way acts as a triggering moment that can make mothers seem less competent and less committed, perpetuating a culture of secretive parenting. Because it remains secretive, these experiences go largely unnoticed. One academic painstakingly chronicled her daily pumping worries, fretting over whether it was more conspicuous to appear in a new shirt or one that was slightly stained exposing her leaky and 'uncontrollable body'. She too had to place her milk in the communal fridge among her colleagues' lunch, which made her feel 'subjected to moral authority and public scrutiny of my lactating body', especially as the maternal body is considered 'taboo' in the professional world.

I pumped less than I should have to maintain supply, because as well as how uncomfortable the whole experience was, physically and mentally, it was also hard to fit it into my working day – washing the equipment before and after also takes time. At first I attempted to work while I was pumping, but in order for milk to flow – for our bodies to provide – we need reminders and prompts that we are mothers to get the hormones working for us – another clash of two selves. Milk doesn't flow easy in a sterile place.

With my second, I did not pump at work.

Pumping at work requires accommodating working hours, but even when parents do take the flexibility on offer, they can be judged for it. When some companies offered paid time off during the Covid-19 lockdowns, they faced a backlash, with comments that they were unfairly putting pressure on non-parents, despite the fact that many were already working three jobs – childcare, homeschooling and paid work. Not only is a full-time job while caring for children at home wholly unsustainable, it is a catalyst for reduced sleep, mental health issues and all the discrimination mothers already face.

Becoming a mother changes a woman's identity and status at work more so than it does for a man, resulting in the motherhood penalty, lower earnings, fewer promotions and increased stress. In this climate, it's no wonder that women often opt to work fewer hours, as even those working full time cannot always keep up with the long hours that some workplaces demand.

Not every country has an overwork culture. Workplace practices differ from country to country, often influenced by the social policies that exist.

My brother, who works in the Netherlands, has two young boys under four, and regularly leaves the office just after 4 p.m. to pick them up (he starts early too). Overtime isn't expected in many companies there. The Netherlands has some of the lowest working hours after Denmark, Norway and Germany. I asked my brother if he ever felt strange about leaving 'early'. No way, he told me, lots of people do the same.

There's a reason for this. In the Netherlands, part-time work is routine. Among OECD countries it has the highest number of part-time workers by far – 37.3 per cent in 2019. Of those who work part time in the Netherlands, the majority are women. In fact, part-time work is often expected for mothers.

The most prevalent work–life set-up among parents is the 'one-and-a-half' income model, where the father works full time and the mother part time. Flexibility and an equal division of labour in the home is expected in many families, but because more women work part time this also leads them to shoulder more of the care work, with other unfavourable consequences. For instance, those who work full time are scrutinised because of the assumption that mothers should be at home with their children for at least some of the working week, a study found. This was especially so among the higher professions showing that we still 'applaud mothers and punish fathers who combine career and care by working reduced hours'. Mothers who worked part time were viewed as more capable and successful than full-time mothers who were the main providers for the family. Fathers who worked a four-day week, the so-called 'daddy track', were viewed as less accomplished and successful than main-breadwinner fathers who worked full time. For a mother the message is clear; part-time working is beneficial because it is the norm. It follows that women also do more unpaid care work, about 22 hours per week compared to nine hours for men.

In the Netherlands, as elsewhere, despite embracing part-time and flexible work, the ingrained societal expectations and norms still put women at a gender disadvantage. Naturally, the culture of part-time work can affect career progression and therefore pay. The gender pay gap of about 14 per cent therefore persists.

Globally, there are many reasons that the gender pay gap exists. To start with, women work fewer paid hours than men. However, we end up working longer hours overall because most of the childcare and housework falls to us. This is so prevalent it has been called the unpaid 'second shift' of work. According to the Bureau of Labor Statistics in the US, women spend an average of 1.1 hours of physical childcare per day for children under six (defined as bathing, feeding and dressing), compared to 26 minutes for men, while 46 per cent of women did housework such as cleaning or laundry on an average day compared to 22 per cent of men. On the days housework was done, women did an average of 2.5 hours compared to 1.9 hours for men.

This occurs even though women make up almost half the US workforce.

There are similar trends elsewhere. An Australian analysis showed that when single, both sexes do roughly equal amounts of housework, with women only doing slightly more. This shifts when couples move in together and is greater still when they become parents. The women's workload increases, while the men's decreases, irrespective of what jobs they have. Parenthood is the moment that the inequality gap of household chores begins to widen, just as it does for the pay gap. A 2016 census put a figure on how much it differs: women in Australia do between five and 14 hours of housework per week on average, with men doing fewer than five. Around the world figures vary but the OECD reports that women do between double to ten times more unpaid care work than men do, and this occurs across the entire economic spectrum, with serious consequences for female 'economic empowerment'. Time spent at home takes time and energy away from careers. The unequal division of care at home is in part fuelled by expectations put upon 'women's work', largely based on the historical and societal constructions of what a women's role is, as well as a recent history of exclusion from the workplace. When women started to enter paid work, expectations at home didn't change enough to follow suit. Or as a *Guardian* article stated in 2020, paying women less than men serves two 'nefarious purposes': cheaper labour and keeps women tied to their higher-earning husbands.

We've talked about biases women face that can prevent them from progressing, but it's worth pointing out that even where women have successful careers, they are predominantly still paid less than men in similar positions. This means those who become mothers drop off the pay scale even further. Take a 2015 survey of over 12,000 MBA graduates, which showed that female graduates with the same level of education as their male counterparts earned less as each year passed, managed smaller teams and were less happy with how their career was progressing.

The impact of this sexism is far-reaching. One 2019 report, looking at over 6,000 Australian working families, found that most employees, male and female, want more flexible workplaces but men struggled to work flexibly – in part because it was viewed as being 'more acceptable for women'. About a quarter of respondents considered leaving the workplace entirely as combining work and family commitments proved difficult, even though many also stated that their jobs were 'satisfying and fulfilling'.

Another report, looking at 2,750 working families in the UK, found that for each child, workplace participation for mothers dropped. With one child, both parents worked 76 per cent of the time, but with three children it was more common for the mother not to be in paid work. It also took an average of two years longer for mothers to get promoted compared to fathers, even longer for women who worked part time.

Those in higher-paid roles have fewer options for part-time work. And as women are already the majority of part-time workers, it can push them out of the market for these more lucrative roles. Without a high income, childcare costs can be prohibitive. Two young children in childcare can easily exceed the average UK salary after tax. The median salary is just over £30,000. After tax this equates to about £24,000. In the more expensive areas in London, a full-time nursery place can cost more than £18,000 for one child.* If the woman is the lower earner and childcare costs more than she earns (easily done with two in childcare), then work doesn't pay. The lower-earning parent may have no choice but to stop work, even though that affects future earning potential as well as widening the pension gap. The longer women are out of work, the harder it is to come back at all, let alone return to a comparable level. For those who consider work as important for their wellbeing, this would only serve to heighten their motherhood complex.

Worse, the motherhood earning penalty hits the lowest-paid workers hardest. Those in precarious jobs are unlikely to get a promotion in the first place and childcare worries make holding onto a job more difficult. This penalty cannot be measured for women who drop out of the workplace entirely. If these were included, it would be even worse. It's a penalty that heightens gender, class and race inequality. Top earners do not see a similar effect, in part because they can afford high-quality childcare and at-home help, which reduces disruption to their career. Or put another way, higher earners can pay lower-paid workers to make their lives as mothers more manageable. This means that the lack of universal paid leave affects the workers who need it most.

Given all that we have explored, the gender pay gap seems an obvious consequence, and, sadly, it stubbornly endures. Among childless young professional women in their 20s, there is a minimal gender pay gap in the US. In the UK the

---

* A nursery in north-west London costs more than £19,000 per year per child. The UK government will pay 20 per cent per child up to £10,000 if both parents are working, but this benefit does not apply if either earns more than £100,000.

gender pay gap is highest among those over 40. Half of this gap has been explained simply by having children. In one large Danish study, women's earnings dropped by as much as 30 per cent after having children, and those who went back to work never caught up.

But career disruption only amounts to part of the reason the gap persists. Declining hours, not going for new roles or promotions or not being able to do as much overtime in companies that demand it, are other reasons.

Disappointingly, mothers have been found to be less desirable for new positions. In one study of fictional job applicants, participants were shown CVs where applicants subtly signalled that they were parents. Mothers were rated as less competent and committed than non-mothers and were offered lower recommended salaries than childless women. Mothers were also judged for being late, while fathers were not. Fatherhood in fact came with a financial bonus as fathers were offered higher salaries than non-fathers. The experimenters then sent very similar CVs to real job openings. Mothers were less likely to be offered potential job interviews. Parent status wasn't overtly indicated either. CVs were almost identical for parents and non-parents, but the parent CVs showed membership of a parent–teacher organisation. That one small signal caused the disparity.

This shows that the assumption is that mothers are less competent and reliable, that they are so devoted to their children they cannot give sufficient attention to their career. Women are already viewed as less competent than men before any mention of children, and this only widens once they become mothers.

This can create a 'feedback loop', in the sense that in any couple, the higher earner's career will be prioritised which – in heterosexual couples – will statistically be the man. If a child is ill it will usually be the lower-paid parent who stays home. This is exactly what researchers found happened when schools were shut during the coronavirus pandemic. Fathers managed to continue to work 40 hours or more per week while mothers worked up to 20 to 50 per cent less. Thousands had to quit work altogether, a common occurrence even in non-pandemic times.

Motherhood not only reinforces gender inequality at work but, because of lower wages or part-time work, women are pushed to do more of the unpaid care work at home, leaving them with less time to focus on career advancement. This has lasting consequences because we know that children are influenced by the roles their parents have, for good and for bad.

It's worth reminding ourselves that many of the motherhood penalties explored are largely a phenomenon for married, white middle-class women. Working-class women and women of colour are statistically more likely to be in low-paid and inflexible, precarious jobs with minimal career progression as it is. For them the penalty is even worse – it doesn't come up in the figures because they are already struggling just to make ends meet. When these families are hit with childcare issues and the jobs are already badly paid, mums often quit.

There are solutions to reducing the motherhood penalty, but they require interventions at a policy level that include equal amounts of paid paternity leave for parents. This must then be backed up by employers who support and encourage it.

Too often, women who do have flexibility state they are 'lucky' to be able to balance their home and work lives, but this sentiment only exists because we are used to far from ideal workplace cultures. Being lucky isn't enough. Instead, training for managers, mentoring and informal networks, would be a good start. Equality is not just a universal human right, it would make for a better workforce. In other words, society as a whole and the next generation would benefit. If this was the norm, I wouldn't have so much to write about when it comes to mothers who work, and the term 'working mother' would seem just as strange as 'working father'.

The problem is that even if mothers want to work part time, it can make them less 'visible' and perceived as less ambitious. Ambition and workplace flexibility do not easily go hand in hand given that many of the highest-paid jobs rarely suit or allow part-time working. This ties back to the importance of social policy. How workplace flexibility is viewed depends on the country and cultural norms. In Germany and the Netherlands, part-time white-collar jobs are more common whereas in the US, part-time work is usually in low paid, low-security blue-collar jobs.

If this all sounds like a bit of a mess, it is. Countries with more paternal leave like Sweden, and in places where part-time working for women is the norm such as the Netherlands, still have persistent gender wage gaps and an unequal division of childcare. There is a good reason why so many of these conundrums exist, despite the apparent ease of the solutions.

First of all, in the industrialised world a problematic narrative is emerging that confuses our ideals with reality. In many European countries, fathers can take paid paternity leave or shared parental leave. If a paternity leave policy exists it is seen as actioning inequality, but it masks the reality of how little change is actually occurring, especially if that leave is not paid. If the 'choice' is available to us but we do not take it, we could be liable to think it's our own fault that gendered structures persist. The current illusion of choice disguises the change that needs to happen, rather than encouraging it. For new policies to be implemented, wider society first has to acknowledge the barriers. This explains why the gender pay gap is so difficult to close even in societies that are heralded for apparent equality.

Other solutions need to come from the top. Leaders are often encouraged to demonstrate boundaries around personal and work time. It rarely happens, but if such behaviours trickle down, more junior employees would feel empowered to follow suit. It's clear that supportive role models make the shift to motherhood more manageable. And a better work–life balance makes for happier, more productive employees.

The very notion of working longer hours in order to 'prove' yourself can set us up for failure anyway. Working more than 40 hours a week is detrimental for productivity and can increase the likelihood of stress and burnout. The 40 hours figure is also problematic considering that for most mothers there are significant proportions of unpaid work that are not accounted for and that they cannot opt out of. That is, the less visible 'second shift', which starts as soon as paid work ends, which women are disproportionately burdened with. It is rarely accounted for except in academic journals and the occasional newspaper article. If the excess work women do was regularly exposed, it would highlight this inequality.

Maintaining a career is not only helpful for mothers, it will benefit their children too. Research shows that daughters of working mothers are more likely to work themselves, hold more supervisor roles, work longer hours for higher pay than comparable women whose mothers did not work. Daughters of working mothers also spend less time on domestic tasks at home. This finding was widespread: the study looked at 29 countries over 11 years and is attributed to a phenomenon known as social learning, where we learn from our environment.

Working mothers therefore help shape gender attitudes that children copy. Sons of working mothers have been found to spend more time caring for their family than sons of mothers who did not work. In dual-earner households, sons are more likely to later expect wives to work. The gender role expectations we express clearly trickle down to our children too.

We've explored some of the issues that new mothers face when returning to work, which explains why it can feel so challenging. It is even harder when employers have expectations that are difficult for those with caring responsibilities to meet, such as long working hours.

An overtime work culture in some industries like banking and law has become an expected norm for what a good worker does. It's no surprise then that the gender pay gap begins to widen as soon as a woman becomes a mother. While there's now an awareness of it, it is likely going take decades to change. In late 2019 the World Economic Forum calculated that it would take 99 years until the gender gap would be closed, revised from 108 years the previous year. This gap is not just in pay, but includes measures such as political influence, education and economic success. The top three countries for gender parity were Iceland, Norway and Finland. Unsurprisingly, these are also countries with supportive family policies.

The competing expectations of work and the home bring to light the clash between the ideal worker and the ideal mother. The ideal worker is a rather rigid view of employees more typical of US corporate culture, of someone single-mindedly devoted to their employer, available to work full time with few disruptions from family or otherwise. Given that women do more of the care work at home, this expectation disproportionately harms them. Obviously, those with families cannot easily subscribe to this 'idealism' without a cost to their home life and wellbeing, given what we noted earlier about optimum hours worked and stress. It's another paradox in a culture where family values are lauded but policy and workplace culture do not tally with that. In the summer of 2020, the US government spent more money on bailing out one airline than it did for the whole problem of childcare, even though schools remained closed.

Ideal worker expectations also explain why companies, including Facebook, Google and Amazon will pay for women to freeze their eggs, creating a culture where it is seen as beneficial to delay motherhood. Make of that what you will, and critics did, saying these businesses are suggesting that a career is more important than a family – promoting the idea that having both is unachievable at worst, or career limiting at best. The policy is meant to help women focus on their career without worrying about their future fertility.

Many mothers therefore feel caught between the pressures of the ideal worker and ideal mother. Sociologist Caitlyn Collins at Washington University in St Louis spent several years speaking to over 135 middle-class working mothers from Sweden, Italy, Germany and the US to understand the factors that help women balance work and family. Her research showed that women who try to achieve both standards tend to fail as they 'categorically cannot live up to either ideal'. This is especially true of capitalist countries and is yet another moment when motherhood guilt comes to the forefront. US mothers were the most stressed, overworked and felt the guiltiest.

Swedish mothers, on the other hand, had few issues with work–life balance. The mothers Collins spoke to were largely happy with their schedule, in part because of the policies put in place to enable them to pursue satisfying careers. In Sweden, it's often a given that children matter more than a job, and that work can flex to accommodate children's needs, not the other way around. Swedish mothers were also confused and amused by the term 'working mother' because all mothers there tend to work. As one interviewee put it: 'I don't think that expression exists in Swedish ... you can't be anything else ... It's not like there's a sort of "non-working mother".'

If ambition and motherhood cannot go hand in hand, a corporate culture that values overwork over personal life holds some of the blame. Working mothers are extremely stretched and this pressure is a driving reason pushing women out of the workforce during their children's earliest years. It occurs so often that these women go by the term 'opt-outers'. Journalists Hana Schank and Elizabeth Wallace painstakingly chronicled this in a series of in-depth articles in *The Atlantic*. The duo tracked down 37 of their high-achieving sorority group from 1993 to find out what happened to them in the years since leaving college. All were high-achievers, but, as soon as they had children, the group followed three clearly identifiable patterns: the aforementioned opt-outers, high-achievers and a middling group (the scale-backers). Notably this was a small, though in-depth insight into one group of women, but qualitative insights like this give a detailed and more personal understanding into what larger data sets show.

The opt-outers didn't leave the workplace just to be with their kids, or because they were disillusioned with their careers. It was a combination of the money not adding up and a lack of workplace flexibility. The knock-on effect for women who opt out is that it is hard to re-enter at a comparable level. Studies show that a CV gap due to childcare is seen as worse than a gap due to unemployment for other reasons. This was found when over 3,000 fictional CVs were sent for real jobs where unemployed applicants and stay-at-home parents both had an 18-month gap in their CVs. The stay-at-home parents were only given 5 per cent call back rates whereas the unemployed applicants were called back 9 per cent of the time. Respondents viewed stay-at-home parents as less reliable and less committed than those who were unemployed. As you can expect, an employment gap has lasting consequences on earnings. Those with several gaps can experience wage discrepancies of about 40 per cent compared to continuous workers, a 2020 study following 6,000 participants showed.

The scale-backers were those who continued to work, but only in roles that gave them the flexibility they needed at the cost of dialling down previous ambitions. Having a family clearly does stall women's careers. An analysis of 25,000 graduates from Harvard Business School aged between 26 and 67 showed that respondents believed the main barrier for a successful career for women was putting family first. About 11 per cent actually left to care for children, but did so reluctantly, especially when they were dissatisfied within their roles or felt penalised for working flexibly.

One respondent said, 'I left my first job after being "mommy-tracked" when I came back from maternity leave.' Another stated, 'There appeared to be preconceived notions about part-time women wanting less challenging work, off track, when I was seeking the more challenging work ... ' There were also fewer females in senior positions than men regardless of whether they had children.

The 'opt-out revolution' as it has been otherwise called, is not a new phenomenon, but has been noted by scholars ever since women started working more. It explains why there tends to be a fairly equal amount of female and male law graduates, but the former are poorly represented at partner level. This pattern is found in many fields and when women opt out they largely blame themselves, not their employers. It's worth pointing out though that opting out is a privileged issue only afforded to higher-earning women. Lower-paid and lower-educated workers, often comprised of already marginalised groups, fare even worse.

Unfortunately, economists point to the idea that capitalist societies benefit from the unpaid labour to raise the next generation, because the work is needed and free, the so-called 'free-rider' problem. Without intervention, market forces will not correct the resulting inequality. Take Italy, where affordable childcare below the age of three is not readily available. The result – women work less; the female employment rate there is only 55 per cent.

There is also more demand than ever for privatised childcare, a reflection that looking after the next generation remains a personal problem. But even here it is only the most privileged workers who can pay for the best childcare, and so wealth begets wealth and lower earners are even more vulnerable. In many places, poorer parents and single mothers (one in five children in the US live with only their mother) are largely left to fend for themselves.

Against this backdrop it's no surprise that mothers are feeling increasing levels of stress from all areas of life. While 'having it all' is not a total myth, it depends on how you interpret what 'all' means. If it's a satisfying part-time job, that is achievable, but the cost is limited pay progression. If it's a high-powered job, the cost may be long hours away from the family and no time to yourself. Something has got to give. For me, writing a book with two young children and a full-time job meant no social outings during maternity leave and rarely an evening or weekend off for a year. But it's a 'sacrifice' I felt compelled to make, especially because I was living the reality of much of what I was writing. To learn more about it was an eye-opening way to understand myself and society at large better.

When it comes to the numerous biases mothers face, many are implicit. This means that change needs to occur at a societal level to be meaningful. If we continue to have workplaces designed and largely catered for men, women are always going to be in second place. Until societal values change, biases will be difficult to correct. An awareness that they exist is a crucial first step.

This illustrates that the split identity I am exploring in this book is, in part, a consequence of the societal expectations of a woman's role. These expectations are pervasive at the very time that women's rights and gender pay gaps are discussed with greater urgency. We are tempted by 'having it all', but society and workplace structures haven't yet caught up to facilitate this. And yet still women largely blame themselves when they can't juggle the career they want with the mother they aspire to be. Even in my home country, the Netherlands, where equality is highly valued, cultural biases remain a potent force that can hold new mothers back. Luckily employers there don't value overtime the way companies do in countries like Japan and the US. In that regard, the burden of the 'second shift' of care work at home doesn't land as fully in the mother's lap.

Although I would have loved to end this chapter on a positive note, it remains the case that when a woman's workplace or cultural expectations, her financial constraints or limited maternity policies override her sense of who she is, or what role she could grow into, it becomes likely she will develop a motherhood complex.

A MOTHER PERCEIVED

When equal parenting is not all that equal

One wintry evening in 2019, after hurriedly breastfeeding my then seven-month-old, I made it out to the pub for a rare social event. An acquaintance had heard I was writing this book and asked me what it was about.

'It's about the science of identity change,' I said vaguely. I then somewhat reluctantly explained in more detail; that, yes, it was specifically about identity change in motherhood, not other types of identity changes.

'Ah, you're one of those,' he said, probably half-jokingly. 'Another mother writing about motherhood.' I laughed, but this was the exact same wording I had used when describing the book to someone else, as it encapsulates the most immediate contradiction and worry I felt about writing the book at all. I didn't want to be seen as 'yet another mother' writing a mother-hood book, precisely because I didn't want motherhood to be my defining characteristic. Don't get me wrong, I love being a mother and have always known I wanted to be one. The love for a tiny living, breathing creature that I nurtured inside my own womb, has seeped its way into every cell in my body.

I am writing about the very essence of the identity I don't want to consume me, even though motherhood is what takes up so much of my time outside of work. I saw no point in explaining this paradox that others may have been oblivious to. The fact that I made it out at all in those early days felt like an achievement in itself. It was hard to even contemplate making plans when sleep-deprived.

I obsessively read articles about motherhood and parenting, trying to validate the importance of it all. One memorable piece in the *Los Angeles Times* struck a chord. 'Why don't people take writing about motherhood seriously? Because women do it,' wrote the author Sarah Menkedick.

It's precisely because motherhood is so 'ordinary' that we need to discuss, write about and validate it, because mothers are still heavily pigeonholed and it's exhausting. Motherhood may be gloriously common, but it is anything but ordinary, and that's why a resulting identity change feels so emotionally heavy and why I was initially hesitant to explain why I chose to devote a whole book to it.

Menkedick found herself explaining her writing, saying, 'It's about motherhood, but not really.' In part, because 'patriarchal culture has reduced motherhood to an exercise no serious artist would tackle as a subject'. Once again, this puts mothers in second place, and marginalises not only the topic itself but also mothers: 'Obscuring the difficulties of childcare, the intensity of birth, the complexities of working and writing as a mother, and the profound ways having a baby changes a woman's life, body and mind.' Or as *Guardian* columnist Eva Wiseman eloquently describes, the love that comes from motherhood 'makes every feeling bigger, even guilt and pain: unattainable ideals appear in the dark of a 5.00 a.m. feed like ghosts'.

I felt this way despite spending every minute of my

limited spare time exploring and understanding the science of how motherhood really does change us, often for the better. And yet I still felt as if I had to justify it, more to myself than to others, who probably weren't thinking about it at all. I thought deeply about identity change because of how it affected me, and that it did so was due to numerous external factors out of my control.

Becoming a mother is clearly only the start of a life-changing journey. There are many different ways to be a mother, and many unwelcome assumptions that follow. The conundrum is that while there remains an appearance of choice in how to 'mother', in terms of the practical day-to-day decisions, this is hard to uncouple from expected gender roles, which impact upon the choices available to us – as Maureen Sherry the investment banker experienced. We are 'free' to choose, but only within the constraints of what motherhood means in our culture, from immediate influences like our own family to those from the outside, such as social norms. How mothers are perceived plays an enormous, almost hidden role.

It starts young. Parents, whether overtly or unintentionally, treat their sons and daughters differently, dependent upon the roles they expect them to fulfil later. At the same time, mothers have been shown to spend more time with their daughters, and fathers with their sons.

Parents unknowingly play a part in the ingrained ideas of what masculinity and femininity means. As soon as we become parents, gender stereotypes become more obvious. Gendered ideas influence our day-to-day interactions with everyone around us. There are the obvious nudges: pink or blue cards, frilly jumpers or monster trucks, but many of our gendered behaviours are implicit. One 2015 study of over 300 families with young children found that parents categorised gender-neutral faces differently depending on their emotional expressions. If the face was angry it was more likely to be labelled as a boy, if it was a sad face it was labelled girl. Happy faces were also predominantly labelled as female. Messages that boys shouldn't cry and girls shouldn't get angry start young.

This kind of implicit gender bias infiltrates into many other areas. Mothers of boys have been shown to overestimate their motor skills for crawling while mothers of girls underestimate these abilities. Perhaps more worryingly, when toddlers were observed in free play, caregivers reacted more strongly to assertiveness among the boys, and less to girls. Before the age of two toddlers can already differentiate gender labels, with girls doing so at 17 months on average and boys at 19 months, as a 2009 study of 82 infants showed. As soon as children understand gender labelling, they are more prone to start 'sex-typed play'. It's not that boys prefer trucks per se, it's that, very early on, boys learn trucks are more associated with being male, and girls learn that shiny sparkly pink things are more female, and so of course they are more drawn to the products that we expect them to like.

When my daughter was about two, she told me that a coat I tried to put on her was for boys and refused to wear it (it was intended to be unisex – meaning it did not look girly). The gendered signs we push upon our children are so subtle that we don't notice it happening. It might be something as simple as telling my daughter she looks cute in a dress. By doing this I could be adding another gendered layer onto her mind. If girls wear trousers, we may not comment much, but put them in a beautiful dress and many will remark on how pretty she looks. Her daily dress demands, despite never intentionally dressing her particularly 'girly', are a case in point. I realise now that her dinosaur coat aged 12 months was actually a futile attempt at being 'gender neutral' – because how can something be 'neutral' if neutral is simply less girly and therefore more boyish? Besides, even this can teach our girls the wrong things too – if we overtly discourage them from wearing the most girly clothes, they might learn that expressing femininity is bad.

Gender is so embedded within our society that attempting to be gender neutral has double standards that inadvertently favour masculinity. For instance, while I sometimes dressed my daughter in boyish clothes, I hesitated to put my son in pink. This is rooted in the idea that masculinity is less fluid than femininity as being male has always carried a higher status. A man who acts feminine is prone to more biases than a woman acting masculine. I was a tomboy growing up, and it was viewed positively by peers; the same is not generally true for effeminate boys. A boy in my class who was a dancer was ridiculed, while to be classed as a tomboy was a sort of compliment.

Similarly, that's why male leaders can be labelled as assertive for the same behaviour referred to as bossy for women, while anger is seen as more negative for female leaders than for males. We view certain behaviours in men as positive and undesirable in women.

Despite my best intentions, these roots go deep. During each bedtime story my then almost three-year-old daughter habitually asked 'where's the mummy' of every character we were reading about. She would point at other women about my age in the street and say 'mummy' because to her all women are also mummies, which is a fairly logical assumption in her world, given that she sees more mummies than daddies on playdates. Until I started writing this chapter, I thought little of it – we don't notice it because we cannot easily undo how gender perceptions are conditioned. When she talked of herself as being older, she said, 'When I am a big mummy.' She even started to categorise animals and inanimate objects as male and female. Seeing four dogs together in the park, the bigger dogs were the 'daddy' dogs while the smaller ones the 'mummy' dogs and the tiniest was the baby doggy, while bigger grapes were daddy grapes and smaller ones were mummy grapes.

While I cannot yet explain that the dogs are different breeds, not mummies and daddies, at least in this instance the categorisation was on the biological difference of their size, rather than the socially constructed division of gender. When she is older, I will explain the laws of averages and delight in telling her that in several species, like spotted hyenas, the mummies are bigger than the daddies and in others (bonobos) the mummies rule the daddies. When she's even older she can learn that some insects' mummies eat the daddies (black widow spiders).

In any case, gender norms are a product of our society and so when girls align with feminine things, they are identifying with a group they understand that they belong to. It would be futile to tell little girls not to dress as princesses, but we should instead encourage the princesses in their minds to be strong, independent and bad-ass, not feeble girls who need rescuing.

We therefore need to be aware of how powerful gender norms are, rather than pretend that they don't exist. Some little girls will grow up to become mothers and will therefore be directly impacted by these norms. Given how deep-rooted gender expectations are, there is no simple way to avoid them. An awareness of our assumptions and biases and talking about these with our children are crucial steps to help prevent them from following similarly rigid expectations. We can explain that not all firefighters are male, nor are all nurses female. We can say that some families have two daddies, two mummies or only one parent. And, hopefully, one day I won't have to change the gender of so many children's books as I read them, where many more characters are male.

In order to understand more about how modern motherhood is perceived in the West, it helps to know how this journey changed from the one-parent breadwinner family to the now more common set-up of both parents working.

My maternal grandmother was a typical housewife. She had been a chemical analyst in a lab before she met my grandfather, but it was abnormal for women from her generation to work outside the home after marriage. She had five children; her husband had a good job with ample income to support them all. There was no need for her to work and, perhaps more importantly, no expectation to do so. She had her hands full running a household, though she had live-in help for childcare and housework.

My paternal grandmother, with 11 children, was not expected to work, but even if she had wanted to, a lack of formal childcare arrangements and the expense of it would have made that impossible. She had trained in domestic affairs (*huishoudschool* – which translates to household school) and was an excellent seamstress. She called her education 'sewing school' and, if time permitted, made clothes for others too. Money was tight and my dad and his siblings would sleep two to a bed, with the older children often watching the younger ones.

Neither of my grandmothers are alive, so I cannot ask them about their experience of motherhood. These were two strong women at the opposite ends of the economic spectrum, but both were expected to stay at home once married.

Across the pond in the US, for a typical 1950s housewife – keeping her house in order and her kids well fed, well cultured and, frankly, better educated than other kids – was almost like a competition nobody signed up for. If women went to work, their kids would surely suffer, the general feeling went, and how children turned out was viewed as directly tied to how they were parented. The idea of being a good mother meant putting the needs of their children very far above their own. Journalist Rina Mae Acosta, co-author of the book *The Happiest Kids in the World*, aptly puts it the following way when reflecting on her upbringing:

> Mothers were indentured servants to their kitchen, their work, their children and their husbands – and, most often, they did it alone. There was a lot of dignity and pride when it came to being a supermom. The more sacrifices you made – including neglecting to look after or take any time for yourself – the better you were at being a mom.

It follows that Acosta wanted a different world for her own family. Gender roles may have had their origin in biology, but the more they permeate the social sphere, the more women became firmly cemented as primary caregivers – even after the earliest biological needs of childbirth have passed.

Today a mother who works is the norm, but women still make up the majority of the part-time workforce. This in turn means that 'working mothers' are categorised in various ways. This includes part-time workers, high-achievers or those whose household income doesn't leave them much of a choice but to work. Then there's the few who have never worked at all. These women, as well as those who stop work to raise their children, are given the somewhat loaded label of a stay-at-home mother, but this doesn't always come from choice. Workplace satisfaction, cost and the illusion of flexibility are all factors that can push and keep mothers out of the work-place. The numerous subtle and overt biases that contribute to the motherhood penalty can make women feel disempowered at work; made worse if they are doing a job they don't like.

Once women are bound to the home, it reinforces the idea that motherhood is a source of power there. That's because it's the one core area where women are in control, as they are the ones who tend to organise most of the domestic affairs. For years mothers have been sold the idea that they can take pride in running their households and being good homemakers. That may be so, but this 'power' is only in place because women can't exert similar power at work. Sociologists have therefore argued that a woman's 'power' at home is not true power at all, given it's an oppressive form of power because of her gender.

This can be explained by the idea that as well as hostile, overt sexism there is a more subtle form of sexism that gives the illusion of positivity: benevolent sexism. This encom-passes the notion that women have certain vulnerabilities or personality traits that make them better carers and, simul-taneously, paints them as inferior in positions of power or authority at work. It therefore undermines gender equality by dividing the idea of what women and men can do into mythical gender-typical traits – remember the whole assert-ive men, bossy women example? That.

This detail is important to consider because whatever kind of mother you are, we live in an age where our decisions are much more visible, often amplified on social media and, in turn, scrutinised, even by other mothers. This happens so often that it's referred to as the 'mummy wars', where women are judged and shamed for the decisions they make for their children. This starts early: breast versus bottle, how we discipline or whether we discipline, how much screen time we allow, and so on. Mum shaming is so prevalent that in a poll of 475 mothers, two-thirds reported feeling shamed, with mums feeling stressed and criticised by comments or advice rather than supported. Discipline and diet were the most shamed topics and it occurred more from family than from friends or other mothers, though a quarter reported being criticised from several overlapping groups.

At the same time there is an ever-increasing awareness and frustration around unequal divisions of care. Dads are doing more than they used to, but it is still mothers who do the lion's share of care work, even when women are higher earners and work full time, which the majority do – in the UK it's 70 per cent while in the US it's 75 per cent.

While men do more childcare today than they did in the 1960s, women do more too, but the rate of increase has been steeper for men, in part because less was expected of them in the past, and more women were at home running their households. A 2016 study analysed time-use data reported across 11 Western countries to put a figure on the time spent on childcare. This is where respondents note down each day how much time they spent on any given task. Whereas in 1965 men averaged 16 minutes of childcare per day, by 2012 it had increased to 59 minutes. Women still do more, even those that work full time. The study found that they did an average of 54 minutes in 1965 and 104 minutes in 2012. We will look at the pitfalls of this increased time spent in the next chapter, but it's important to highlight here too, because the burden of this extra unpaid care can exacerbate gender inequality as well as limit career advancement.

Therein lies a related conundrum; there's the motherhood penalty in the workplace, but there's a secondary penalty related to that. High 'ideal worker' standards directly clash with the high standards that are expected of motherhood. If women are caught between the expectations of being ideal workers and ideal mothers, something has to give as it is impossible to live up to both ideals. While most mothers want the best for their children, the unspoken message is that they should settle for less than best themselves.

That implication is that good mothers sacrifice their own time. The great irony of this is, when asked, would any mother want their own child to settle for less in the same position? The answer, invariably, is no. As children learn from their parents, by settling for less in terms of our own career and ambition, we could be unintentionally implying that our daughters should do the same later on. Of course, we intuitively want to give everything we can to our children to ensure they get the best start in life, but there has to be a balance. If this comes at the expense of our own happiness, they would not be growing up in a happy environment either. Unhappy mothers can make for unhappy children.

So much of a mother's body and time are given to her children, and what's left of her is open to scrutiny from society too. A conflicted identity when a woman becomes a mother then starts to look alarmingly inevitable.

That motherhood is so normal and even expected, means most of us just carry on. It can be exhausting to think too deeply about it anyhow, and motherhood tends to be so all-consuming that it can feel frustrating to ruminate about identity loss – which is why I am writing this book – to help understand exactly why we do. Especially because the more that the possibility of equality is dangled in front of us, the greater the frustration is that we are the ones penalised for attempting to achieve it.

Media portrayals of gendered expectations don't help either. Despite men doing more than ever before, especially in liberal circles, today there are still immediately apparent examples where men unashamedly take on the role of provider rather than carer. In 2017, one well-known UK politician, Jacob Rees-Mogg, caused a stir when he stated, after the birth of his sixth child, that he had never changed a nappy. His reason for this? He was not a 'modern man'. He didn't imply it was left to his wife, but that the nanny could do it better, so why should he? Nor reportedly, did Donald Trump or UK comedian Russell Brand change any nappies. When Brand admitted this in 2019, he said that his wife 'does all of it. It turns out that she is extremely well versed in the nuances and complexities of child rearing.' These men may be outliers, but the examples point to the obvious: there is still an underlying assumption of 'parental essentialism', where many aspects of childcare are believed to be best left to women because they are deemed better at it. When you consider the amount of unpaid work women still do compared to men, you see this perception remains a reality. And when women do more, then of course they become better at it more quickly.

It gets worse. The reported extra hours of unpaid work do not include a mother's mental load. This is the less-obvious time spent on just thinking about what is needed for child-care and household tasks and it cannot easily be quantified. Another term for it is 'cognitive labour'.

It is real and women do most of it. It's not the result of

constant multitasking (it's a misconception that women are better at multitasking, everyone is terrible at multitasking), we just do more of the 'second shift'. To some it might appear as if we are doing several tasks at once, whereas we are constantly switching between tasks quickly. That we have to, comes at a cost to our paid work and free time.

When you think about it, it is easy to recognise mental load: the invisible tasks needed to make family life function. Remembering an appointment, or when to buy new shoes or clothes before they get too small, or what ingredients to cook for a dinner plan made earlier. It's packing sufficient clothes for holidays, enough snacks for playdates, organising after-school clubs, researching childcare, schools ... You get the idea. Thinking about and juggling these tasks is largely somehow typically a mother's job, and it usually happens with no overt conversation about dividing such tasks. While the time spent on housework and physical childcare is easy to account for, the planning involved in making ordinary life function is unseen. If the mother is the one to take any amount of leave from work, she will also spend more time with her baby and therefore do the necessary childcare admin early on. But even when she's back at work, this load remains hers, presumably because there's no 'handover' to the partner, and so patterns that start early, linger.

I certainly didn't attempt to explain the details of my daughter's wardrobe and food preferences to my husband when I went back to work, knowledge I had acquired by spending ten or more hours a day alone with her during weekdays for over six months. It somehow seemed easier for me to pack for holidays and to prepare food, than to delegate. Initially, I wasn't aware I was mentally doing more; I unthinkingly just did it. Research on mental load shows this is not only common, it is the norm.

In a 2019 study, Allison Daminger of Harvard University interviewed 70 individuals from 35 couples. She asked them to fill in diaries and questioned them about their thought processes around tasks. Given what is already known about women taking on a significant part of the mental load, she was looking for specific gender divisions of cognitive labour. She found that there were four key stages:

- Anticipating needs.
- Identifying options for filling these needs.
- Choosing and deciding among the options.
- Monitoring the results.

All these processes are largely unseen and would not appear on the type of time surveys that economists use to assess how households spend their time on specific tasks. We cannot easily quantify the time spent organising playdates or researching after-school activities in the same way as we do for obvious physical tasks, like cooking or a trip to the playground. Daminger found that these four steps are gendered in subtle ways. Women do more cognitive labour on all of them, especially anticipating needs and monitoring them, but, for step three, both couples were almost equally invested in making the decisions, say on school places, it just happened to fall to the women to do the legwork in terms of researching options, scheduling visits and so on. The steps that were most gendered were also the ones that were most invisible, so much so that the couples themselves didn't notice the division of this cognitive labour until it was pointed out.

Interestingly, when Daminger asked the couples about this, their own perception of why these tasks were split was not at first attributed to gender among the college-educated participants, but those in the lower socioeconomic group were more likely to explicitly describe certain tasks as 'women's work'. This may be because the college-educated parents had a stronger sense of their idealistic and feminist intentions to divide this work, and that it was unequal was in conflict with that identity. They therefore sought other ways to explain it, such as mentioning differing workloads, masking the fact that it was more easily explained by gendered work.

Rarely did the couples in the study specifically divide tasks, they simply 'fell into them'. It was often due to the absence of deliberate choice that the tasks were split into typical women's work and men's work (cooking and childcare versus DIY). This shows that when we don't overtly decide on how to divide tasks, gender norms often make those decisions for us. I do the bulk of the laundry, my husband fixes bike punctures. We now joke about this and he'll do the laundry anytime I ask, and, in truth, I'm happy not having to fix any punctures, but I could (and have done) if I needed to.

Naturally there are exceptions to who does most of the care work, but, overall, the assumption is that the organisation around a child's needs are more the mother's domain than the father's.

There was the time my husband took the kids to an activity on a Sunday morning and the female organiser asked, out of politeness or curiosity, where their mother was. My husband replied that I was having a much-needed break, to which the response was, 'Yes I can imagine that she needs one after looking after these two all week.' Sure, she was a woman in her 60s and our youngest was not yet one, so it was not an absurd assumption to make by any means, just yet another one that assumed I was the one at home, when I had been back at work for over a month already. Or how about the fact that trains going up and down the UK's west coast show a symbol of a woman changing a baby's nappy on gender-neutral toilets, an apparent oversight lost on whoever designed, approved and ordered the signs. Or how schools will often call mothers when a child is sick – I've heard this done even where the father is listed as a primary contact. These are but a few recent examples and they are not a coincidence, but a product of powerful cultural influences that start from birth.

Sharing the burden is not as easy as it seems, given that so many of the tasks mothers do are invisible. If women's unpaid care work was valued and acknowledged, it would help, as would closing the gender wage gap. By acknowledging the very real gender divides we fall into both on cognitive labour and actual physical tasks, couples could make choices to be more collaborative. Since researching this chapter, we certainly have.

It's not easy given that many of those in Daminger's study didn't attribute cognitive labour to gender. If anything, the illusion of equality, or attributing cognitive labour to other forces, such as personality: *'She's just better at that sort of thing'*, or the fact that a member of the household (usually the man) works longer hours, pushes gendered patterns under the radar even further.

If a mother's cognitive work sounds exhausting, now consider 'mother's worry', the disproportionate amount of everyday worries and concerns a mother has about her children, often tied in with emotional concerns about how a child is doing. When interviewing new mothers and fathers, sociologist Susan Walzer noticed that mothers spent much more time worrying than fathers. This was in part because they were expected to, and, more surprisingly, because it tied

to the pressures they felt to be a 'good mother'. One respondent worried that because she was working long hours, she
was not able to live up to a 'good mother image' of being
'all nurturing and all present and always there'. But, for her,
worrying itself made her feel like a better mother, because by
worrying, she was at least doing what was expected.

Mothers also worry because they 'experience their children as extensions of themselves', while, at the same time,
how a child behaves might reflect on how we mother. I know
many who feel embarrassed when their toddlers throw tantrums, as if it's somehow our fault (it very rarely is). But, in
the moment, it can feel as if we cannot control our children.
A mother's worry, then, in some ways comes from this conflict, and from constantly being expected to act a certain way.
The problem with this type of worry is that so much of it is
invisible and tied up with a woman's identity as a mother.
And, because it's expected, we don't always notice that it is
an additional burden that only mothers carry, even in otherwise seemingly equal households. All this feeds into the
constructed idea of women as 'selfless caregivers who serve
their families'.

These gendered roles may in some part be formed because,
as the psychologist Diane Ehrensaft noted, men experience
fatherhood as something they do, whereas women experience motherhood as something they are. Or as my husband
said early on, it seemed unfair that his life stayed much the
same in his first year of fatherhood, at least at work, while
mine was so immeasurably different. Motherhood is something that nestles into our very identity and lived experience
from the get-go, meaning the mother's worry that is expected
of us is a recognisable consequence.

Many women are aware of this on some level. A friend
recently confided in me that her fear of becoming a mother

came from the 'constant judgement that people pass on you all the time', because such strong ideas exist about what it means to be a mother. One of the participants in Walzer's study noted something similar – that people don't look at you and say 'oh there's a good mother' but they will quickly judge a mishap that could make you look like 'a bad mother'.

If what we do is so powerfully shaped by our expectations, then this has other consequences. Take the phenomenon known as 'maternal gatekeeping', which is when mothers, knowingly or not, restrict their partner's involvement with their child. Gatekeeping can be extremely subtle, such as small criticisms, or redoing a task again after the father has done it. I've been guilty of the latter on occasion. For example, as I start work earlier than my husband, I finish earlier too, so I do the pick-ups while he drops the children off. On the occasional days we switch, I still feel compelled to check that he has remembered. I don't need to do this, it's unlikely he would forget, but as I feel it's my 'role' I still remind him. Or smaller acts like dressing our toddler in different clothes after my husband has already dressed her (I definitely never do this now), or leaving detailed instructions for mealtimes when I was away for the weekend instead of allowing him to figure it out for himself.

Gatekeeping may sound like an abstract term, but it's extremely relatable. We've no doubt all heard our own parents, friends or colleagues moan about a task and say, 'I may as well do it myself.' When it comes to parenting, disabling our partners from doing tasks disrupts, disempowers or demotivates them.

In a 2015 study looking at maternal gatekeeping in 182 dual-income working couples, mothers who had overly idealistic or perfectionistic standards of what the father should do were found to be more likely to 'close the gate'. Mothers with psychological issues or those with difficult relationships had higher instances of gatekeeping. This was especially so if the relationship had ended. The team also noted that when both parents are trying to balance work and family life, they tend to show more progressive views on equality whereas stay-at-home mothers with more traditional beliefs about gender roles might naturally be more likely to 'close the gate' as they already do more childcare.

Interestingly, the authors proposed that gender attitudes could be a consequence of maternal gatekeeping, not always a cause. The reason could be due to what psychologists refer to as 'cognitive dissonance', where, if what we do day-to-day, such as more childcare, is inconsistent with a belief (the desire to do equal amounts of care) then a person may change their beliefs to match the behaviours they are experiencing. Both mothers and fathers could be affected by this. Take a mother with egalitarian views about her role: if she experiences a gendered world that does not match her mindset, it may result in her changing her views to become more traditional in order to remove this feeling of inconsistency, so that her identity no longer clashes with her ideology. This would be especially likely to happen if she was also showing gatekeeping behaviours.

Gatekeeping naturally has downsides. The quality of a father's involvement in childcare could be affected. Putting this extra burden of care onto the mother could push her to gatekeep even more. An attitude change around gendered roles may then be an inevitable consequence.

The same could happen to fathers. If he is less involved than he expected to be, it may actually change his expectations to prevent feelings of unease. We all tend to avoid discomfort whenever we can and changing our attitudes could be one consequence. A father may therefore start off with equal views on gender roles but if, for whatever reason, he is not as involved as much as he wanted to be, his views could shift to become more traditional.

Even framing it like this is uncomfortable, as it is hinting that women are to blame for 'gatekeeping' when, in reality, it again ties into what we saw with mother's worry and mental load. If expectations are so ingrained, it can have the unfortunate result of mothers doing more. The fact that men generally work longer hours while women earn and work (for pay) less, perpetuates the cycle. In one study, looking at over 600 women from dual-earning couples, the 21 per cent who were classified as gatekeepers did five additional hours of housework and childcare per week compared to those who were not showing gatekeeping behaviours. Gendered expectations can even impact upon marital happiness. Gatekeeping is more likely when a relationship is in trouble. If a father is subtly pushed from contributing to everyday childcare, it could lead to even more conflict and isolation.

It's hard to establish cause and effect of such a phenomenon, given that gender attitudes are often hard to pin down. The consequence of maternal gatekeeping shows that perfectionistic ideals are not just problematic for a mother's own sense of who she is as a mother and a woman, but when this ideal extends to what a father's role should be, it exacerbates a mother's load.

Fortunately, just as gates can easily close, they can be opened too. This can be helped by greater collaboration as well as asking our partner's opinion on activities or decisions relating to childcare. Or, even better, mutually identifying tasks each can take ownership of can also ease cognitive load, especially if the tasks are end to end – planning and doing.

It's no use offering to cook if someone else has to ensure you have all the ingredients. There are positive benefits when a mother relinquishes control. If she has been at home with a child more, she may know the ins and outs of their routine, but that doesn't mean she needs to dictate the schedule all the time. The more a partner does without any input could lessen the negative effects of gatekeeping and help improve a father's relationship with his children.

Now that I understand more about gatekeeping, I will never again leave a list of meal options when I'm out. We become more confident as parents with time, by learning from experience and failures. New parents already find it difficult to know whether what they are doing is 'right' – as there is so much conflicting advice. A bit of flexibility in allowing failure, or less-than-perfect parenting, will go a long way, but close the gate too often and a father may be inclined to continue doing less, with the mother picking up the leftovers.

I'm including these analyses of the perception of gender and the assumptions that go with it, in no way to criticise a father's contribution, especially considering that many want to be more involved with their children's lives, but long work hours can impede that. I'm highlighting that gender impressions impact upon what we do and how we are judged. Even splitting overt tasks 50:50 doesn't solve imbalances such as the mental load. To alter this, we first need to change how mothers are perceived, as well as reframe the expected stress and worry that can be a result of these burdens.

If nothing else, when childcare is equally shared between couples, it could even result in more sex. In heterosexual couples, men who are more involved have reported more satisfying sex lives while those who stated that their female partners did most of the childcare showed least satisfaction in several areas – sex, childcare and relationship contentment overall. When fathers did least, the mothers were also less satisfied. Though take note, doing more childcare is not a magic trick that will improve your sex life. We have to remember that this was a correlation; it could simply be that couples that have more sex have a better relationship generally, and not to mention that women are happier, more rested and less stressed when more of their childcare burdens are eased.

Of course, while the male–female parent model is still in the majority, family norms and social attitudes along with them are changing. Boys from single-mother households perceive their mother's role differently to boys from mother-father households. The former are expected to help more with housework and, in turn, do so more willingly. They also tend to be more egalitarian in later life. The motherhood and fatherhood experience is also different for LGBTQ+ parents and single-parent households, where entrenched social views can feel even more alienating because the language used around parenthood is so often limited to expected social norms.

While the scientific literature largely focuses on heterosexual couples, all the different ways a family is formed are no less valid and need to be better understood in order for all versions of motherhood, in all its beautiful or stressful reality, to be respected.

For instance, a female friend of mine in a same-sex relationship carried and gave birth to her partner's biological child. She described how this led to quite intrusive and personal questions from minor acquaintances and even strangers. People were curious and would ask her why she carried a child that was not biologically hers or how they chose who would get pregnant. By transgressing norms of motherhood, her personal affairs were somehow open to scrutiny.

Stigmas like these remain difficult to change, especially because motherhood is so expected for women. Non-parent friends have told me of judgement they feel for not having children; as if they have to explain themselves, even though this is a very personal choice – if it is a choice at all. Women who are not mothers have reported that it makes them feel 'other' and 'weird' after a certain age. Studies show that non-mothers are stigmatised, pitied and viewed as desperate, regardless of how they themselves feel about it.

At the same time, the number of childless women in their 40s has doubled compared to the 1970s, in both the US and the UK. In 1946, only 9 per cent of UK women were childless at 45, classified as 'the end of childbearing years'. As of 2018, a generation later, 19 per cent of women who were born in 1973 were childless (in Germany it was 22 per cent). Those that do have children, delay it, with an average starting age of 31 compared to 24 a generation earlier. While childlessness is becoming more prevalent, the idea of it as a lifestyle choice is slow to catch up. One friend who adamantly states she doesn't want children says that almost everyone she shares this with tells her she'll change her mind.

In short, women are penalised when they do become mothers, and stigmatised when they don't. The motherhood penalty we explored earlier is, in fact, a penalty on all women. On a societal level, we are damned if we do, and damned if we don't.

Despite the many implicit biases, I was pleased to discover that deep-rooted assumptions as well as behaviours can change when the father stays at home but the mother works.

This role reversal is rare – in the US it's about 5 per cent, but this is a lot higher than a generation ago. Noelle Chesley at the University of Wisconsin-Milwaukee analysed family dynamics in heterosexual couples when fathers stayed at home while the mothers worked. First, as expected, she found that breadwinner mothers did reduce housework and childcare during working days. Although this is good news, overall more pressure was still on women. While they did less on days they went out to work, just as men do, it was still more than a breadwinning father.

Additionally, at weekends, gender roles resumed. Breadwinning women once again did more than men and their weekend workloads looked no different in terms of household division of care than stay-at-home mothers. However, an interesting pattern emerged: the stay-at-home fathers did different types of housework on weekends compared to breadwinner fathers – that is, they were more involved in parenting and other types of more female-specific tasks, likely because they had become more in tune with their children's routines and needs during the week. One participant said of the change: 'It's more of a team environment ... it's become what it is supposed to be.' Another, commenting on her husband's attitude, said, '[Oscar] would say to me "I can't stand not knowing what my little boy is doing every minute of the day." [This was] just how I felt when I had to leave Keith at daycare after I'd been home with him for six months.'

These positive changes took place despite the fact that it was largely not by choice that the men did not work, but due to job losses or relocating for work. Just by spending more time on day-to-day family activities, the fathers valued their involvement more while showing a renewed appreciation for their working wives. Previous assumptions of a woman's role were altered because they were doing more themselves.

It also encouraged longer-lasting change. Once back at work, some of those who had been stay-at-home fathers reported a greater understanding of the difficulties of work–life balance for mothers. Those at management level said they were more likely to show support for parents. Others also found they talked about their children more.

It's a relief that gender roles can change, but a two-breadwinner model remains the norm for Western countries, so these types of mind shifts wouldn't easily occur for the majority of couples. Working mothers still often feel guilty when they are the main earners; 52 per cent of the female breadwinners showed jealousy and guilt as they felt that, when working full time, they could not live up to a perfect parenting ideology. Chesley argues that it was no accident that a culture of intensive mothering (which we will learn more about in the next chapter) increased right at the time when women were entering the labour force in greater numbers. The hard-to-reach ideals of the stereotypical 'good mother' are heightened when a mother feels like she is unable to follow them by carving out a career.

Even where change is occurring on an individual level between couples, the rest of society is slow to catch on. Sociologists refer to a phenomenon known as 'structural lag' which means that individuals tend to change quicker than institutions or cultures.

Men often report wanting to be more involved, but society is set up in a way that makes it harder, which reinforces all the gender expectations discussed. It's not that change isn't happening, it unfortunately takes time to infiltrate institutions, especially when it comes to entrenched, emotional views about the family. One stay-at-home father I recently bumped into told me that another man laughed when he explained he had quit work to look after his children. He reacted this way because he thought it was a joke or, worse, couldn't imagine a father would take on that role.

Though institutional change will take time, many small alterations can have an impact, be that being more vocal about work–life balance or holding each other to account for childcare tasks. If behavioural change is shaped by doing, women clearly need to do less, more often. This could in turn help them reduce the pressure to achieve perfection and the associated guilt that goes with it.

THE SECRET TO SUCCESS

On the pitfalls of trying to be a perfect mother and the toxic idea that you can 'have it all'

Bénédicte, a mother of two, prepared fresh vegetables for her babies every day – she would even wake an hour early to do so if they had a day trip out. Ready baby meals were not an option. She felt an intense pressure to be perfect, though she was also plagued by self-doubt and guilt, which only pushed her to attempt to achieve perfection even more. This was especially on her mind because she felt a strong sense of responsibility that her children's future happiness depended on how she behaved.

She recalls feeling scared that her children would think she did not 'care enough' and, even when doing her best, she still felt she was not doing enough.

What an ideal mother would do weighed heavily on her mind, especially as 'it seemed normal to exhaust myself for my children, because my mother had exhausted herself for us'.

Bénédicte's pursuit of perfection contributed directly to her feeling burnt out. It started with being consciously overinvolved but quickly transgressed to being completely overwhelmed. She eventually received help from a clinical psychologist, because it got so bad that she stopped engaging completely.

> I was not aware of my children any more. I think I did not want to admit it to myself ...
>
> I felt so guilty not to play with my children. Because it is widely accepted in our society that a mother should not leave her child sitting in front of the television.

As is clear in her case, intensive parenting comes at a cost. The pursuit of 'having it all' as well as the pressures to achieve perfection are unrealistic and can set us up for failure. The secret to success is to do less, worry less and love just as much. It's not easy, but it is important for our own sense of self. As Voltaire famously said, 'the best is the enemy of good'. In this chapter, we will see that the mindset of aiming to be perfect is toxic on a personal and societal level.

If there is anything I have learnt about the 'secret' to success, it is that the first thing we can do is cut ourselves loose from the expectations thrust upon us in many areas of life, which is a challenge in itself. To be 'successful' we need to be less perfect. Being 'good enough' is more than sufficient.

The idea of a 'good enough mother' first gained prominence in the 1950s, coined by the influential psychoanalyst Donald Winnicott. It referred to the idea that a mother can and should fail at least some of the time, as she cannot possibly attend to her baby's needs all of the time. 'Failing' now and again is better in the long term, he figured, as it would help to build up resilience and an understanding that the world is imperfect. Bear in mind that these are little failures: not getting there in time to prevent one child pushing the other, or the other having his hair pulled, or forgetting to take water or snacks to the park or giving in to requests like yet another outfit change to avoid a tantrum.

Many of us intuitively know that the pursuit of perfection is pointless, but when we have children, the bombardment of internal and external pressures for what we should be doing is unparalleled in its intensity. This may include any combination of the following: preparing nutritious meals with fresh organic food, no screen time, adequate socialisation, quality time with parents, a good mix of culture and so on. Then there's the after-school activities or listening to the right kind of music and reading enough stimulating books, but at the same time, fostering independent and creative play while also carving out enough quiet time. In other words: too much.

Perfect parenting is a toxic fallacy, dangerous for our own mental health and the wellbeing of our children. It is the strive for perfection that can contribute to feelings of fatigue and guilt, precisely because of unrealistically high standards parents at times expect of themselves. If our identity ties to the idea of being a perfect mother, we cannot live up to the reality. Expecting perfection will leave mothers feeling less and wanting more.

Throw in the fact that many mothers also work, and it's readily apparent that there are not enough hours in the day to pursue 'ideal mother' standards while doing anything for ourselves. It's a cognitive and emotional burden that weighs on Western mothers' shoulders.

This pursuit of the unachievable can quickly backfire and is directly linked to parental burnout, a chronic stress disorder that is being diagnosed among parents in greater frequency and with lasting negative effects. Parental burnout is more serious than the general sense of fatigue common among parents. Tiredness will abate after rest, whereas burnout prevails even after plenty of sleep.

The symptoms include feeling physically and mentally exhausted, leaving parents feeling detached from their children. They lose a sense of fulfilment and, in the worst cases, this can result in neglect. Burnout increases suicidal thoughts even more so than depression, research has found. That's because there's no getting away from it: those who burn out at work can take leave, resign or find another job. But parents cannot go on sick leave from their children; it's the same early start day in and day out.

One mother in a 2018 report on accounts of burnout talked about how she felt a sense of 'failure' when striving for perfect behaviour. 'If I had been able to let go instead of wanting everything to be perfect, maybe I would not have gone crazy . . .'

Once a parent experiences burnout they can be stuck in a toxic situation. In the most extreme cases, it can lead them to believe they only have two options: leaving the family or suicide, the latter of which is the leading cause of death for new mothers. Another mother in the same 2018 analysis recalls just how bad it got:

> At that time, I felt I should either kill myself, or leave the girls. It was one or the other . . . I was so much trapped in it, that I was not able to take the smallest step back. At the height of the crisis, everything appears as disproportionately difficult.

Isabelle Roskam and Moïra Mikolajczak from the University of Louvain lead several large-scale burnout studies, which started in Belgium but have since expanded to more than 40 countries involving 15,000 participants. They found that burnout occurs in up to 10 per cent of parents in several Western countries. In the US, the most conservative numbers indicate that at least 5 per cent of parents are affected, equivalent to well over three million parents.

In a 2020 study the team found that parental burnout can be much more serious than other types of stress. In the first biological study of parental burnout, they looked at the cortisol level of more than 100 patients diagnosed with the condition. Cortisol was measured from hair samples, which gives an indication of accumulated stress over time. The results were unexpected – the level of the stress hormone found was double that of other parents and higher than for individuals who suffer from chronic pain. These burnt-out parents felt prolonged and overwhelming levels of stress.

Bénédicte, who we heard from at the start of the chapter, finally sought help when she found herself screaming angrily at her daughter to get dressed, eventually punching a hole in her wardrobe.

There are other factors that can contribute to burnout. One is the individualistic quest for happiness, usually influenced by cultural values. A large-scale study currently under review looked at the causes of burnout in a combined total of 16,685 parents from 40 countries. The prevalence of burnout varies significantly between countries and the strive for individualism, common in the US and the UK, was found to be a strong predictor for parental burnout, even more so than financial stress, which is another risk factor for burnout.

It's especially challenging when our quest for individual

happiness or success directly competes with our children's needs. It can be difficult to pursue hobbies or focus on our own whims and interests when parenting and work already take up all of our time. Even when we do carve out some rare alone time, we are prone to feeling guilty for prioritising ourselves. When we have competing goals but not enough time for any of them, that's when identity clashes feel most stark. If we prioritise a hobby, our mother identity might suffer, but if we prioritise motherhood at the expense of everything else, our pre-parental identities are at risk of fading or disappearing altogether.

Subtle messages that our children are all we need to make us happy and make life complete are not helpful either. Happiness often dips for new parents. Even thinking of time spent with my children as taking away my 'free time' is enough to make me feel guilty, but the reality is that free time looks very different than it used to. It usually comes with a child or two in tow and a lot more noise and mess.

Of course, mothers do usually put their children's needs first, and it frequently comes at a cost to their career. That may solve one element of motherhood guilt but leave another brewing unhappiness of unfulfilled potential. This can contribute to a decline in wellbeing as well as a greater risk of burnout, heightened when our parental identity interferes with a professional or personal identity. When a parent experiences this as a regular tension, such as the conflicted feeling of working late to stay on top of deadlines, versus being back home for bedtime, it makes things more difficult because prioritising one often means sacrificing the other. It's a constant juggling act to balance different and competing needs, which becomes even harder when parenting is treated as an individual pursuit with little outside help.

Given all this conflict, it's a natural consequence that

burnout is a common Western phenomenon, precisely because of our perfectionistic expectations. In fact, it's so clearly driven by societal pressures that culture was shown to be a key driving factor for burnout.

The way cultural pressure becomes an individual problem is revealing. Perhaps surprisingly, mothers who held the most egalitarian beliefs with regards to parenting were found to be more vulnerable to burnout. That means mothers living in the very countries that claim to be improving gender equality and the gender pay gap are more prone to burning out, in part because those goals are hard to reach.

Parents in countries with a strong emphasis on 'positive parenting' are ten times more likely to burn out than those who live in societies with less pressure. It's not that the number of children necessarily increases stress either – African mothers with eight or more were less likely to show symptoms of burnout than a mother with one or two children in Belgium or the US. That's because in the West, mothers believe parenting will be shared but, in reality, it isn't. It is expected for mothers in countries such as Togo or Cameroon in Africa to do up to 90 per cent of all parental duties. There, mothers reported being happy with the little help they got, even if it was less than 10 per cent. A Western mother, however, often has an expectation of dividing tasks equally and is frustrated when she inevitably does more.

Stay-at-home mothers have been found to be at a greater risk of burnout than working mothers. This seems counterintuitive as the latter are stretched at work and at home, but it happens because stay-at-home mothers spend the most time with their children. This can mean that the pressure to be 'perfect' all the time is higher, making them more vulnerable. This is especially likely if being a mother becomes their primary identity, intensifying the need to do everything right all the time, to be an entertainer, carer, chef, chauffeur, educator, cleaner and so on.

At the same time, research shows that work is actually less stressful for parents than being at home with children. The economist Emily Oster explains how long days with our children are so challenging in economics terms – the marginal value of time spent decreases extremely quickly. Three hours of time per day with her kids is the optimum.

Assuming we have had a good night of rest, our base level of happiness during the first hour or two with our children is likely to be higher than it is when at the office – we love our children and so spending time with them makes us happy, for a while. Eight hours later and the decline in our enthusiasm is steep as exhaustion sets in and our resilience drops. Another demand for a snack, pasta thrown on the floor, a sibling rivalry, refusing to get dressed, a one-year-old who fusses 80 per cent of the day. A three-year-old who screams in your face when you don't give her a third glass of milk, or howls when you leave the room for one minute during a particularly clingy phase. These minor incidences are that much harder towards the end of the day. Persistent cries can feel like a stress trigger leaning ever heavier on our brain. It becomes easy to snap.

Contrastingly, and assuming you like your job, think of the time spent at work. The first hour might not be as rewarding as that first hour with your children, but the decline seven hours later is not as steep. Perhaps you are a bit more tired at the end of the workday than at the beginning, but our energy won't have dropped as dramatically. Conversations are not interrupted by cries, while coffee breaks are normal, enjoyable and the drinks can be drunk while still hot. A full day of parenting is far more tiring than a full day of work.

This means for Oster and likely many other parents, it is optimum both for her own happiness and for more meaningful time with her kids to spend her days working, with a few hours with her children before or after. It's not about prioritising work over children, but about optimum time spent in both domains.

This resonates. I have so much more love, patience and energy when I see my children at the start and end of the day. On workdays I usually have just over an hour with them before the bedtime routine. I adore this hour and I find the snack negotiations and stories about my toddler's day endearing. I remind her she can have one snack and she consistently manages to negotiate both raisins and nuts, and sometimes even a rice cake or biscuit too. If this happens after a day alone with both, I have no patience left to find it amusing – instead it feels like she's been prodding me with an invisible stick. There's only so many times you can deny a snack to an increasingly loud moan or cry in a jovial manner, or be patient with a 13-month-old as his frustration builds when his repeated 'requests' for the Play-doh, which will go in his mouth, are denied. The problem is, an hour or two before and after work isn't quite enough time, but all day is too much. Sadly it's not often in our gift to change the hours we work and so the resulting work–life conflict is frustratingly inevitable. That's also why it's so important to have time for ourselves. However, there still appears to be an expectation that we always want to spend more time with our children. It really is the quality time that matters more than the quantity, even if the quality time is limited. Everyone would benefit. I feel this pressure too and it's why I felt guilty for not really enjoying the time alone with my children during the earliest days as a mother of two. If my cortisol levels had been measured, I don't think it would have been good news.

There's another reason why the pressure to be perfect is so widespread. It's due to a style of parenting often referred to as intensive mothering, which has been slowly spreading predominantly among the middle classes. It's rooted in the idea that the time a mother spends with her children is believed to be sacred and irreplaceable, because mothers are uniquely sensitive and attuned to their children's needs. This idea is especially common in the US. Think soccer or ballet moms, making home-made Halloween costumes and cakes for a bake sale. Add a full-time job to the mix and there's not much time left.

This ideology of intensive mothering swept the US in the 1990s and strengthened the idea that mothers who spent most time with their children were better mothers, while those who went off to work were in some way neglecting their offspring.

The prevailing criticism of working mothers is that it could be detrimental for children's wellbeing if they are away from their mothers, that they will in some way suffer. Research does not back up this claim, making it a frustrating and damaging judgement.

Studies that consider the effect of childcare as well as time survey data give little indication of adverse issues. In fact, it's quite the opposite; there can be positive outcomes when children spend time away from their parents, provided they are well looked after. One analysis of over 69 studies of working mothers from 1960 to 2010, found that aside from a 'few exceptions', there were no negative effects on academic achievement or behavioural problems later in life. When teachers looked at academic performance, they rated the children of working mothers as higher achievers, finding that those who worked when their children were young was 'rarely associated with children's later outcome'.

One thing that did have a negative effect was when a mother worked full time in the first year: later achievement scores were then slightly lower compared to mothers who did not, but were higher for children whose mothers worked after the first year. Going back to work too soon can be detrimental, but after the first year the effects were positive.

This overview shows that we cannot attribute achievement or behavioural issues to the fact that mothers work when their children are young. Links between working mothers and later issues were small and largely explained by the type of childcare setting as well as less-sensitive parenting. That is, aside from quality of childcare and social background, having our children looked after while we work is not going to be harmful.

Childcare has to be high quality, though. Other research has shown that spending over 30 hours at childcare is linked to slightly worse than average behavioural problems such as more aggression. This is from US data, which is important to note because childcare starts so much earlier given the lack of universal parental leave, and the quality of childcare available differs.

It sounds counterintuitive, but children do not necessarily benefit from more time with their parents. A 2015 study analysing time survey data found that total time spent with children made less of a difference in the earliest years compared to teenage years. That's in part because parental time itself does not necessarily equate to quality time. The researchers divided time survey data into engaged time (doing activities together) or accessible time (being there while the children are entertaining themselves). This can be further split up into quality of engaged time, and so on (though this wasn't done in this particular study). Reading a book is a better form of engaged time than sitting on the sofa watching television, but both are technically time spent together. The team found that between three to eleven, the amount of engaged time mothers spent with children actually mattered less than it did for adolescents aged 12 to 18, where more maternal time reduced the likelihood of behavioural problems.

At first it's hard to see why maternal time at older ages is more beneficial than for the younger group. Break it down and it becomes more apparent. First, older kids are generally at home less, meaning time together is more on their terms and spending time with their parents helped teenagers feel that they mattered. A time diary study published in late 2020 found that both parents and teens had a better emotional experience and felt less stressed when they were together compared to when they were apart.

Second, unstructured time – including passive activities like screen time – is not particularly beneficial or engaging, meaning younger children could be better off in childcare as some families can find it difficult to replace the type of structured group activities children receive in pre-school.

It follows that children of working mothers have been found to spend less time in unstructured (passive) activities than children of stay-at-home mothers, in part because it's impossible to structure entire days around our children when other life admin has to happen too. Income level clearly plays a role, but so does the idea that the 'marginal value' of the time we spend declines during the day – that is, we can't keep up morning energy levels all day long.

Working mothers seem to make up for their lack of time while they are at work by increasing the intensity of what they do with their children when at home, for good and for bad. In short, they are dropping unstructured time, meaning the time they spend with their children can feel more rewarding in short bursts compared to an exhausting, full day. And for some, because they feel guilty for 'missing out' on seeing them for most of the day.

What this shows is that 'time spent' doesn't capture what type of time is valuable. Time alone does not make as big an impact early on as we might believe it does. Young children need sensitive and attentive carers, but it does not have to be the mother who does everything; other caregivers matter too. The pressure on us to be constantly present during the earliest years is an unhappy consequence of the expectations of the perfect mother, especially as time away is also detrimental during adolescence, when our children might appear to be more independent but, emotionally, they still clearly need us.

The intensive interpretation of motherhood feeds into many of the issues that come about from the pursuit of perfect parenting that we have explored. For mothers who work, there are not enough hours in the day to follow intensive mothering ideals. Intensive mothering is therefore more likely to lead to mental health issues. A 2012 survey found that those who followed intensive motherhood standards were more prone to stress and depression. This can naturally have an impact on children, resulting in lower quality and warmth of parenting. That's why reducing the most intensive type of mothering when our children are young would benefit us all – otherwise it will exhaust us, and that is of no help to our children.

Despite this, and tying directly into intensive motherhood ideals, both parents actually spend more time on childcare activities now compared to 50 years ago. As we heard, in the 1960s women spent 54 minutes per day with their children compared to 104 minutes in 2012. University-educated parents spent the most time on childcare, 123 minutes for mothers and 74 for the fathers. For less-educated parents this dropped to 94 minutes for mothers and 50 minutes for fathers. This is despite the fact that average family sizes are much smaller today so you might expect time pressures to have eased. This hasn't happened, especially as the freedoms of the past have dwindled. During my father's childhood, being one of 11 in a small village where everyone knew each other, children could be left to play outside on the street. In another small Dutch town, my mother walked to school alone when she was not yet five. Similarly, in my north-west London neighbourhood, one elderly local told me that when her kids were young they would be sent out to play in the park by themselves for hours at a time.

Today, most parents wouldn't dream of letting young children go out alone, for obvious reasons. We even tend to supervise their play inside, though this varies enormously between individuals and cultures. In the Netherlands it is normal for families with a baby to have a wooden playpen in their living room called a 'box'. The baby can play there freely without having to be watched constantly. The idea is they get used to this semi-constrained environment as a safe and fun space. It enables the mothers to get things done without having to follow a crawling baby around and it also encourages free play, which we know is important for creativity and independence. I haven't seen as many similar set-ups in the

UK. That's not a surprise given the type of intensive, child-led parenting that is becoming more popular here.

As we have seen, the overall increase in time we spend with our children isn't necessarily as beneficial as we might believe, for them or for us. It's the warmth of the relationship that is important, as well as the quality of activities. This again adversely falls to the mothers who still do more child-care even when working full time.

Researchers believe that the increased load that comes from intensive parenting is another factor that contributes to burnout. This has been difficult to study, given that there's no data on burnout from past generations, in part because it was rarer and not yet recognised as a serious condition. To study the prevalence of burnout 50 or so years ago, Moïra Mikolajczak and her team had to come up with a slightly unusual method of 'time travel'. They visited old people's homes and provided residents with a list of symptoms of parental burnout. They asked if they could recall experiencing similar feelings, but burnout was still found to be rare. The figure aligned with the number who experience burnout in some African countries today, only 1 per cent, even though some of these participants had up to 11 children.

Taken together, the studies on the downfalls of intensive mothering and the data on burnout show that by aiming for the best, mothers can be setting themselves up for failure. Although intensive parenting is on the rise in Europe too, it is far more relaxed than the all-consuming mothering expected in the US. In the Netherlands, parents seem to have a more realistic balance with less of a focus on doing it all, as Chapter 10 will highlight. Families there also score high on happiness and wellbeing – they ranked sixth in the world for happiness in the 2020 World Happiness Report, coming after Finland, Denmark, Switzerland, Norway and Iceland.

If a family is set up without the idea of intensively mothering or the worry of fulfilling social comparisons, everyone seems to benefit. By not aiming to be perfect, we can begin to let go of some of the toxic mum guilt, which is never far from our minds.

THE PSYCHOLOGY OF MUM GUILT

How guilt makes us feel
we never do enough

It was early October 2019 and I was alone all weekend as my husband was travelling. My kids were then five months and almost two and a half. I promised my husband I would try not to stress-text him, as I called it; when I pour out my most immediate and raw thoughts on how hard it can be.

In the earliest weeks this often happened during biting incidents – the toddler would routinely bite the newborn on his fingers, his face and, occasionally, his feet. She'd go in for a kiss and it would sometimes turn into a bite, even if I was right there. This made me feel a level of despair unlike anything I had felt before. I felt anger towards my toddler, guilt that I hadn't protected my baby and despair at my inability to prevent some of these moments. I hated shouting, but to protect one I had to be stern with the other.

My toddler was jealous and acting out to get attention, even if that attention was negative. She would purposely ask to go in 'time-out' when she hurt him. She knew what she was doing was wrong, which made it harder to deal with, especially as she was likely doing so because she felt she wasn't getting enough attention from me.

On this October morning it was not yet 8.30 a.m., and Sanne had already bitten Arjen on the head, leaving the familiar imprint of toothmarks that started white and would slowly turn to red. Shortly afterwards, she hit him with my hairbrush. I was right beside them but wasn't close enough to prevent it; I couldn't police every kiss that turned savage. Later on, when he was sitting on his bouncer and I turned my back to make lunch, it went momentarily quiet. I ran over and saw that she had placed her entire body weight on him, most of it resting on his head and neck, causing it to arch back into a dangerous-looking position. It looked bad and I panicked. I ran over, dropping her lunch on the floor, grabbed her off him and shouted, more out of panic than anger. I comforted Arjen who was by then howling, and, in the shock of the harm she could have caused him, I burst out crying myself. When I did that, she walked over to me with a look of quiet concern, stroked me and asked if I was OK, gently patting me as if nothing had just happened. I guiltily felt ashamed at how angry I was at my toddler for acting in a seemingly manipulative manner; naughty one second, consoling the next. Babies are resilient, I told myself. It wasn't as dangerous as it looked. Still, I called my husband, tearful, and told him I couldn't do this parenting thing any more.

Later on, watching her eat with a smirk on her face, looking extremely cute, angelic almost (she has an ability to charm everyone in a room), I reflected on the stress of the day and momentarily wondered how it was possible to love someone so much, but not really like being with them.

I know this came from the fact that I was feeling protective over her more helpless little brother. Still, I quickly banished this thought from my head. She's my own flesh and blood, my beautiful baby, my *liefste meisje in de hele wereld*. And surely if she harmed the baby, it would have been my fault anyway? She knew she was being naughty, testing me, but can I blame her when all she wanted was more attention, something I was unable to give? Although she knew what she was doing was wrong, she hadn't yet developed a 'theory of mind', the ability to infer the mental states of others. Still, it made me question my patience and competence as a mother. How could I let my firstborn hurt my second? Even if she wasn't aware that what she was doing caused pain.

This was temporary,* she was testing boundaries, and observing cause and effect. When Arjen became more responsive and could crawl and walk, she started to see him more as an ally than a competitor, aside from outbursts when she told me to put him down or jumped in his buggy and howled when we removed her, or told us that 'we need a new baby because this one is crying'.

Hearing my mother's tales of how my brother acted when I came along, I also realised that this type of jealous behaviour is a common occurrence and that children sometimes do whatever they can to get attention, even if that attention is negative.

Moments like these meant that when I was on maternity leave and the baby was fussy, or on days I had both kids on my own, I sometimes secretly wished I was already back in the office. Even writing these thoughts in my notes made me feel guilty, would I have the nerve to include them in my book? What if my children later read this and saw that I

---

* At the time of editing, a year after this anecdote took place, be assured that she stopped this – and her robust 18-month-old brother is now equally capable of fighting back. He's the one we now have to remind to be gentle – and now she enjoys telling him to go into 'time-out', then asks him to say sorry, giving him a big hug after he does so and tells him it's OK.

wasn't enjoying myself, that spending time with them made me so stressed?

On reflection I also realised that it was my irrational 'mother voice' always aspiring for perfection and largely conditioned to think this way. In other words, I was experiencing more of the never-ending mum guilt. I remembered how I loved hearing anecdotes about my own childhood from my mother, about my tantrums and how she dealt with them, and how badly my brother and I could behave around each other. I also relished the knowledge of how strong-willed my toddler can be, how demanding for my attention and how she cannot see past her own immediate desires. It comforted me to read a psychiatrist's take on the feelings I had during the most intense days. Philippa Perry in *The Book You Wish Your Parents Had Read,* writes that we should all acknowledge our feelings, good and bad, and accept those of our children. It was no use telling my toddler she should love her brother and be nice to him all the time; she clearly does love him but she had other, very real and immediate feelings of jealously (or curiosity) that were causing her to lash out. If we tell our children to feel the opposite of how they are really feeling, then they may learn from an early age that their feelings are inappropriate and they could lose the ability to react accordingly. That doesn't mean it is ever easy – nobody enjoys being screamed at by someone as noisy as they are irrational several times a day.

One thing mothers have in common is that feeling of guilt, that we are never quite doing enough. There are so many forces at play that make this almost inevitable, from the pressures of intensive mothering, to the pursuit of perfection to our ever-present mother's worry. Guilt is another contributing factor for burnout – the feelings stem from how high our expectations are for ourselves, coupled with social comparisons. It's ingrained. Mum guilt has almost become synonymous with being a good mother. You can easily imagine why. Mothers today may run from one extra-curricular activity to another, feel guilty if they work too late or do not cook fresh food daily. It's a cognitive and emotional burden that weighs heavily on us.

I'm a rational science journalist and I aim to take an evidence-based approach to parenting, but this can feel impossible when it comes to dealing with guilt, as it comes from an emotional place. I have felt 'mum guilt' often – take the white noise we used with Sanne because it helped her to nap at specific times; as if that predictability was key to living an ordered life with a baby. Months later, at a conference I interviewed an auditory neuroscientist, Nina Kraus from Northwestern University, about the importance of rhythm and noise in daily life. This led to me ask about the rise of white noise apps for babies. She told me that white noise is meaningless, and by providing a baby with mean-ingless sounds when the neurons in their brain are forming new associations, it is akin to blunting the auditory parts of the brain as it searches for meaningful sounds. What we hear is clearly often full of meaning; it is key to how we commu-nicate and understand each other. I quietly added this onto the list of things to feel guilty about, especially as many of these white noise apps are too loud for delicate ears.

Or there were the 5.30 a.m. wake-ups for weeks on end, when the only thing that would calm her down was a video of a Dutch children's song-and-rhyme-time show. We felt OK about that as it was in Dutch, but felt terrible again months later when constant requests for our phones led to almighty tantrums if we didn't give in. We attempted to enforce a blanket screen-time ban to stop the tantrums, which sometimes worked (out of sight out of mind?), then felt less guilty – except we lied to her about the TV being 'gone' and therefore still had an inkling of guilt. We would tone down the fact that we rarely allowed screen time to friends so we did not appear judgemental or opinionated about it. The last thing I wanted to do was have my choices make someone else feel guilty about theirs. And, besides, many of these rules went out the window during the Covid-19 pandemic.

Now, as a mother of two, I have a recurring feeling of never quite being enough for either. As the introduction to this chapter highlights, on days alone I was outnumbered, my time and heart split in two, swelling with love and frustration, at times in equal parts. Frustration at the more able one throwing tantrums, or at the less able one being so helpless. On the numerous nights I start bedtime alone, the second child rarely gets a bedtime story, it is rushed, a time-bomb before his sister acts up. Before he managed to self-settle to sleep, he would have to wait, often howling, while I put his sister to bed. Only then could I breastfeed him peacefully.

While these early days could be extremely stressful, I knew that they would soon pass, and that other challenges would appear. I felt like I should be enjoying my time with them when they were so tiny, but that didn't mean I always did. Sending them to childcare was a welcome relief, but then, especially the first time round, I realised she spent less time with us than at childcare. Another stab at my mother heart. I worried about missing her first crawl, her first steps, her first words. Later, when she became more vocal and told me it was a 'mummy day' today, when it wasn't, stab number two. I reduced her hours there to four days a week when on leave with Arjen, but even that felt like I was robbing her of time with me, as she had to share me with a helpless baby. It was one day a week, but I used to dread it, on constant alert all day long, adrenaline pumping. My husband would feel guilty for leaving me to go to the office, knowing he would have an easier day.

When I felt relief at being back in the office after yet again prising her baby brother's milk bottle and dummy out of her hands to another almighty tantrum, guilt stab number three. It got easier as the baby became more mobile and the toddler more vocal, her tantrums ebbing softly away, but never far from returning and coming back with a vengeance when we switched her to a new nursery. So much change made her even more attached to me; she would sometimes scream even if I left the room.

These conflicting emotions of intense love, avoidance or guilt were confusing. I can't count how many times I mentioned 'mum guilt', as routinely as I might say what I'd eaten the night before and would often hear other mums do the same. It is pervasive, it is all-consuming, it is expected. It's also toxic and exhausting.

I've discussed the importance and positive influence working mothers have on their children, and still we feel guilty when at work, and stretched and rushed when at home. Weekends are therefore spent over-compensating on missed time or worrying that spending yet another Sunday afternoon at home is inadequate stimulation, but sometimes the mere thought of leaving the house for further than our local park, and potentially ruining nap times or a new potty-training routine, seemed equally stressful. The guilt became worse when we had no option but to stay at home due to strict coronavirus restrictions. No playdates, no relatives, no grandparents, but visiting the same park for days on end.

Passive comments from others also feed into motherhood guilt. My own mother frequently reminds me that my children will only be young once, and I should really consider working part time as is so routine in the Netherlands where she lives. This is further cemented in my mind as an implicit expectation when many people asked me whether I would be returning to work full time after maternity leave. A well-meant question, but yet another example of benevolent sexism so subtle and ingrained that it's almost hard to see it for what it is.

Or there's the fact that every decision we make is open to scrutiny, which can make us feel guilty simply by comparing ourselves to how others do things. Something as simple as 'Jonnie doesn't eat any sugar yet', could make another parent feel bad if their child does have the occasional sugary treat, or citing the risks of co-sleeping to a mother who is doing just that, or espousing the benefits of a 'natural' birth to someone who has had a C-section.

Sociologist Caitlyn Collins, who has studied motherhood guilt in depth, reminded me of something I realised from experience – that expectations of mothers are unachievably high. This causes us to feel guilty when we are not living up to those imposed ideals. Motherhood is often seen as an all-consuming, hugely rewarding, positive experience. If we feel different to this norm, we feel guilty for it. Guilt is therefore tied to what it means to be 'a good mother', one who cares more about her children than anything else. Obviously it need not be either or; we can love our children but also enjoy other parts of our life. This comes at a cost though: mothers who put themselves first are seen by others as cold and unfeminine. And yet the expectation to martyr ourselves continues, as Glennon Doyle wrote in *Untamed*: 'We have lived as if she who disappears the most, loves the most. We have been conditioned to prove our love by slowly ceasing to exist.'

This obligation then only serves to propel women to work even harder to achieve those ideals, or, as Collins says, is like 'grease on the wheels on the uneven division of household labour'. While men don't feel these intense feelings of guilt, women's guilt is nested into the perception of a good and proper woman. Similar to mental load, our guilt then becomes an internalised way that we process the expectations put upon us, which results in changing our behaviours to reflect these ideals. Guilt is therefore more than just an internal feeling about how we mother, it has broader implications for gender inequality. Even when it comes from outside pressures, guilt makes us feel bad.

Unhelpfully, some have argued it is useful, claiming that it serves as a good evolutionary motivator to change the behaviour that caused those feelings, resulting in mothers doing anything they can to avoid guilt. Sociologists like Collins strongly refute this, especially as guilt is 'not gender neutral' but is yet another aspect of parenting that is reserved for only mothers and closely tied to the Western construct of what motherhood means.

During in-depth interviews with women in Germany, Sweden, Italy and the US, Collins found that many of her participants believed that being 'a good mother' meant that their own needs mattered less than their children's. She also noted that feeling guilty in itself became a signal for being a good mother, making maternal guilt a form of internal oppression that 'plays into a culture of blame and diverts attention away from the larger structural inequalities'. Even the mothers that accepted a lack of perfection around parenting still expressed feeling guilty, but, fortunately, their guilt didn't feel as bad.

I too have stopped feeling so guilty about sending my children to childcare, a place they adore. Of course I love my children, but having a sense of purpose at work is necessary for me too, and it means they get a better version of me when I see them.

The problem is, a feeling of guilt is almost inevitable, given that it can be impossible to combine the ideals of intensive mothering when also working full time. While guilt might lead a mother to reduce focus on her career, we know that opting out of the workforce has all sorts of other trickle-down effects on the gender pay gap. Besides, if the mother's salary is an important addition for the household, it could have financial consequences too.

I have always wanted to work, but it's equally valid that some women would rather quit work if they can't spend as much time with their children as they would like, finances permitting, as many would not have the luxury of this choice. But if that leaves them with little time alone, it can also cause stress or dissatisfaction. That's why it should come back to the quality time we spend, rather than feeling guilty about the quantity, which is often out of our control.

There's also the consideration about what's important for our own wellbeing and how we can be the best version of ourselves. Mothers who don't live up to perfect parenting ideals and therefore feel guilty show more stress, anxiety and have lower self-belief.

If we focused on what is most important for our own family, and spent less time and energy on outside influences, not only would we feel less pressure, we might feel less stress too, and our children would surely pick up on that. We may even be happier as a result, and our motherhood identity could benefit in the process.

HAPPY CHILDREN, HAPPY MOTHERS?

On why having children doesn't necessarily make us happier

I spent my first six years in the Netherlands on the tiny island of Texel, so small you could cycle around it in less than a day. We were at walking distance from a beautiful sandy beach, past picturesque sand-dunes and numerous blackberry bushes. We rarely had to drive anywhere. Dutch parents tend to transport their children in front of or behind them on their bikes, sometimes one on each end. As soon as they are old enough to learn, children cycle alongside their parents. Special cycle paths are largely cut off from the road, making safety a given. Cycling so young encourages confidence and independence early on. I have fond memories of growing up there, through that lens of perfect and innocent idealism that childhood allows itself to be seen through. A moment in time that felt like it might last for ever, both yearning to be bigger but loving being small. I remember my older brother and I once agreed that if there was a pill that could make childhood last for ever, we would take it.

Dutch children experience a fairly liberal and cooperative upbringing. Even the school system tends to focus on pass or fail, rather than an emphasis on what grade is achieved, and the universities and schools have fairly equal rankings. The class divides seen in the UK and the pressure on what school or university to go to, are less prevalent in the Netherlands. There are divides, of course, but for the most part society is slightly more equal.

Children in the Netherlands have been dubbed some of the happiest kids in the world. Now that I am a mother, I wonder how this could make for a different type of motherhood identity. Without the pressure to be everything for their children, mothers are freer to pursue some of their own needs, which benefits the entire family. While we know there is still a considerable gender pay gap in the Netherlands, the lack of overwork culture and emphasis on family life means there is less pressure on mothers, who are generally happier too.

On the whole, Dutch mothers are less obsessed with achieving perfection and cultural norms help explain why. A common phrase: *doe maar gewoon dan ben je al gek genoeg* translates to: be normal and then you are already crazy enough.

The underlying message we can take from this is that we are imperfect, being average is fine and what will be will be, so what's the point of imposing your ideals on others. A scientist friend explained how her professor had once mentioned that it would be hard to reach 'the top' in her field if she stayed in the Netherlands, because individual success there is not typically appreciated. This is also reflected by the saying *de zesjescultuur*, referring to the grade system where a six out of ten – a pass – is seen as perfectly fine and there is no huge cultural pressure to be top of the class.

That being said, recent insights show that the more relaxed European approach to parenting is waning, with the intensive American style coming into play. The hallmarks of this are putting in more time, money and resources into children's lives – say an abundance of structured after-school activities. A 2017 report showed that while Dutch kids remain fairly happy overall, there has been an increasing feeling of pressure at school, which has doubled compared to 2001. But, fortunately, these Dutch children showed resilience in face of this added pressure. There was no corresponding increase in mental health problems and the cited reason for that was a positive relationship with their parents.

Dutch parents score high on happiness and so do their children, and it starts from birth. Dutch babies have been found to be more smiley, they laugh more, are more cuddly and easier to soothe than US babies. When it comes to happiness, there are many things we can learn from how the Dutch parent.

To start with, six-month-old Dutch babies have been shown to sleep for about two hours more per day compared to American babies. Dutch adults also sleep longer than most, at an average of eight hours 12 minutes a night, almost an hour more than Japan and Singapore, who rank lowest on the scale of sleep length. Women aged between 30 and 60 tend to sleep 30 minutes more than men.

We know that sleep is intricately tied to wellbeing, mental health and therefore happiness. Surprisingly, parenting styles give a clue as to why the Dutch are so well rested. They emphasise the following key qualities – the three Rs:

rust (rest), *regelmaat* (routine), and *reinheid* (cleanliness). This focus on rest clearly pays off.

Even the way we talk about our children is informative and reveals just how much our culture influences the way we see our children and ourselves. In several cross-cultural comparisons looking at how parents described their children, a group of international researchers led by Sara Harkness and Charles Super, from the University of Connecticut, found that while the Dutch were more likely to describe social traits, saying their children were agreeable and enjoying life, parents in the US were more focused on how intelligent or smart their children were, and spent the most time on activities relating to academic development.

Italian parents were more prone to comment on their children's emotions, describing them as easy and well balanced or 'simpatico'. The word happy was used by Australian, Dutch and Swedish parents, but rarely by US parents. Swedish parents were similar to the Dutch, in that they mentioned persistence. They also highlighted traits such as being well balanced, agreeable and secure, while the Spanish described the good character and social nature of their children, with an emphasis on 'proper decorum', and learning how to be a social and successful member of society.

Intriguingly, in stark contrast to the US, Dutch parents found that there were downsides to focusing on intelligence, with one mother saying: 'The ultimate goal is that they be happy with something that they can do later in their job.' To some, overwork pressures have conflated the idea that success is tied to their career. For the Dutch, being happy is success in itself.

*

How we parent naturally varies across cultures. Harkness's studies reveal why the motherhood experience can be so vastly different from country to country. It explains why a US friend worried whether she was providing *enough* stimulation to her three-month-old baby. This would rarely concern Dutch mothers, who would be more likely to be worried about *over* stimulation. It runs deep, as one US mother said:

> I think he needs to be warm, to be fed, to be clean, dry, that kind of thing, but I also think he definitely needs some stimulation. There are times when he is in a chair and we're not paying attention to him or, you know ... he needs some stimulation, something of interest to look at, something to, you know, just for him to play with.

We know that parents spend more time with their children than several decades ago. This is not necessarily a good thing, as working hours have not reduced – more mothers are in paid work now than a generation ago. We have fewer children on average, so it means this time is more concentrated on smaller families.

The more intensive the time with our children is – if we take them on mesmerising, expensive activities every weekend – the more they will come to expect it. A reason parents do this is tied to the intensive parenting ideals we have explored. Intensive parenting itself is not as selfless as you might think, as researchers point to the idea that it acts as a status symbol that separates social classes. But these added pressures make mothers less happy. That's because, as the sociologist Sharon Hays put it, it is 'child-centred, expert-guided, emotionally absorbing, labour-intensive and financially expensive'.

We know that letting children play creatively by themselves helps increase their imagination and curiosity and acts as a buffer against stress. Children don't need to be spoon-fed or constantly entertained and while quality time is definitely a good thing, over-parenting is not.

Dutch parents, on the other hand, are more inclined to let their babies entertain themselves in their playpens or highchairs and are not worried about providing stimulation, instead 'maintaining a calm, positive state of arousal in the baby'. This is similar advice that my mum often shared with me, and why she insisted I buy that large wooden baby box that takes up a significant amount of space in my living room.

Those who are trying to do too much by creating additional expectations for their children and themselves, can become time-stressed and are more likely to burn out. When Harkness and Super lived in the Netherlands, they obtained cortisol samples from mothers and children, and did the same in the US. These samples confirmed what survey data had already hinted at: Dutch mothers are less stressed than their American counterparts – though these were middle-class participants who didn't have additional poverty-related stresses that many lower-income families face.

Our parental approach and what we expect and observe from our children not only impacts them but reflects our mothering style – which in turn is intricately tied to the societal expectations that shaped us. If we describe our children with words that indicate how we wish them to become as adults, it puts additional pressure on them, but also on us.

And, anyway, there is more than one way to be intelligent. For starters, among one ethnic tribe – the Kipsigis, in Western Kenya – Harkness and Super noted in the 1970s that there is a word for intelligence, used only to describe children: 'ng'om', meaning a particular type of helpful and responsible intelligence, largely at home. To be ng'om was expected of Kipsigis children. Being smart at school versus showing intuition at home were seen as separate traits. The ng'om type of intelligence is not usually expected in the cognitive-loaded meaning of the word 'intelligence' in the West. If we don't expect our children to be ng'om, they will not learn that it is important, and so culture begets culture and we risk continuing to parent in a way that puts emphasis upon certain types of intelligence – namely academic ability, something that many Western cultures clearly value more than other forms of intelligence.

The stark irony of that is while we may not encourage ng'om, we do value play, but play has been injected with steroids and laced with products that seek to harness cognitive advancement. Even some baby books are sold as being able to 'stimulate the baby's brain' when in fact our day-to-day environment stimulates the brain all the time. Adopting a stimulation mindset for play again brings it back to encouraging a narrow kind of intelligence. If children are given constant attention they may not learn how to be bored and this can further intensify their need to be entertained at home. If they are used to their every waking hour being micro-managed, they will not as easily learn how to entertain themselves when the world is already a natural playground, and play is how we learn.

How a nation views intelligence matters when it comes to happiness. In the Netherlands, for instance, the education system gives a unique insight into why they often rank so highly for happiness. To consider how this helps mothers, we need to rewind a bit and understand how this culture is embedded early on.

Professor of happiness Ruut Veenhoven of Erasmus University Rotterdam, has an enviable title as director of the World Database of Happiness. He has found that a key component of eventual life satisfaction starts at school. In a 2014 study, his team observed that when children are taught in a hierarchical environment with a strict emphasis on achieving certain grades, their self-esteem suffers because only a select few reach the top and the rest are 'losers'.

We spend a lot of our formative years at school and so over time, children in countries with a highly competitive school system have been found to be less happy as adults. The most striking examples were France and Japan, where school is extremely top-down and competitive. In such an environment it can be very difficult for those who don't reach the top. Anyone stuck behind can feel as if they have failed. Veenhoven found that collectively the French had lower self-esteem than other European countries. And a low self-esteem in adolescence has lasting effects on life satisfaction.

In the Netherlands the education system is fairly horizontal and what he refers to as 'participatory' with lots of cooperative group work. There is not such an emphasis on grades, passing is sufficient (*de zesjescultuur*), and children are streamlined into academic appropriate schools with clear career pathways.* Veenhoven explains that alongside feeling more valued in school, children are heard and are free to express opinions. This helps develop a higher self-esteem and a greater sense of freedom, which generally makes people better at making decisions that can improve happiness later on. Our choices are more constrained when we are less confident or have lower self-worth. All this goes to show

---

* This streamlining has come under increasing scrutiny as it happens at such an early age (12). Who really knows what career they want to follow so early on?

that prioritising intelligence ahead of wellbeing can make children more insecure and potentially less happy as adults.

We want to be good mothers. This can mean we spend more time with our children than there is time available, leaving little left for ourselves. There are obvious downsides to this. In fact, becoming a parent is the start of a happiness dip in numerous countries.

Many people expect that children will make them happier but that is not necessarily the case. Rachel Margolis, a sociologist at the University of Western Ontario in Canada, began to study parental happiness when she noticed that many of her peers who had children were miserable and stressed. This was despite the prevailing idea that having children leads to happiness. Her collaborator from Finland, noted that this was completely different in his country – the same stresses are not felt. That's why in 2011 she embarked on a cross-cultural study looking at happiness data from over 200,000 respondents from 86 countries. The team found that around the world, happiness decreases with the more children you have, but only up to a certain age. Parents under 30 were a lot less happy than child-free people the same age, and happiness declined even more for those who had more children. Between 30 and 39 this downwards trend disappeared and above the age of 40 parents were found to be happier than non-parents. This was found for both sexes regardless of income, though lower earners experienced greater unhappiness, likely because of how expensive children are and how money can help 'alleviate the burden'.

In a follow-up study Margolis wanted to see why the changes in happiness occur and whether this had an effect on having a second child. Her team analysed survey data from 1984 to 2010 featuring over 2,000 respondents three years before and two years after their first child. Each year they were asked, 'How satisfied are you with your life, all things considered?' The answers could range between 0, meaning completely dissatisfied, to 10, meaning completely satisfied. As participants were asked the same question over time, the researchers could track whether responses changed year on year.

The results were clear. Right before parents had a child their happiness went up, perhaps due to the anticipation of a new baby joining the family. But just as the 2011 data had suggested, after a child was born, parents experienced a happiness dip. Those who had a greater wellbeing drop were less likely to have a second child. The parents who did have a second child generally had a higher baseline level of happiness to begin with, meaning another happiness dip after this child wasn't as consequential as it might have otherwise been. Well-educated parents with reduced happiness scores were also less likely to have second children, thought to be due to incompatible work-life pressures and the stress of juggling work and parenting.

While we know that marital satisfaction decreases after the birth of a first baby, it's now abundantly clear that it continues on a downwards trend after each additional child, a decline often called 'the parental happiness gap'. This dip is greatest in the US where parents are reported to be 12 per cent less happy than those without children. Marital satisfaction is also lower for parents, with mothers of young infants experiencing the largest drop.

Similarly, when comparing 22 countries, looking at their policies of childcare costs, paid family leave and work flexibility, researchers found that US parents had the highest 'happiness penalty'. In several countries such as Hungary, Norway, Sweden, Finland and Russia, parents were happier than non-parents. There, even non-parents had higher baseline levels of happiness as clearly all of society benefits when there is adequate social support early on. Work-family policies were found to be the biggest contributor of this effect. The lack of help for families in the US makes parents significantly less happy. That shouldn't come as a shock – once our basic needs are met, if childcare isn't prohibitively expensive, is high quality, schools are free, and motherhood isn't so scrutinised, then there are fewer barriers to happiness.

The decline in marital happiness, like the life-satisfaction dip, is greater among those with more children and affects more educated, higher earners most. In a 2003 meta-analysis looking at almost 100 studies totalling 47,692 respondents, researchers showed that mothers from higher income levels had lower overall marital satisfaction. This is no coincidence as mothers have long been over-burdened with childcare. Better-educated mothers tend to expect equality and if this doesn't happen, these women are dissatisfied as they 'experience more role conflict and greater reduction in freedom'. These women have fewer children and also tend to have their first child at a later age.

This dip occurs due to many of the reasons we have already explored, including chronic sleep deprivation, confinement to the home, guilt and worry about physical appearances, restriction of freedom and being pushed into typical gender roles. Reduced sexual intimacy was also a cited reason. Overall those who were the primary carers, usually women, also experienced a greater marital satisfaction decline.

Intriguingly, as the analysis tracked almost three decades, the researchers noticed that later generations experienced a greater reduction in happiness levels. They put this down to the fact that a generation ago, social conformity, close family and community ties were highly valued. Having children was the done thing, it wasn't seen as a choice, it was just the next logical step in life. First comes love, then comes marriage, and so it went. The idea of equality wasn't really on the agenda the way it is now.

Now though, women have more choice in terms of prioritising career over family, and perhaps this puts a greater value on our freedom. This choice and the knowledge that it exists, makes us less happy. At the same time, we are becoming parents later and later so the loss of freedom feels more painful. In the nineteenth century, children were viewed as an economic asset but now they are an emotional asset, or in economic terms, our children have changed from being economically useful to being useless. Parental discontent is not their fault, nor is it ours, but it can be seen as another unfortunate consequence of the treadmill pursuit of success in so many competing areas of life.

A major reason happiness decreases with more children is that marital satisfaction also goes down. There is less time for each other, less sleep, less sex and more stress. Not exactly a winning combination. Rather than focusing on each other, the focus often turns to the children. Rather than talking about our own interests, we plan and organise our children's lives.

As marital satisfaction contributes to happiness, having children impedes both. In a 2009 analysis of declining marital happiness after the birth of a second child, researchers found that after the initial adjustment period, negative feelings towards a spouse increased. The study looked at over 200 families from the second pregnancy right through until their second child was 12 months old. By four months the majority returned to 'positive marital relations'. This was not the case for some of the groups, who experienced what researchers referred to as a 'crisis model'. These couples showed a dramatic decline in satisfaction, suggesting it would be difficult to return to pre-birth levels of happiness. Fortunately, after a few years it evens out – and parental happiness increases again years later – in particular after children have left the family home, a finding that is consistent in the US and in Europe.

If this all sounds like bad news, that's because it sort of is. A decline in marital satisfaction is alarmingly inevitable given the additional parental burden that comes with a growing family, especially so for mothers. But fear not, it doesn't have to mean our happiness is doomed for ever as soon as we become parents. There are some ways that couples could adapt to mitigate the negative effects. The solutions are straightforward, such as a more equal distribution of childcare and housework. We know this is a simple adjustment to make, but it remains difficult because the change means swimming against a patriarchy-infested tide. Frequent, honest conversations between couples would help. As mothers make the majority of the everyday decisions as well as take on most of the cognitive load of parenting, if this goes unchecked it will continue to build resentment. There's also the finding that men and women tend to have higher life satisfaction in countries with more egalitarian policies and views. Obviously if women are less burdened, they will be happier too. Improving gender equality elevates us all, and would not result in fewer opportunities for men.

*

I can see also why happiness shifts from having one child to two. One Friday evening I found myself telling my husband just how awful the evening and bedtime routine had been. Arjen was almost nine months and Sanne a few months away from three. When he queried what aspect was hard, I couldn't put my finger on it. She had moments of intense outbursts when she didn't get her way, like when she stole his bottle, his dummy or climbed into bed with him while he was napping – precious quiet that allows me a moment to breathe, shoving an old bottle of cold milk into his closed mouth. It wasn't one thing, it was a build-up of lots of little outbursts. A baby's cry is intensely irritating for a good evolutionary reason; we do our utmost to comfort them and attend to their needs to stop it. When children fuss, shout or tantrum it instantly activates our brain's stress triggers.

This in turn can also make our empathy response go into overdrive, essentially resulting in us becoming overly empathetic (referred to as empathic over-arousal), meaning not only are we physically experiencing an increased heart rate and higher blood pressure, we also take on our children's feelings of stress, making us more emotionally anxious, hampering our ability to parent effectively. Like when I raised my voice a little too high and Sanne said to me: 'That's a tantrum, Mummy,' and I responded with, 'No, you're having a tantrum,' which went on for a few rounds. Not an optimal emotional response, but when she screams unreasonably and often, it hurts my soul, as my husband says.

I can also see how marital satisfaction drops. After being climbed on by two children all day and catering to their every need, when they are finally asleep I sometimes just want to be alone. When I have to give so much of myself away, day in and day out, there is nothing left. Affection can easily be rediscovered, we just had to make a concerted effort not to give in to our tiredness now and again and talk about something other than the children.

How do mothers with more than two do it, I wonder, with a jolt of new amazement at my grandmother and her 11 children. Well, one thing that makes it easier is obvious but not necessarily easy to action: support and sharing the load equally. Or having more people around, as our ancestors did. We need a village, a support bubble. It's a uniquely Western phenomenon that parents are solely in charge of raising their infants; it wasn't always this way and it's making us less happy.

On days when both of us were around, I could focus on the cute moments, the giggles; there was enough attention to catch a bite, and if we missed it, one of us could console the one that was crying. When it's just me, however, I couldn't always stop it, I could not feed both the baby and the toddler at the same time. I couldn't fetch her a fresh cup of water while simultaneously changing a nappy, and her concept of patience was non-existent.

If this all seems a bit negative, it's not intended to be. It's a reflection of the constant demands, the constant tugs for me, my time, my help, that sometimes leaves little left for the glimpses of joy and love: the whispers in my ear, dancing for the baby to make him laugh, bringing him toys when he's crying. Telling me she missed me first thing in the morning, singing songs in the bath.

The pressures put on mothers are another contributing factor to the motherhood complex. It tugs at our mother heart and makes our days more stressful than they could or should be. That's why our happiness drops more notches than our partners', and then they wonder why their wives have changed.

*

When it comes to happiness, children may not be the answer, but they do give us meaning and purpose. Meaning and happiness are not the same, because however meaningful children are, that doesn't get us away from the daily grind of feeding, tidying, homework and discipline. A stand-off with my three-year-old on the hottest day of the year about visiting the same old playground for what felt like the 10,000th time, won't live on in my happy memories. She won, by the way. And this day will happen again, and again. But I still look at her sleeping face at night and wonder at her smallness, her perfection.

It also comes down to how we define happiness. Sociologists define it as 'life satisfaction', psychologists call it mental wellbeing, while some schools of philosophy consider happiness as the absence of pain and suffering.

If it's in the moment, parents may lose out. We have many meaningful snippets at the cost of general satisfaction. Life with young children *is* stressful and tiring, but if we start to question our grander sense of purpose or ask what it is that makes life worth living, that's where we can hope for future happiness. If our children provide us with long-term fulfilment, at the cost of temporary misery, it explains why those who are voluntarily childless score higher on wellbeing, see themselves as independent masters of their world, and do not regret their decision when compared to involuntarily childless individuals. While those who delay children but do want them, have been shown to experience regret, powerlessness, as if they are at fault.

In old age, those with children report higher levels of happiness than those without. Ruut Veenhoven paints an interesting picture – he says childless people tend to have more friends, and these contacts provide a 'functional equivalent' to the happiness that children give empty-nesters later in life, but only up to a point. It turns out that when the comforts of friendship whittle away in old age due to people moving away or passing away, childless people can feel less happy and more isolated. Clearly this may differ between the voluntarily childless and those who wanted to but did not have children. That's why in old age, the long-term bene-fits of parenthood pay off. It just takes a lifetime to get there.

Think about it another way; being happy is not a universal right anyhow. In pure biological terms, a mother and birth represent renewal, nourishment, and the survival of the species. We are incessantly sold the idea that we deserve happiness and we need to chase it, but perhaps children are nature's way of surpassing that. They are our genetic ticket to the future, a bond that ties us more closely into caring what world they will grow up into. Her perfect smile, his unexpected giggle, the tantrums, screams, moaning and clever manipulation to get the best snacks. The bins full of soiled nappies. Our rocky, happier future.

TECHNOFERENCE

How technology changes relationships

Katie has recently had a baby. With nobody around to social-ise with during strict lockdown measures, she is isolated, even from family. She hasn't made friends who had babies at the same time, and she's now worried about missed oppor-tunities to develop a social circle of mums. Katie turns to the Instagram community. She finds herself following baby group hashtags with detailed stories about sleep patterns, routines or attachment parenting. Each new hashtag leads onto another one, and another set of beautiful mothers with picture-perfect lifestyles. She also starts to post cute photos of her baby and even buys new outfits for that very purpose. #SoBlessed, she writes, but feels even lonelier.

Many of the issues of new motherhood were once very private. How we were viewed as mothers was limited to who we interacted with day to day. Now though, should we wish, we can broadcast our highs or aggrievances at the touch of a button. Many people do, leaving us even more open to scrutiny. Take 'sharenting' – a word that describes how parents routinely post photos of their children on the internet without consent, which is heavily scrutinised. Some parents post hundreds of pictures each year, creating digital identities for their children before they can even walk, with the associated privacy concerns. Many children have a social media presence before they are two.

We all intuitively know that social media doesn't show real life, but what we post is still how we are seen. In a world of instant updates, sharing feels compelling, fun and creates a momentary sense of community. It is also addictive and can be terrible for our mental health, and yet we plough on. #motherhood has over 19 million posts, #mommylife over five million. It's tempting to look for more, but that's not time well spent.

How mothers are perceived can clearly shape our behaviour; this in turn will influence our choices. Social media intensifies this. Even for those who don't habitually use or look at social media, it's hard to step away from the expected perfectionism around motherhood that bleeds onto our screens. If you were to browse a social network and look up some of the aforementioned parenting hashtags, an alternate reality quickly emerges. Mummies with clean, beige houses, musing about the psychology of parenting, wellness and staying on top of it all, their children dressed in similar quirky outfits, standing in a row facing the camera and a little essay about the ups and downs of that particular day. Many such posts are sponsored, which is usually fairly transparent with a reason why the poster is in partnership with a brand, and how it ties into their lifestyle. There's an expected level of honesty, but it's often tied to reflections on how to overcome daily hardships, worth it all for the love. This juxtaposition of a postcard-perfect image and a story about a struggle makes the latter seem less difficult, or real. And, besides, if images are the first thing we see, they can paint a more powerful impression than any words underneath, which may not even be read.

Social media also has an unfortunate way of blurring the line between the personal and the promotional. It's rarely mentioned how these women make a living, or an explicit statement about how much money they get from being 'mumfluencers' apart from the obviously gifted items they are paid to promote. If social media motherhood hype is temporary, then we haven't yet hit the top of the bell-curve, as likes for these kinds of pages grow in their thousands.

For those who can make a living out of it, they will be using their brand knowingly. The problem is that for every account with thousands of followers, there are numerous others like it with very few, attempting to emulate their success.

The occasional post might feel helpful and offer a sense of solidarity, but for the most part, these accounts are a unique kind of toxic. With captions such as 'feel energised' or 'ready for the day', if someone scrolling through dozens of posts like this doesn't feel energised, hasn't got themselves or their child dressed yet, it could make them feel like a bad mother.

Aspiration can be motivating, but those who can't reach these 'perfect' ideals presented online may think they are failing. For instance, perception of postpartum bodies has long been skewed by celebrity mothers and is now amplified by the social media generation. Despite what we know objectively, it feels compelling to join in – maybe some of my posts infuriate others too. Posts about running, getting my fitness back or baking – maybe nobody cares about that sourdough bread I baked, or how fast I can run five kilometres.

Other than switching off from it completely, it's hard to be immune to the social comparisons we make, as comparing ourselves to others is a normal human experience, as is sharing information. These two forces are colliding constantly, so if we remember that large parts of social media are filter-tinted performances of reality, it may help us view these images with a bit more perspective or, better still, tune out.

At the other end of the spectrum, posts about the more mundane aspects of the reality of parenting are also popular. Take books such as *Why Mummy Drinks*, or the TV shows *Workin' Moms* and *The Let Down*. Though these are fictional, many can relate to the anecdotes of the comical stresses and pressures of daily life, which offer more realistic representations of motherhood than glossy mummy influencers, albeit with a sharper focus on how unpredictable, messy and chaotic parenting can be. While neither extreme quite represents reality, we crave a justification of what we are going through while we also long for a version that seems easier, calmer or more blissful.

To understand more about this, we only need to consider our enduring fascination with celebrity. Even the ancient Greeks were obsessed with the pursuit of physical perfection, holding beauty competitions and idolising ideal bodies in their sculptures. We've seen how a similar pursuit of perfection exists for motherhood, and this potentially unachievable quest leaves mothers open to exploitation.

Take the fact that multi-level marketing schemes (MLMs) invariably target women, presenting them with the idea that they too could be rich, successful and spend more time with their children. In truth it doesn't quite work like that. Only a select few at the top will make a comfortable income.

Many of these schemes target women and they are encouraged to grow their network using social media. One analysis noted that MLM schemes intentionally exploit stay-at-home mothers in traditional gender roles who seek to generate extra income. These mothers want freedom to work when it suits them as well as 'meaningful employment'. Interviews with women from MLMs show that they can make women, in particular mothers, feel as if they have power and control over their lives when, in fact, companies are largely exploiting them. One participant stated: 'There was a time when I felt guilty because I couldn't do everything … it was me having this perfect idea of what a wife and mother should be.'

The idea presented to her was that she could 'have it all' but, instead, she was working extremely hard for little reward. The way these schemes are set up is that rather than giving women freedom as promised, they anchor them even more firmly into a gendered role at home. Some of the language used even softens the idea that this is work, making the women who partake in these schemes merge their seller and personal identity – again blurring the lines between work and home. A lot of MLMs are reliant on technology, so it can result in more time online. This ironically takes attention away from the family; a key thing these companies had promised would be a benefit of joining them.

Social media use has only intensified the pressure to be seen doing the right thing. In one 2016 study looking at how 127 mothers used Facebook, researchers found that 98 per cent had uploaded photos of their children online, and 80 per cent included their infants in their profile photos. Those who were concerned about how they were viewed and valued as a mother spent more time on the network, were more likely to include a picture of their child in their profile and found it stressful if their pictures were not liked or commented on as much as expected. These mums were seeking outside validation as 'good mothers' through their social media use. The mothers who posted most also showed more perfectionistic tendencies. For them, social media helped to show the world they were 'the best mothers possible for their children'.

The team also looked at how social media tied to a new mother's identity, in particular how socially expected perfectionism played out in their behaviour online. The participants who identified most strongly with their motherhood identity were also most sensitive to reactions to their online posts and were most likely to have featured their child in their profile picture.

Mothers who sought more validation in the form of comments and likes were most sensitive to how others viewed them and, in turn, had more symptoms of depression. This reveals that those most consumed by their motherhood identity find the accompanying expectations and pressures more difficult. This is all the more damaging in our heightened digital world, where a reflection of our lives, true or not, is easily amplified.

This comes back to what sociologists have long known: when women conform to expected gender norms they are often praised for doing so, which only serves to perpetuate these norms. Put like this it's glaringly obvious how this occurs, and these expectations start young. Take my dress complimenting behaviour mentioned earlier – my daughter prefers dresses in part because she sees other little girls in dresses and she gets called cute or pretty when wearing them. Add up the numerous incidents like this throughout a woman's lifetime and it becomes near impossible to escape similar expectations of what femininity means, even if we are unaware of how it started.

We know that the more time a person spends on social media, the more they show depressive symptoms in general and the lonelier they feel. When vulnerable people are exposed to highly curated lifestyles, it can lead them to think that these lives are happier or better than their own, resulting in even more feelings of isolation. We don't know the direction; depressed mothers may be seeking more validation online, or those that spend more time online could become more depressed. Most likely a bit of both occurs. There's also a clear link between social media use and reduced quality and quantity of sleep, which is a risk factor for depression in itself.

Once again this shows that the effort to be perfect, the pressure of intensive mothering and the socially expected values that go along with it, can act as a feedback loop that make mothers feel worse about themselves. This is only amplified by spending *more* time online. Equally, some mothers could be posting unrealistic photos to confirm and take ownership of their maternal identity, and thereby unknowingly perpetuating the problem for others.

It's hard to escape. There is no shortage of social media channels, from mum forums to chat groups with both friends and strangers. During my first maternity leave I was on three different ones, some were more useful than others, and at times it was too much.

In the right environment, being part of such groups can provide key social support, especially for those who are already feeling stressed. In one study, women in Kenya who joined a WhatsApp group with other pregnant women felt more confident, more companionship and were more likely to seek health advice when needed. They also made friends. Another study found that spending time online, in the form of blogging, helped new mothers feel more positively connected to friends and family. This shows that it's the type of interaction with supportive individuals that is more important than how it occurs.

Naturally, there is always a balance. If social networks veer into boasting, whether intended or not, that's where it has potential to become damaging, especially when the people we interact with are similar to us. We compare ourselves to real-life acquaintances more than we do to influencers and celebrities, so are therefore more likely to be envious of those who are most like us. We latch onto things we have in common and immediately notice what sets us apart, from our hair, height, skin colour, food preferences, to whether someone is a parent or not. It is an important skill as it allows us to foster stronger social bonds and helps us understand how to relate to others, but it's also what causes the more negative consequence of social comparisons – envy and feeling inferior.

Envy can be benign – we can appreciate a trait or quality someone else has and it may inspire us to achieve a similar goal. We might be envious of another mother's seamless life organisation skills, healthy cooking habits or fitness regime. If this is benign envy, then it acts as a useful motivator, but if we are envious of a trait or covet something (a house or job) that we cannot ourselves reach, it creates division, a feeling of the other as superior, and this is when envy becomes malicious. In Dutch there are even two words for these different forms of envy – *benijden* – benign envy – and *afgunst* – malicious envy. The latter form of envy, inspired by social comparisons, explains why spending time on social media can be so detrimental. Envy can propel us forwards or bring us tumbling down. This highlights why some forms of social media can have positive effects for some but be harmful for others.

In the social media age, our experiences can easily feel heightened. If we find ourselves making frequent social comparisons to mentions of night nurses, extravagant holidays, expensive equipment or other forms of subtle bragging, this can be damaging as it once again puts a mirror up to ourselves in already uncertain times. While social networking apps can be a vital source of interaction, when these groups make us feel bad too often, it might be time to disengage or leave them altogether.

There is another consequence of being switched on all the time. It can isolate us from the very people who we are posting about.

A friend once posted an inverse image of what his baby must have seen in its first few weeks of life. The happy faces of his parents beaming down at him, check. But, in most of them, a square black object obscuring their faces. The constant presence of phones can tempt us to capture many precious moments, but at what consequence? Like most parents I take plenty of photos of my children, often rushing to capture something one of them did or said that was new, in order to share it with family. When my daughter became more mobile it was clear that seeing me on my phone so much made it an object of extreme interest to her. And when she got older still, she would regularly ask to 'play' with my phone, delighted at taking 'pictures' with her toy phone, just like we did. This made me realise I needed to limit my own screen time in front of the kids as much as possible, something difficult to do when it's used for video calls with grandparents, online shopping, organising playdates and so on. I try to hide my phone when the kids are around, but this remains a challenge. Even my now ten-month-old (at the time of writing) tries to grab my phone whenever it is nearby and intuitively seems to know how to swipe. Researching this chapter has made me re-evaluate my own smart-phone use even more.

I love having information at my fingertips, but I am on my phone far too much and this comes at a cost. If parents are distracted too often it could impact their relationship with their children.

Take a tired mother sitting beside her child on public transport. Rather than engaging with her, she is looking at her phone while her infant sits absent-mindedly in the buggy. Or how about the mum watching out for a baby's first steps. Instead of enjoying it directly, she carefully watches through the lens of her phone, so she can share it with her partner later. This wasn't far from my experience of Sanne's first steps – I caught her wobble the second time she walked on camera. I was the only one with her and I wanted to share this milestone.

One or two missed moments of communication in favour of looking at our child through our phone, fine, but add that up over time and it may become the norm. During my first maternity leave, I used my phone a lot. Contact with the 'outside world' felt important, necessary as I had so many questions about every developmental milestone and this was largely communicated virtually.

It's so difficult to uncouple ourselves from technology that it seeps into every part of our life. Of course, there are benefits of staying connected to others, but spending too much time on our phones can distance us from our infants. This can make it even more unnatural to foster good communication habits, such as frequently talking to our baby about everyday things. Research says we should be doing so from birth. Infants whose parents engage in more quality turn-taking 'conversations' rather than just talking at or around them, perform better at school, a finding replicated many times irrespective of socioeconomic status.

Studies show that a baby's brain is literally in tune with its caregivers during conversations. Scientists have measured the brains of infants as their carers were talking to them and found that when they were engaged in a back-and-forth dialogue (in as much as a baby 'talks', that is), their brain waves aligned. If the baby and carer were involved in separate activities their brain waves did not converge this way.

As mothers tend to be the primary carers, especially early on, it once again reveals that even outside the womb just as our identity becomes linked to them, so do our brains in a duet-like dance. Humans are extremely social beings and it shows – those neglected as babies have lifelong adverse effects.

It is important to note that ignoring your child in favour of your phone is not the same as sustained neglect, but the former is not without its consequence, albeit very subtle effects that could reduce learning moments and make the mother–child relationship weaker.

To show how, let's turn to a now-famous experiment first undertaken in the 1970s when psychologist Edward Tronick conducted a study that highlighted how vital positive social exchanges were between a mother and child, and how dramatic it felt for children when parents stopped paying attention. In the experiment a mother was asked to remain unresponsive to her baby for three minutes as they faced each other. Quickly, her child tried to get her attention, but the mother did not react. After repeated attempts the baby would start to withdraw, and Tronick wrote: 'rapidly sobers and grows wary' showing a 'hopeless' facial expression. Although babies did initially try to attract their mother's attention, when this didn't work, they lost composure and showed distress. At this point in the experiment, mothers were allowed to comfort and respond to their infants. This still face experiment has since been replicated numerous times and reveals just how quickly and instinctively a baby becomes upset when their social needs are not met.

When a baby acts distressed in real life, a mother usually has little choice but to stop what she is doing to comfort her child. However, if she is continuously distracted by her phone and, as a result, doesn't pick up on subtle social cues, babies may socially withdraw. Even two-month-old babies can detect when their mother becomes less responsive for as little as two minutes.

Focused contact matters and technology can impede this. For instance, it's been shown that a child did not learn a new word if an interaction was disrupted by a phone call whereas those who were not interrupted did learn the new word. Children learn best when we respond to them and expand or elaborate on what they are communicating about.

It is the turn-taking interaction that is vital. In a similar experiment adding in a video call element, when toddlers were presented with new words either live, via a video call or in a pre-recorded clip, they learnt best in the first two conditions as both had immediate back-and-forth interactions. The conclusion was that screen time can be beneficial to a point, but passively only watching clips did not help the children learn as well. Other studies have shown that children under three years old struggle to learn new words from videos alone; older children can, but not as well as during a real interaction.

If our communication with our children is interfered with too often, a mother–child bond might be at risk because, as we know, interaction is a key part of our social development. We learn through social exchanges; a baby learns meaning about the world from its parents, but we also learn to take cues and respond to our infants.

Ironically, while technology allows us to be in constant communication with each other online, throw it into the mix of day-to-day parenting and it has the potential to impair these social bonds. Research shows that a mother–child interaction is compromised during joint play with an electronic toy compared to a non-electronic toy, in part because the noise of an electronic toy reduces interaction, and the mothers relied less on their imagination while playing.

Another study of 143 women found that using technology affected relationships when couples were together, largely during leisure time but also mealtimes and bedtime. The women showed lower relationship satisfaction, increased depression and more conflict. The researchers dubbed it 'technoference', a somewhat self-explanatory term.

We are rarely switched off. Many of us have our phones with us constantly, even during meals. For instance, in a study of 55 caregivers eating in a fast-food restaurant with one or more of their children, over 70 per cent of them used their phone during the meal.

Our work life bleeding into our personal life makes it even more difficult to switch off. If we constantly have a phone or smart watch on us, it's hard to resist the temptation to check each time we hear or feel a notification. We are so dialled into the virtual world, but it comes at a cost of dialling out of reality.

It's not that technology is all bad, far from it. It's more that it is inescapable and intrusive. That's why noticing when it interferes too much is key to creating a positive balance. Knowing this now I'm more motivated to keep my phone in another room at least some of the time. My toddler used to bring my phone to me if she saw it somewhere and would throw a tantrum if someone else held it. Even my husband was not allowed and she would shout: 'That's Mummy's phone.'

Our relationships with our family, and therefore our own happiness, may immensely benefit from us letting go just that bit more. If we don't, it can increase stress, perpetuate that toxic motherhood guilt and feed back into making mothers feel even more strained, judged and worried about being good enough.

DIFFERENT MOTHERS

How culture shapes us

We're often told there's no right way to be a mother, that we simply need to be 'a good enough' mother, but there's a constant array of conflicting advice about what to do and what not to do. Don't praise your child too much, don't praise them too little, don't send them to childcare too early, don't work full time, don't work part time, don't sacrifice your career, don't prioritise your career while the kids are young ... the list goes on. There's an overwhelming bombardment of information and misinformation in various parenting books that is not necessarily helpful. It's confusing at a time when everything else is already changing.

In the first months as a new parent, you may not give much thought to what type of parent you will be, except a broad-brushstrokes notion of wanting to be a 'good mother'. And yet an array of different parenting styles and ideas have come in and out of fashion, from tiger mums to helicopter parents, from attachment, naturalistic or free-range parents. This matters though, because how we act informs how we see ourselves and our changing identity.

It was all such a blur in the first year that I didn't even

realise what specific parenting styles meant or what they represented. We followed a fairly scheduled feeding and nap routine with Sanne. Were we therefore 'routine parents'? Before having her I remember hearing that some parents followed strict routines, and I thought this sounded a bit much. I was sure I would not want to miss playdates or coffee groups because it was the baby's nap time – and that I would just go with the flow.

When reality hit, we swung the other way. I quite liked knowing when and how often she fed, as it meant I could plan my day accordingly. Crucially, I knew her bedtime was 7.00 p.m. each day. We followed a fairly flexible 'routine' as we had the misguided idea that she might sleep through the night by 12 weeks, which a book we read as good as promised. If this had succeeded, I think we may have been a bit smug but it didn't work. She did not sleep through the night regularly until she was 15 months and, even then, there were frequent 5.00 a.m. wake-ups.

The routine was hard work – it required scheduling naps and stretching the time between feeds, which logistically meant finding ways to comfort a fussy baby with other means than milk in case she got too used to 'snacking' all day long. When our second was born, I didn't bother with the same pattern. His routine was much more fluid, with semi-regular feeds and the same bedtime. He fell into a routine of sorts without the arduous work it had taken for the first. Aside from two months of struggling with hourly wake-ups eight times per night, he slept through the night much earlier than his sister.

With Arjen, instead of a nap routine, my rule, if you can call it one, was that we both slept whenever he did for his first nap, the second or third I would use for writing. The one thing I remain thankful for is that we stuck to bedtimes, largely because it worked, and it has meant we have had evenings to ourselves since Sanne was born.* This came at the cost of being the type of parents who could rarely take the kids out past 7.00 p.m. Our children become unmanage-able if we break the bedtime routine – that and we value our evenings too much to risk it.

My two experiences vary, but so does each child. It goes to show that whatever gets us through the day when the baby feeds every two hours is fine. If there was one key 'method' that helped babies sleep better, eat better and made parents happier, then the parenting book industry would not have flourished the way it has, but there is no quick-fix or easy answer. Those early weeks are confusing enough. The illu-sion of a solution in a book may appear as though it will help or be a crutch to lean on in an otherwise mystifying time. If it does, fine, but if we try to follow advice and don't manage to, it has the potential to make us feel like bad par-ents. Books that make loose promises can more easily set us up for failure and leave parents feeling confused or seeking another method to follow.

Parenting trends and 'how-to' books have always been around, from the unthinkable to the outright bizarre. Cover your baby in butter every day, have them sleep facing north, don't spoil a crying infant by attempting to comfort it, are some memorable pieces of antiquated advice.

A 1916 book stated that a mother's worry or anger was a contributing reason for colic, that 'nothing dries up milk so

---

* Aside from the occasional evenings where the baby would not settle for hours on end, or took much longer, especially prevalent in the first two months. But for 95 per cent of the time, the children are down between 7.00 and 7.30 p.m.

rapidly as worry, grief, or nagging', and so mothers should be in a happy, carefree state. Mothers who have 'uncontrollable tempers' should not breastfeed at all, the book went on to advise.

In 1920, a handbook of advice to 'maiden, wife and mother', pregnant women were instructed to 'avoid thinking of ugly people, or those marked by any deformity or disease' as well as to 'avoid ungraceful position and awkward attitude'. The same book advised to 'diminish a baby's food the minute signs of illness appear. Most babies are overfed anyway.' And that 'babies thrive on cuddling but they can get along on a lot less kissing'. A few years later, advocating an extremely frosty style of parenting, the influential psychologist John Watson wrote: 'Put it out in the backyard a large part of the day', and advised against hugging and kissing them.

It was common for these century-old books to be written by men (though the first mentioned was by a husband-and-wife team) with the onus often put on women when things went wrong. And now sometimes we wonder where the persistent self-blame stems from when it comes to parenting. If these outdated and misleading patriarchal books made women feel bad, so too do the vastly more accurate (and certainly more politically correct) ones of today.

That's because following 'advice' in an attempt to find order in a chaotic time is not always helpful. Trends change with greater scientific knowledge, but as true answers on the pros and cons of specific baby rearing styles remain hard to come by, there will always be polarised views of what is best for each family.

Even routine versus child-led approaches were talked about decades ago. In the 1980s a psychoanalyst called

Joan Raphael-Leff found key differences in how mothers viewed themselves depended on what parenting style they followed. The idea was that there were two types of parents: regulators and facilitators. Regulators are what we now refer to as routine-led, while facilitators are much more fluid and follow a child's lead. Regulators were more likely to cling onto aspects of themselves that remained the same, and felt that their identity was at stake, while facilitators embraced every new moment of pregnancy, enjoying the change of the growing infant inside them in a way that enriched their identity. Raphael-Leff wrote that 'the Facilitator mother adapts to her baby while the Regulator mother expects the baby to adapt'.

This goes some way to explaining what I have always felt – there are different 'camps' of motherhood. Other mums have often seemed more 'mumsy' and natural to me, perhaps because they seem to have managed better to mould their motherhood identities with themselves, whereas I have often struggled to do so. That, or appearances are deceptive; friends have shared similar worries, but of course, both identities can co-exist. We can feel like a mother but also want to hold onto a form of ourselves that is not 'mummy'. As motherhood is so all-consuming, this can feel like an impossible feat, especially if the two identities are in conflict and, naturally, we have to prioritise our infants.

How we feel has little influence on how we are viewed by others, which contributes to the complexity of our own feelings towards motherhood too. We have our own internal validations coupled with external expectations, and these do not always align. When expectations don't match reality, that is a driver for self-conflict in its most basic form. Raphael-Leff's original observations are still at play today: routine versus baby-led. Following one style over another has the potential to create divides early on, and whichever method is followed is often framed as the one that holds the answers.

The routine supporters paint a picture of two types of mothers in a bid to showcase the pros of establishing a predictable schedule. The mother who doesn't follow one is depicted as late for appointments or playdates because she feeds her baby on demand and so never knows when she will come and go. When her baby cries, she doesn't know if it's from hunger or tiredness, and so might feed her baby more often, meaning the baby is 'snacking' all day long or doesn't drink enough to feel full, and so a cycle of constant feeding continues. Meanwhile, the routine mum can make appointments safe in the knowledge that her baby will have slept and have been fed on cue. Her baby will feel more settled as he or she will know what to expect, as will the parents who can therefore get more done in the day.

On the other hand, the baby-led followers suggest routine mums are militant and selfish, moulding the baby to fit into their own, perhaps unnatural, schedule at the cost of missing the baby's needs. According to the more extreme attachment-parenting philosophy (which differs from baby-led, though attachment parenting is usually *also* baby-led), the view is that unless you co-sleep, carry your baby or be their sole provider for their first few years, your child is at risk of becoming insecurely attached. This is where children struggle to form social bonds, often as a consequence of neglect, or where an infant's basic needs of attention, love and care are not met.

The attachment-parenting philosophy is not as old as you might expect. It originated in a book published in 1993 by a devoutly religious doctor called William Sears, who, with his wife, advised parents to take a baby-led approach, including baby-wearing, co-sleeping and breastfeeding on demand until the child was at least two years old. They also urged readers to avoid science-based parenting advice, claiming that this meddled with our natural instincts. The idea was that attachment parents follow a 'natural' process, because of how parenting has been documented in traditional societies, despite the fact that this isn't the key to a securely attached baby. It is sensitive caring, rather than time spent in close proximity, that is key to a securely attached child. We can adopt very different styles and still parent sensitively.

Following an attachment-parenting style may suit those who can spend every waking hour with their baby, but it is not compatible with holding onto a job. To be a good parent of the type the Sears family proposed would keep women at home. To get around that for those who might have jobs, they suggested that mothers could wear their babies at night for several hours or co-sleep for the whole night to make up for lost time.

'Natural parenting' is not actually practised in all indigenous groups the way that attachment evangelists suggest. In fact, parenting looks completely different wherever you look. In Tajikistan, it has long been a cultural norm for infants to be restrained in wooden cradles called a gahvora for long stretches of time, until aged about two. It has a hole with a bucket underneath instead of a nappy and only the baby's head can move. Mothers can even breastfeed with the baby still strapped in, they simply lean down. There have been some reported motor-skill 'delays' compared to other children, but by age four there is no documented developmental issue due to having been bound in such a device.

Meanwhile, in the Bolivian Tsimané tribe in the Amazon,

babies are not named until after they turn one and parents barely talk to them, nor do they seem to require much soothing. Compared to Western standards there are some language delays, but many are bilingual and show no cognitive impairment in later life. Researchers believe this initial avoidance comes from a high infant mortality rate, explaining why parents do not invest too much time in their infants when roughly 13 per cent do not survive. Similarly, in the Hausa-Fulani tribe in West Africa, mothers are forbidden to make eye contact, play or talk with their infants due to a strict cultural norm called 'kunya', meaning kin avoidance. Some even send their children to relatives after they are weaned and will not see them for several years.

This highlights that there are many ways to raise children, and how we behave is heavily dependent upon the culture we inhabit.

In a chapter about parenting styles, it feels fitting to address one of the most criticised and agonised approaches parents face: letting the baby 'cry it out' in order to encourage them to sleep through the night. This is otherwise known as sleep training.

Those who are against it warn it could damage the child for life and cause attachment issues. However, the citations of these claims often link to cases of severe neglect documented in Romanian orphanages in the 1990s. These children were neglected in every way you could imagine and had little or no meaningful contact with adults. Years of sustained neglect are not comparable to letting your baby cry for a few minutes in a safe and loving environment.

Opponents of cry-it-out believe that there's a sliding scale, and while sleep training is not akin to severe neglect, they suggest we can't know how it truly affects children.

In the moment, that may be so, but as for lasting effects, the research paints a clearer picture. One 2006 review of several different sleep training methods found that sleep-trained children were more secure, predictable and less irritable, with no adverse outcomes. Longer-term studies have found that sleep-trained children showed no positive or negative effects when followed up five years later. That is, there were no observable sleep problems, stress or deficiency in child–parent closeness, compared to those who were not sleep-trained.

What we can clearly see are positive effects for the parents. When we sleep better we also parent better. Parents of sleep-trained babies are less likely to be depressed, are less stressed and show better physical health. Whether we opt for a sleep intervention or not comes down to our own preferences. Scaring parents into following one particular style without balanced evidence to back it up is yet another guilt-inducing exercise.

Attachment disorder is a serious issue, and many of us will have heard about the damage caused to insecurely attached babies, and how it has lifelong consequences. Attachment theory was first brought into the mainstream by British psychoanalysts John Bowlby and Mary Ainsworth. Bowlby noticed that neglected children developed emotional issues, whereas those with strong ties to their parents or caregivers did not.

It isn't only the mother who is important for childhood attachment. In many societies a child is raised by several other members of their family and wider network. In the Aka tribe of hunter-gatherers in the Central African Republic (who we will hear more about later) infants can be transferred between people up to eight times per hour and show attachment to several adults from their group, forming rich and meaningful social connections.

This shows that the style we follow doesn't matter as much as we may think. Parental involvement contributes to about a third of any eventual attachment issues. Our personality, genes, and how our own parents interacted with each other also plays a role. Individuals whose parents divorced when they were children, for instance, are less securely attached as adults. Fretting over every element of parenting is also likely to make us more anxious, and fretful parents have more anxious children.

When I first read that babies who are separated from their mothers could have attachment issues later, I panicked. We sent Sanne to childcare at just over six months, part time initially and full time from when she was one. Would she be at a loss without me, would she be insecure for the rest of her life because of this decision, I naively wondered.

Luckily this was a misconception. Young babies certainly need love, care and attention, but, as long as they have that in their surroundings from a parent, trusted carer or grandparent, that child will usually be fine.

Quality care is what matters most. Well-cared-for children are not more likely to be insecurely attached. This was shown by a longitudinal study following 1,153 children and their mothers over time both at home and at childcare. It was only if the childcare was poor quality and if the mothers showed low levels of 'sensitivity' – if they were not in tune with their children's needs – that the children were less securely attached.

I knew the facts and yet I still initially felt guilty for leaving her for so long, a worry that friends have voiced too. Our emotions are so powerful that it's hard to make objective judgements when it comes to our children. It's therefore comforting to know that in many of the Nordic countries, like Denmark and Sweden, most children attend partly state-funded nurseries when parental leave ends. As this is a cultural norm without a hefty financial cost, it puts less pressure on the mothers to have to think about 'choosing' to stay at home. If nurseries have adequate state funding as well as high standards of care, it empowers more women to work and society benefits in countless ways. Maybe we can stop feeling so guilty about it too.

Suggesting that babies could have attachment issues later in life by putting them into childcare is not only misleading, it is yet again damaging to a woman's sense of her competence as a mother. This could fuel a mother's guilt and, if she has the option, could drive her to opt out of a potentially fulfilling career with all the resulting gender imbalances that we have explored.

What we do know is that rigidly following parenting advice can be damaging. One study of 354 new mothers found that those who read strict routine-led parenting books were more likely to have postnatal depression and lower confidence. This was a correlation, so the mothers could have been anxious before and read more parenting books, or the sheer scale of the advice contributed to their lack of confidence as a parent. Given that the very idea of following strict routines means parents can expect the baby to follow suit, it could be detrimental to consume so much advice when expectations are not always likely to be met. A subset of the participants, about 22 per cent, did find the books useful, but 53 per cent felt more anxious after reading them. It was those who found the books unhelpful that reported feeling greater anxiety.

That parents – specifically mothers – continue to invest in practices and follow advice even if it's not helping, makes sense when you consider a common psychological bias known as the 'sunk-cost fallacy'. If we put time into an event, relationship or job, we mistakenly plod on, as otherwise all the time we have already invested feels wasted, even if continuing comes at the cost of our own wellbeing. It's why we will often finish a meal at a restaurant even if we are full, which only makes us feel worse. The money has already been spent, so whether we eat it or not cannot change that cost.

Most of this book so far has focused on infancy and new mothers, but it's worth considering how we act around our children as they get older. For instance, in one survey of 401 teens, a study found that parents who were authoritative (strict and warm) and permissive (loving with low demands) had a better impact on an adolescent's wellbeing and happiness compared to authoritarian (strict and cold) parents. Those with authoritative parents were more likely to score high on wellbeing and life satisfaction. On the other hand, authoritarian parents had well-behaved children who performed well at school but showed higher levels of depression and had lower self-esteem. Children of permissive parents did not perform as well in school but were more confident. Crucially this study was based on the teens' perception of their parents rather than how the parents saw themselves.

As they rated both parents, the researchers could see

which parent had a stronger effect. For self-esteem and life satisfaction, the outcome was much the same. When it came to happiness there was a difference. For the teens to be happy, it was more important for the mothers to be authoritative (warm) than authoritarian (cold). A mother's parenting style has a greater influence on their teen's happiness than the father's. This could be a reflection of the added time that mothers spend with their children, or that more emphasis and pressure is put on women to be good mothers.

Other studies show that authoritative mothers have the best-adjusted children overall. This matters because, as we know, happier children also make for happier parents. There are other outcomes too: happier children tend to try harder at school, drink less alcohol and are less likely to be depressed. While we may not knowingly adopt a parenting style early on, what is clear is that more pressure is on the mothers for children to be happy.

Take, for instance, the now-infamous description of a helicopter parent. This is a type of intensive parenting which is exactly as it sounds: parents hovering above a child, rarely out of earshot. These parents have high expectations, schedule educational activities and tend to be overprotective and overbearing in order to shield their children from anything bad that might happen to them.

There are numerous downsides to helicopter parenting. If children never have to face any hardship because their parents cushion them from stress, when they finally fly the nest real life will undoubtedly come as a shock. Children of helicopter parents have been found to be worse leaders, show lower confidence and find difficult situations more challenging. They have worse psychological wellbeing and are more likely to take medication for anxiety or depression. In one study of 377 students, children of helicopter parents had more emotional problems, were poorer decision-makers and performed worse academically. In a 2019 survey of over 1,200 adolescents in China, the more overprotective the parents were, the worse others rated them as potential future leaders. This was directly attributed to their lower self-esteem and confidence.

With so many downsides, why would any mother choose to be a helicopter parent at all? The answer is they may not. It could simply be an unfortunate downside of wanting to protect their children too much and do everything for them. Culture plays a role too: in individualistic societies where there is a greater emphasis and pressure on achievement, parents push their children harder.

Similarly, intensive parenting of this type could be a result of greater economic uncertainty, making parents worried about the future. If it's harder to get ahead in the job market, then what parent wouldn't attempt to give their child the best start in life in order for them to succeed in an uncertain future? It just so happens that by doing so everyone feels a bit more stretched in the process. Perhaps we can learn more from the Dutch, where being average is perfectly fine, and trying to be the best or the top is a cultural faux pas.

We've already established that there is no such thing as a 'perfect mother' and that the ideals of a 'good mother' are largely culturally conditioned. Sadly, as we've seen, our motherhood identity doesn't always stem from our own choosing, but is intricately tied to how we are perceived. Veer too much into one parenting style over another (or a few combined, as they can overlap) and we either lose important aspects of ourselves or tamper with crucial connections to our children.

This brings me back to the Dutch mothering culture. Although there is a greater trend towards competitive and intensive mothering, parenting there still is more relaxed. From the physical environment we create for the children – a baby box in the front room where babies can 'play' independently – to less emotional hand-holding. If we anticipate and try to intercept each issue, our children would never learn to do so for themselves.

Intriguingly, even if we don't consciously attempt to parent in a particular way, many aspects of how we parent are not entirely within our control. We are often driven by instinct, for good reason. Consider this scenario. Your baby is struggling to reach a toy just out of grasp but cannot yet crawl. Do you let him or her struggle and leave it out of reach, or do you instinctively pass the toy? Perhaps the 'thrill' is in the chase, and the baby might get bored once they have the toy, but we don't tend to think twice about how we respond. These seemingly minor exchanges are important. How we respond to our children could change the structure of the brain almost from birth.

In a 2015 study, researchers looked at how responsive mothers were to their six-month-old babies in such scenarios, considering how they comforted their babies, whether they suggested toys to play with or let them choose things for themselves. The team also scanned the babies' brains and found that when parents were less responsive to their babies, they had a slightly larger hippocampus. This area is important for memory and emotion, such as how we learn to deal with distress. These results suggest that the babies that are left to manage minor day-to-day challenges for themselves become more resilient by doing so, shown by their larger hippocampus, whereas those with more sensitive carers did not need to develop this extra buffer.

A harsher environment tends to result in less-sensitive parenting, and babies' brains respond to that. This is not a bad thing, per se, but a reflection of infants adapting to their environment. In another lab-based study, researchers exposed three-and-a-half-year-olds to an unexpectedly jumping toy lizard, presented as the real thing. Many children were startled when the lizard 'jumped', but those who had experienced sensitive parenting at six months learnt to regulate their emotions better by the fourth jump, whereas those who had faced insensitive parenting either became more afraid from one trial to the next or stayed as afraid as they were the first time. That is, less-sensitive parenting made children on higher alert at each exposure.

One of the authors, Anne Rifkin-Graboi of the National Institute of Education in Singapore, explains that these findings could reflect the idea that in a more 'dangerous' world children have to mature more quickly (shown by hippocampus growth) and less-sensitive parenting accelerates this, but potentially at a cost of other things. It's worth pointing out that the effects are small and Rifkin-Graboi reassures me that though small effects are bad for scientists like her who 'want to find the key to everything', they are great for parents who tend to worry too much about how small interactions affect their children later in life. Besides, the type of 'sensitive' parenting measured in these experiments was subtle. Parents may not be aware of the nuances of sensitive parenting, but it largely means providing a safe environment for them and being attentive to their emotional needs. Fortunately, sensitive parenting can easily be improved by tested interventions. Overall, it leads to better-attached children while in a more uncertain environment with less-sensitive parenting children's brains adapt accordingly.

Parents who worry about how sensitive they are as parents are probably doing just fine already. It is reassuring that in numerous non-Western cultures, parents don't seem to fret about how they parent nearly as much as we do in the West. Many don't even worry about providing too much or little stimulation. This is a good thing.

In fact, parents may unknowingly be making life harder by providing too much 'stuff'. It's clear, for instance, that too many toys are overwhelming. Children with fewer toys have been shown to partake in better play with a single object for longer, more intently and more creatively than those with more to choose from. Too much choice is stressful; we've no doubt all encountered the dizzying effect of being spoilt for choice and children feel this too.

During the coronavirus restrictions when playdates were limited or schools shut early, sometimes my daughter played with a ball, her comfort rabbit or her brother's tiny carry cot – making herself small enough to lie in it (these are meant to be suitable up to six months). At times, this was enough to entertain her for hours, while her baby brother delighted in simply following her around or chasing a balloon. If this paints a rather rosy picture, of course we also had our fair share of tantrums and incessant demands for snacks, but more toys would not have solved this.

I became even more convinced of the case for fewer toys and less stimulation as a coping strategy for play when I read the work of the late anthropologist Jean Briggs, who lived among a small Inuit community in Canada's Northwest Territories for 17 months in the 1960s. She noticed that the children needed little more than their imagination and could keep themselves entertained for hours with simple objects, such as a blanket or piece of cardboard. She wrote that 'the peacefulness of the children, lying together in bed, and their ingenuity in entertaining themselves on such occasions was amazing to me ... ' One of the Inuit words for play, 'pinnguujaqtug', even means 'to pretend to do'. The elder child in the family she stayed with barely demanded any attention at all. Briggs also reported hearing few dos or don'ts uttered by parents. A striking contrast to my own experience and many other mothers I know, where there are constant tugs for our attention, and incessantly we say 'no', despite our best intentions. It was one of the first words both my children learnt.

A similar pattern that Briggs observed among the Inuit has been seen in other indigenous groups. Among Mexican and Guatemalan families with indigenous backgrounds, researchers observed that parents provided little planned entertainment to the children. One-year-olds would play without much attention and older children happily partook in family chores without needing to be asked, even as toddlers. In one study comparing indigenous Mexican families to 'cosmopolitan' Mexican families from the same city, Guadalajara, six- to eight-year-olds from the indigenous families helped more and were involved in more self-play compared to the families who lived a Western style of life. The former helped from their own initiative, while the 'cosmopolitan' children had to be asked to help out.

Likewise, in the Maniq nomadic hunter-gatherer group in Thailand, play often mimics adult tasks like preparing food, which the children help to hunt and collect. They have no words for 'learning' or 'teaching'; instead children learn by doing. The Maniq also allow their children to use real knives from a young age. By four years old they learn to use them to skin and prepare meat. This is common among tribal societies, where knives, machetes and other practical tools are used by children around the world, also observed among the Amazonian Matsigenka and Parakanã and the Hadza of Tanzania. Children naturally copy what they see adults doing – it's why mini brooms and toy kitchens are such popular toys and why, before he was even verbal, Arjen would grab our vacuum or broom whenever he saw it and happily walk around the house 'cleaning'. He even cleans up spills with a cloth, while Sanne loves to 'wash up' at the kitchen sink, which inevitably results in large puddles of water all around her. It's tempting to ask her to stop as it creates additional mess, but I refrain – even allowing her brother to join in.

Children don't require structural teaching to learn such life skills. And there are benefits to reap. If we don't wrap our children in cotton wool and let go of some of our more deliberate child-rearing methods, our children could become more resourceful, creative, show more willpower and 'grit', as the anthropologist David Lancy has learnt first-hand when observing traditional societies.

Play is important. It may not seem like learning as we define it today, but play is the way children first learn about the world, from creativity (make-believe) to problem-solving (hopscotch), to numeracy (counting the toys in an animal picnic), to collaboration (sharing out plates of pretend biscuits). Starting academic learning too young is therefore not necessarily a good thing. In a study looking at children who learned to read and write at age five, a team found that they were no better at 11 than children who only started to learn two years later. The later readers not only caught up but had slightly increased comprehension skills than the earlier readers. This is thought to occur because understanding the meaning of words is important for reading, so having more time to develop language through creative play helps reading later on. Many European countries start teaching literacy skills much later than they do in the UK for instance, with no observed impact on achievement as adults. Learning to read and write earlier does not necessarily lead to improved academic success in later life, but prioritising play early on has countless strengths. It is proven to help children learn better, reduces stress and even leads to beneficial brain changes. It shouldn't be either or, but the benefits of play show it's worth highlighting just how important it is.

Helpful behaviour in childhood must be encouraged at a young age for it to continue in a meaningful way. Toddlers are born helpers; they kick up a fuss if they can't help us break eggs into a pancake mix or cut carrots while cooking, even when we explain that a sharp knife is dangerous. They will pick up fallen objects for us even when it takes them away from playing with a new toy. They have been shown to be more motivated to do this for verbal praise alone rather than for a reward. Children will try to help adults before they can even talk, leading to the idea that humans have an inborn desire to help, as we need to form strong social bonds.

It has to be real help, too. Many Western parents often let their toddlers do so-called 'mock work'. This is where we let children pretend to sweep the floor after it has already been swept, as a trick or distraction method so that they think they are being helpful. This type of mock work has not been observed in US families with Mexican indigenous heritage backgrounds, where children are expected to help from a young age with ability-appropriate tasks. Children are intuitive: research shows they quickly realise when they aren't really helping, thereby gaining little satisfaction from this pretence. That's why mock work could unknowingly be demotivating kids to do real, helpful work.

If we want helpful *ng'om* children as we saw in the Kipsigis, it requires a mind-set shift in how we see toddlers. In the West we may first and foremost think that they want to play all the time or need to be entertained. But we can reframe it – perhaps they want to help more too. In many ways help and play at an early age are the same thing.

Andrew Coppens of the University of New Hampshire, who has studied indigenous groups in Mexico, observed that a lot of this helpful behaviour comes down to how much children are integrated into the adult activities in their community. In societies where this is more likely, the boundary between adult and child activities is blurry or non-existent, with children expected to help in age-appropriate ways. This is also true of the Chillihuani people in the Andes, where play and work are one and the same and children are raised with respect as fully fledged members of the community, whereas in the West being called childish is an insult. Children are completely separate from adult life, from the food they eat, to the games we buy for them and how we talk to them.

Of course, in many parts of life this is needed. Adults go to work and children go to school. This segregation is less necessary during leisure time, but still it persists. As Coppens puts it, 'it's taken for granted so we don't notice how strange that is'. He argues that how integrated our children are in conversation, play and in the productive work they do, makes a difference psychologically and physically. When adulthood and childhood is segregated, as it so often is in Western families, children become politically marginalised as well. The consequences are that we assume children can't easily partake in adult activities. Some of that is true, but it's a sliding scale. Children can cut carrots and cook them, they can sweep and help to paint with supervision, it just takes them ten times as long. That's far from convenient as hectic schedules do not easily allow time for their meaningful participation.

Less-helpful children naturally results in more work for parents later on, and these children may well need more stimulation and entertainment. If children are more integrated, feel more valued and less infantilised, they could be expected, and therefore be more motivated, to contribute more in all areas of life.

This isn't easy to implement. We are all a product of our culture and the great irony of this is that in the West, we are 'Weird', literally. That is, we are a Western, Educated, Industrialized, Rich, Democracy. And Weird parents are the ones who can unknowingly extinguish potentially helpful behaviour. Both Coppens and Lancy have observed that in non-Weird groups, natural helpfulness is 'carefully nurtured', while in the West, at the very age that we would like children to take on more of their own responsibilities, such as tidying rooms and helping to prepare dinner, we often see a pushback.

Although it can be a challenge, it would benefit us to capitalise on this natural inclination to help. It's slower, messier and can be hugely frustrating, but it's worth it. Recently, while baking some brownies, my daughter asked to stir the flour and pour the sugar. It went everywhere, and she got angry when I took over, but, largely, she enjoyed the process. One weekend when she had just turned three, we let her help paint the back of our house. She got paint on the patio and herself, it took longer to do, but it washed off afterwards and she enjoyed taking part. Adult tasks are often deemed too difficult, or a toddler can get in the way (and this can sometimes be dangerous), but involving them in small tasks could make for more natural helpers. If children are frequently discouraged from helping (even subtly, with 'mock work', or by distracting them with play when they slow us down), it could reverse an instinctive desire to help.

It's difficult to compare children across cultures as many factors contribute to their development. We can't easily pluck desirable practices we see in other cultures and apply them to our own, as different worlds breed unique habits and motivations. However, we can learn reassuring insights into helpfulness and play. By cultivating our children's lives less and giving them real autonomy, we can encourage better creative play, more helpful behaviour, stronger imaginations and, in turn, be prevented from micro-managing their lives. This reminds me of Sanne using nothing more than a blanket and her favourite toy bunny to play with, cradling it in her arms, putting it to 'bed' on the sofa, covering it up, shushing it and pretending to breastfeed it.

We've discussed why play is so important, and yet 'play' has become problematic in other ways. There's a difference between self-play and the type parents sometimes encourage, where we are the ones on hands and knees, playing with or entertaining them. It's true that guiding play can help coax my child out of a meltdown, but if I did this all the time, she'd come to expect it and I'd never get anything done. Nor would she gain an important sense of independence that boredom can foster.

It wasn't always like this, but play seems to have intensified in the post-Second World War era. As early as 1951, the psychologist Martha Wolfenstein wrote of a clear shift in American culture, from play being an indulgence to an all-encompassing obsession, where it has become 'obligatory', and 'fun has become not only permissible but required'. From then, the pressured compulsion to entertain our kids has grown, with all the marketing of toys to boot and the resulting motherhood guilt, anxiety and burnout we have already explored. There's even a term David Lancy coined to describe this: neontocracy, encapsulating the *Weird* style of parenting where life largely revolves around our children. If we focus on them, put them first and ourselves second all the time, then they will be happier, right? ... or so the thinking seems to go. Not only would this become a vicious cycle at the expense of parents' own happiness if they follow this trend, but cross-cultural analyses suggest it's not optimum. In all the societies he has observed, none were as child-focused as we are in the West. At the same time, children and teenagers here feel more pressure than ever before, many are riddled with anxiety, insecurity and depression, and research shows that in some places like in the US, this has been steadily rising. That's why Lancy advocates for a more 'benign neglect' form of parenting, simply meaning less hands-on.

While play is obviously fundamental to a child learning how to navigate the world – it's the intensive all-consuming pressure to be playing, entertaining, educating and caring for our children all at once that has downsides. It could lead to a child becoming worse at independent play later on. Independent play helps them to explore, observe and therefore better entertain themselves.

It's something my mother often stressed to me: 'Your children don't need to be constantly entertained. Put them in the box and let them play.' She would tell me I had to do this when they were young enough, only months old, so that the baby box became their fun and safe space, not an environment to contain them. There are photos of me and my older brother in the box aged around three and one, with a makeshift tent above us, seemingly quite content. We would play there for hours with simple, hand-made wooden toys (hipster before it was cool). She warned me that if I gave my own children too much attention, they would become dependent upon it. By all means, the idea is to involve them in all areas of family life, be it cooking, cleaning and so on, but not the other way around – for us to constantly pander to their wishes. We'd never get anything done. I used to think she was being over-dramatic, but she has a good point.

My laid-back approach to joining in with play was far from strategic at the time, but at least I can stop feeling guilty about it. At the time of writing, early May 2020, it's the end of a busy Sunday that started at 5.00 a.m., with Arjen waking early before going back to sleep. No such luck for Sanne, she was up, bright-eyed and full of energy before 6.00 a.m., and the morning 'shift' was mine. Subsequently closing my eyes on her bedroom floor while she played, then being told to: 'Open your eyes, Mamma, don't sleep', was not a proud moment of my weekend, but I feel better with the knowledge that a little independent play without supervision will do her good in the long run.

Given such an emphasis on play, intensive motherhood and stimulation, to ease our motherhood complex it would do us all good to remember Donald Winnicott and his notion of being a good *enough* mother. If we consider that the '*good mother*' ideal and all the pressures that go with it are largely Western constructs, it goes some way to explaining what much of this book has already addressed; that the standards we are held up to strongly depend upon the culture we inhabit.

For instance, among the Aka group gender roles look quite different. Men will hold the babies while the women hunt, though women also carry their babies during hunts, temporarily placing them on the ground as they get close to catching their prey. Women are such proficient hunters that sometimes they go alone, even when heavily pregnant. The Aka men care for their babies more than fathers in any other observed society and are in arms' reach at least 50 per cent of the time in a given day. They hold the babies while the mothers prepare food and gather firewood, even where there are older siblings on hand who could help. The fathers also hug and kiss their children more than the mothers and, on occasion, offer a nipple to babies who are rooting for food. At night, it is common for fathers to sing to their fussing babies. They will take their infant for a walk or even a dance to soothe them more than the mothers do. Overall, the caregiving appears to be equal in many domains and it is never seen as a burden for men, nor does it penalise their status to spend more time caring.

The idea of the 'good mother' norm holds us back. Most mothers are already good, striving for an impossible construct, which contributes to more fear, anxiety and pressure, and inevitably leads to a motherhood identity complex.

Taking all the contradictions around motherhood we have explored, it becomes apparent that women are sold the idea from politicians and from their workplaces that we live in an equal society. That itself sets us up for failure. If we are told we can empower ourselves at work, and that companies are minimising the gender pay gap, it puts the onus of 'failure' on ourselves, when in fact we are operating in an unfair society from the outset. At the same time, the endeavour to succeed in one area just to feel equal to men, can mean our motherhood identity loses out as we push our professional identities to the forefront. That's for those of us who have the choice to do so. If this is a struggle for white middle-class women, consider that it's even worse for working-class women and for women of colour, who are marginalised in many other ways, combating classism and implicit and explicit racial biases. Middle-class women can rely on more paid help to ease this discomfort and clash. Others are not so fortunate.

It goes back to the reality that workplaces were not initially designed with women in mind – meaning we feel forced to prioritise work or the home because being an 'ideal worker' directly clashes with being a 'good mother'. This is why aiming to do both often comes at a cost to our career, our children or our sense of self.

Considering all the evidence explored in this book, I would argue that neither should have to take a step back. Choosing to do so is not a real 'choice' when it comes from social pressures or minimal governmental support for families. If our society was more equal from the get-go, there wouldn't be as much pressure on mothers and the identity shift so many of us experience wouldn't feel as stark.

Our identity as a mother is tugged at, pushed, pulled in many directions, from our own critiques to outside pressures. Protecting ourselves, our wellbeing and therefore our true self, to put it in somewhat grand terms, is of utmost importance for the long run. It may seem selfish to think this way, but, given the contradiction that we are constantly doing more out of a worry of not doing (or being) enough, our children will thank us later for putting ourselves first at least some of the time. If we are happier, they are bound to be too.

ACKNOWLEDGEMENTS

I have wanted to write a book for ever, since I was a teenager, but somehow something always got in the way. In a sleep-deprived haze three months after my second baby was born, with barely any time to myself at all, I decided to go for it. A strange sense of urgency filled every spare moment and I lived and breathed this subject in a way that allowed me to write fast, which was very necessary as I had about ten months to do so.

However, this book would never have happened without my agent Catherine Cho. Your reply the day after I submitted my proposal made me more excited than you will know. I literally thought I was dreaming and had no idea when I sent my query letter that you had written a memoir about your own journey into motherhood – and what a book it is, serendipity indeed.

My editor Holly Harley, you took such supportive care of my words and gave every wild idea or tangent I had a lot of thought, helped me find more confidence in my words and made the mistake of giving me your number so I could ask questions at any time of the day – I can't wait to celebrate with you and Catherine soon. Oh, to have actual drinks in a bar again one day.

So many people have shaped and helped me improve as

a journalist, which no doubt played a part in making this book happen. My colleagues at the BBC have been key to this journey: Jonathan Amos, Richard Fisher, Victoria Gill, Zaria Gorvett, Sarah Keating, Michael Marshall, Rebecca Morelle, Pierangelo Pirak, Paul Rincon, Amanda Ruggeri, Dhruti Shah, Matt Walker, Griesham Taan and Rosie Waites. All of you have edited my words or worked with me in some form and each edit no doubt improved my writing.

For supporting me into the opaque journey of the book world – David Robson – where would I be without your wisdom and encouragement, putting up with my regular questions and spurring me on from the very moment this book was still only a vague idea in my mind. To my friends who I over-burdened with the details within the book and to some of you who kindly read some early chapters: Frouke Engelaer, Catherine de Lange, Cathy Mitchell, Agata Slater, Lucy Arrowsmith, Saffron Thain, Naomi Ozretich, Jane Bradley, and Jodi Mishcon, who unknowingly planted an early seed of the idea when she interviewed me. To the other fabulous mothers I know or have since met that help make playdates a joy: Julia, Michelle, Davina, Ross, Tess, Mathi, Helen, Ingrid, Ekin, Elizabeth, Melissa, Brit, Fiona, Lauren and Ailbe. And to Aga, whose magic touch and child whisperer ways make our lives infinitely easier and our children are so happy in your care.

To the dozens of academics who talked to me, explained their work and so generously gave me their time, I thank you for this but also for the important research that makes us understand ourselves so much better – Michelle Budig, Caitlyn Collins, Andrew Coppens, Allison Daminger, Alison Fleming, Roberta Golinkoff, Sara Harkness, Elseline Hoekzema, Melissa Milkie, Rachel Margolis, Lee Nelson, Kathy Hirsh-Pasek, Noya Rimault, Meredith Rowe, Sarah

Schoppe-Sullivan, Ruut Veenhoven and dozens more. I can only hope I have done your work justice.

Of course, I would be nowhere at all without my own family for bearing with me during a very unsociable year. Your support when I spent evenings writing instead of socialising means the world. That the second half of my book was finished during the pandemic meant I at least wasn't missing out as we couldn't see each other anyway. Mum, Seb, Mich, Mau, Trisha, you are the absolute best family to have in my life – the same goes for Mike, Helen, Jo and Andy. And a special mention for my dad Piet, gone from this world too soon, I will always miss your unwavering love and support. How special you made me feel. Even as we were losing you to a cruel disease, you still recognised me and how happy we all are that you met and held your four grandchildren before you left us.

And lastly, but perhaps most importantly, to all mothers out there, whether this resonates or not, this is for you, especially my own mother Marga van den Eijnden who shaped my early idea of what motherhood feels like: unconditional love and belief in your children – and my mother-in-law, Helen Parker, I feel so lucky to marry into a family with another writer and to have you look over so many of the early words.

Oh and of course, my partner in life and love – Stephen Parker – thank you for your constant encouragement, for cheering me on and for helping me talk through every aspect of my motherhood identity journey with our chaotic, adorable cherubs. We may lament our lack of free time, but almost every night we talk about how much we love them.

NOTES

INTRODUCTION

Roberts, S., Havlicek, J., Flegr, J., Hruskova, M., Little, A., & Jones, B. et al. (2004). Female facial attractiveness increases during the fertile phase of the menstrual cycle. *Proceedings of the Royal Society of London. Series B: Biological Sciences*, 271(suppl_5).

Arslan, R., Schilling, K., Gerlach, T., & Penke, L. (2019). Using 26,000 diary entries to show ovulatory changes in sexual desire and behavior. Correction to Arslan et al. (2018). *Journal of Personality and Social Psychology*.

Cusk, Rachel (2008). *A Life's Work*, London: Faber & Faber, pp. 61–62.

Ireland, M. (1993). *Reconceiving Women*, New York: Guilford Press.

CHAPTER 1

Hoekzema, E., Barba-Müller, E., Pozzobon, C., Picado, M., Lucco, F., & García-García, D. et al. (2017). Pregnancy leads to long-lasting changes in human brain structure. *Nature Neuroscience*, 20(2), 287–296.

Hoekzema, E., Tamnes, C., Berns, P., Barba-Müller,

E., Pozzobon, C., & Picado, M. et al. (2020). Becoming a mother entails anatomical changes in the ventral striatum of the human brain that facilitate its responsiveness to offspring cues. *Psychoneuroendocrinology, 112,* 104507.

A brain scan can show changes in grey matter but we cannot know for sure what grey matter reduction involves, as grey matter changes could be reflecting changes in the 'number of synapses, glial cells, dendritic structure, vasculature, blood volume and circulation' as Hoekzema et al (2017) report.

Davies, S., Lum, J., Skouteris, H., Byrne, L., & Hayden, M. (2018). Cognitive impairment during pregnancy: a meta-analysis. *Medical Journal of Australia, 208*(1), 35–40.

Macbeth, A., Gautreaux, C., & Luine, V. (2008). Pregnant rats show enhanced spatial memory, decreased anxiety, and altered levels of monoaminergic neurotransmitters. *Brain Research, 1241,* 136–147.

Crawley, R., Grant, S., & Hinshaw, K. (2008). Cognitive changes in pregnancy: mild decline or societal stereotype? *Applied Cognitive Psychology, 22*(8), 1142–1162.

Logan, D., Hill, K., Jones, R., Holt-Lunstad, J., & Larson, M. (2014). How do memory and attention change with pregnancy and childbirth? A controlled longitudinal examination of neuropsychological functioning in pregnant and postpartum women. *Journal of Clinical and Experimental Neuropsychology, 36*(5), 528–539.

de Lange, A., Kaufmann, T., van der Meer, D., Maglanoc, L., Alnæs, D., & Moberget, T. et al. (2019). Population-based neuroimaging reveals traces of childbirth in the maternal brain. *Proceedings of the National Academy of Sciences, 116*(44), 22341–22346.

Abraham, E., Hendler, T., Shapira-Lichter, I., Kanat-Maymon, Y., Zagoory-Sharon, O., & Feldman, R. (2014). Father's brain is sensitive to childcare experiences. *Proceedings of the National Academy of Sciences, 111*(27), 9792–9797.

Reynolds-Wright J. J., Anderson, R. A. (2019). Correction: Male contraception: where are we going and where have we been? (2020). *BMJ Sexual & Reproductive Health, 46*(2), 157.1–157.

Roberts, M. (2019). Male pill – why are we still waiting? Retrieved 2 January 2021, from https://www.bbc.co.uk/news/health-47691567

Petersen, N., Kilpatrick, L., Goharzad, A., & Cahill, L. (2014). Oral contraceptive pill use and menstrual cycle phase are associated with altered resting state functional connectivity. *Neuroimage, 90,* 24–32.

Skovlund, C., Mørch, L., Kessing, L., & Lidegaard, Ø. (2016). Association of Hormonal Contraception With Depression. *JAMA Psychiatry, 73*(11), 1154.

Anderl, C., Li, G., & Chen, F. (2019). Oral contraceptive use in adolescence predicts lasting vulnerability to depression in adulthood. *Journal of Child Psychology and Psychiatry, 61*(2), 148–156.

Nielsen, S., Ertman, N., Lakhani, Y., & Cahill, L. (2011). Hormonal contraception usage is associated with altered memory for an emotional story. *Neurobiology of Learning and Memory, 96*(2), 378–384.

Birnbaum, S., Birnbaum, G., & Ein-Dor, T. (2017). Can Contraceptive Pill Affect Future Offspring's Health? The Implications of Using Hormonal Birth Control for Human Evolution. *Evolutionary Psychological Science, 3*(2), 89–96.

Birnbaum, G., Zholtack, K., Mizrahi, M., & Ein-Dor, T. (2019). The Bitter Pill: Cessation of Oral Contraceptives

Enhances the Appeal of Alternative Mates. *Evolutionary Psychological Science, 5*(3), 276–285.

Cohain, J., Buxbaum, R., & Mankuta, D. (2017). Spontaneous first trimester miscarriage rates per woman among parous women with 1 or more pregnancies of 24 weeks or more. *BMC Pregnancy and Childbirth, 17*(1).

van den Bergh, B., van den Heuvel, M., Lahti, M., Braeken, M., de Rooij, S., & Entringer, S. et al. (2017). Prenatal developmental origins of behavior and mental health: The influence of maternal stress in pregnancy. *Neuroscience & Biobehavioral Reviews, 117,* 26–64.

Laplante, D., Brunet, A., & King, S. (2015). The effects of maternal stress and illness during pregnancy on infant temperament: Project Ice Storm. *Pediatric Research, 79*(1), 107–113.

Weinstock, M. (2008). The long-term behavioural consequences of prenatal stress. *Neuroscience & Biobehavioral Reviews, 32*(6), 1073–1086.

Brannigan, R., Tanskanen, A., Huttunen, M., Cannon, M., Leacy, F., & Clarke, M. (2019). The role of prenatal stress as a pathway to personality disorder: longitudinal birth cohort study. *British Journal of Psychiatry, 216*(2), 85–89.

Bailey, L. (2001). Gender shows – first-time mothers and embodied selves. *Gender & Society, 15*(1), 110–129.

Bainbridge, J. (2006). Unsolicited advice: A rite of passage through your first pregnancy. *British Journal of Midwifery, 14*(5), 265–265.

Cahusac, E., & Kanji, S. (2013). Giving Up: How Gendered Organizational Cultures Push Mothers Out. *Gender, Work & Organization, 21*(1), 57–70.

Pregnancy multivitamins 'are a waste of money'. (2016). Retrieved 2 January 2021, from https://www.bbc.co.uk/news/health-36765161

Hodgkinson, E., Smith, D., & Wittkowski, A. (2014). Women's experiences of their pregnancy and postpartum body image: a systematic review and meta-synthesis. *BMC Pregnancy and Childbirth*, 14(1).

Upton, R., & Han, S. (2003). Maternity and Its Discontents. *Journal of Contemporary Ethnography*, 32(6), 670–692.

Morley-Hewitt, A., & Owen, A. (2019). A systematic review examining the association between female body image and the intention, initiation and duration of post-partum infant feeding methods (breastfeeding vs bottle-feeding). *Journal of Health Psychology*, 25(2), 207–226.

Kirk, E., & Preston, C. (2019). Development and validation of the Body Understanding Measure for Pregnancy Scale (BUMPS) and its role in antenatal attachment. *Psychological Assessment*, 31(9), 1092–1106.

Sacks, A. (2017). The Birth of a Mother. Retrieved 2 January 2021, from https://www.nytimes.com/2017/05/08/well/family/the-birth-of-a-mother.html

CHAPTER 2

Dikmen-Yildiz, P., Ayers, S. & Phillips, L. (2018). Longitudinal trajectories of post-traumatic stress disorder (PTSD) after birth and associated risk factors. *Journal of Affective Disorders*, 229, 377–385.

Anokye, R., Acheampong, E., Budu-Ainooson, A., Obeng, E., & Akwasi, A. (2018). Prevalence of postpartum depression and interventions utilized for its management. *Annals of General Psychiatry*, 17(1).

Sriraman, N., Pham, D., & Kumar, R. (2017). Postpartum

Depression: What Do Pediatricians Need to Know? *Pediatrics in Review, 38*(12), 541–551.

Hahn-Holbrook, J., Cornwell-Hinrichs, T., & Anaya, I. (2018). Economic and Health Predictors of National Postpartum Depression Prevalence: A Systematic Review, Meta-analysis, and Meta-Regression of 291 Studies from 56 Countries. *Frontiers in Psychiatry, 8,* 248.

NIMH Perinatal Depression. Retrieved 2 January 2021, from https://www.nimh.nih.gov/health/publications/perinatal-depression/index.shtml

Qiu, A., Anh, T. T., Li, Y., Chen, H., Rifkin-Graboi, A., Broekman, B. F., Kwek, K., Saw, S. M., Chong, Y. S., Gluckman, P. D., Fortier, M. V., & Meaney, M. J. (2015). Prenatal maternal depression alters amygdala functional connectivity in 6-month-old infants. *Translational Psychiatry, 5*(2), e508.

Pawlby S., Hay D. F., Sharp, D., Waters C. S., O'Keane V. (2009) Antenatal depression predicts depression in adolescent offspring: prospective longitudinal community-based study. *Journal of Affective Disorders.* 113(3), 236–243.

Beck, C. (2004). Post-Traumatic Stress Disorder Due to Childbirth. *Nursing Research, 53*(4), 216–224.

Dekel, S., Stuebe, C., & Dishy, G. (2017). Childbirth Induced Posttraumatic Stress Syndrome: A Systematic Review of Prevalence and Risk Factors. *Frontiers in Psychology, 8,* 560.

Farren, J., Jalmbrant, M., Falconieri, N., Mitchell-Jones, N., Bobdiwala, S., Al-Memar, M., Tapp, S., Van Calster, B., Wynants, L., Timmerman, D., & Bourne, T. (2020). Posttraumatic stress, anxiety and depression following miscarriage and ectopic pregnancy: a multicenter, prospective, cohort study. *American Journal of Obstetrics and Gynecology, 222*(4), 367.e1–367.e22.

Moses-Kolko, E. L., Perlman, S. B., Wisner, K. L., James, J., Saul, A. T., & Phillips, M. L. (2010). Abnormally reduced dorsomedial prefrontal cortical activity and effective connectivity with amygdala in response to negative emotional faces in postpartum depression. *American Journal of Psychiatry, 167*(11), 1373–1380.

Esposito, G., Manian, N., Truzzi, A., & Bornstein, M. (2017). Response to Infant Cry in Clinically Depressed and Non-Depressed Mothers. *PLOS ONE, 12*(1), e0169066.

Laurent, H., & Ablow, J. (2011). A cry in the dark: depressed mothers show reduced neural activation to their own infant's cry. *Social Cognitive and Affective Neuroscience, 7*(2), 125–134.

Morgan, J. K., Guo, C., Moses-Kolko, E. L., Phillips, M. L., Stepp, S. D., & Hipwell, A. E. (2017). Postpartum depressive symptoms moderate the link between mothers' neural response to positive faces in reward and social regions and observed caregiving. *Social Cognitive and Affective Neuroscience, 12*(10), 1605–1613.

Barba-Müller, E., Craddock, S., Carmona, S., & Hoekzema, E. (2019). Brain plasticity in pregnancy and the postpartum period: links to maternal caregiving and mental health. *Archives of women's mental health, 22*(2), 2 89–299.

Barrett, J., & Fleming, A.S. (2011). Annual Research Review: All mothers are not created equal: neural and psychobiological perspectives on mothering and the importance of individual differences. *Journal of Child Psychology and Psychiatry, 52*, 368–397.

Fleming, A. S., Steiner, M., & Corter, C. (1997). Cortisol,

hedonics, and maternal responsiveness in human mothers. *Hormones and Behavior, 32*(2), 85–98.

Stallings, J., et al, (2001). The Effects of Infant Cries and Odors on Sympathy, Cortisol, and Autonomic Responses in New Mothers and Nonpostpartum Women. *Parenting, 1*(1–2), 71–100.

McKinnon, M.C., Palombo, D., Nazarov, A., Kumar, N., Khuu, W., & Levine, B. (2015). Threat of death and autobiographical memory: A study of the passengers of Flight AT236. *Clinical Psychological Science, 3*(4):487–502.

Lovett-Barron, M., Kaifosh, P., Kheirbek, M., Danielson, N., Zaremba, J., & Reardon, T. et al. (2014). Dendritic Inhibition in the Hippocampus Supports Fear Learning. *Science, 343*(6173), 857–863.

Redondo, R., Kim, J., Arons, A., Ramirez, S., Liu, X., & Tonegawa, S. (2014). Bidirectional switch of the valence associated with a hippocampal contextual memory engram. *Nature, 513* (7518), 426–430.

Ramirez, S., Liu, X., MacDonald, C., Moffa, A., Zhou, J., Redondo, R., & Tonegawa, S. (2015). Activating positive memory engrams suppresses depression-like behaviour. *Nature, 522*(7556), 335–339.

Ford, E., & Ayers, S. (2009). Stressful events and support during birth: The effect on anxiety, mood and perceived control. *Journal of Anxiety Disorders, 23*(2), 260–268.

Lothian, J. (2004). Do Not Disturb: The Importance of Privacy in Labor. *Journal of Perinatal Education, 13*(3), 4–6.

Zielinski, R., Ackerson, K., & Kane-Low, L. (2015). Planned home birth: benefits, risks, and opportunities. *International Journal of Women's Health*, 361.

Hannah, M. E., Hannah, W. J., Hewson, S. A., Hodnett, E. D., Saigal, S., & Willan, A. R. (2000). Planned caesarean section versus planned vaginal birth for breech presentation at term: a randomised multicentre trial. *The Lancet, 356*(9239), 1375–1383.

Berhan, Y., & Haileamlak, A. (2015). The risks of planned vaginal breech delivery versus planned caesarean section for term breech birth: a meta-analysis including observational studies. *BJOG: An International Journal of Obstetrics & Gynaecology, 123*(1), 49–57.

Hauck, Y., Fenwick, J., Downie, J., & Butt, J. (2007). The influence of childbirth expectations on Western Australian women's perceptions of their birth experience. *Midwifery, 23*(3), 235–247.

Macfarlane, A., Blondel, B., Mohangoo, A., Cuttini, M., Nijhuis, J., & Novak, Z. et al. (2015). Wide differences in mode of delivery within Europe: risk-stratified analyses of aggregated routine data from the Euro-Peristat study. *BJOG: An International Journal of Obstetrics & Gynaecology, 123*(4), 559–568.

Kjerulff, K., & Brubaker, L. (2017). New mothers' feelings of disappointment and failure after cesarean delivery. *Birth, 45*(1), 19–27.

CHAPTER 3

Breastfeeding guilt experienced by half of mothers – BBC survey. BBC News. (2019). Retrieved 13 January 2021, from https://www.bbc.co.uk/news/uk-england-south -yorkshire-46989489.

O'Connell, M. (2021). After giving birth to my first child, I wondered: would I ever want sex again? Retrieved 9

February 2021, from https://www.theguardian.com/lifeandstyle/2018/apr/12/sex-after-pregnancy-meaghan-oconnell-now-we-have-everything-extract

Bailey, L. (2001). Gender shows – first time mothers and embodied selves. *Gender & Society, 15*(1), 110–129.

Alder, E. (1989). Sexual behaviour in pregnancy, after childbirth and during breast-feeding. *Baillière's Clinical Obstetrics and Gynaecology, 3*(4), 805–821.

Hyde, J., DeLamater, J., Plant, E., & Byrd, J. (1996). Sexuality during pregnancy and the year postpartum. *Journal of Sex Research, 33*(2), 143–151.

Postpartum Sexual Dysfunction: A literature review of risk factors and role of mode of delivery. British Journal of Medical Practitioners. (2010). Retrieved 19 December 2020, from https://www.bjmp.org/content/postpartum-sexual-dysfunction-literature-review-risk-factors-and-role-mode-delivery

Walzer, S. (1996). *Thinking about the Baby*. Philadelphia: Temple University Press.

Nygaard, I. (2008). Prevalence of Symptomatic Pelvic Floor Disorders in US Women. *JAMA, 300*(11), 1311.

Mant, J., Painter, R., & Vessey, M. (1997). Epidemiology of genital prolapse: observations from the Oxford Family Planning Association study. *BJOG: An International Journal of Obstetrics and Gynaecology, 104*(5), 579–585.

Dheresa, M., Worku, A., Oljira, L., Mengiste, B., Assefa, N., & Berhane, Y. (2018). One in five women suffer from pelvic floor disorders in Kersa district Eastern Ethiopia: a community-based study. *BMC Women's Health, 18*(1).

Hodgkinson, E., Smith, D., & Wittkowski, A. (2014). Women's experiences of their pregnancy and postpartum body image: a systematic review and meta-synthesis. *BMC Pregnancy and Childbirth, 14*(1).

Bainbridge, J. (2006). Unsolicited advice: A rite of passage through your first pregnancy. *British Journal of Midwifery, 14*(5), 265.

O'Donohoe, S., & O'Donohoe, S. (2006). Yummy Mummies: The Clamor of Glamour in Advertising to Mothers. *Advertising & Society Review, 7*(3), 1–18.

Centers for Disease Control and Prevention. (2015). QuickStats: gestational weight gain among women with full-term, singleton births, compared with recommendations–48 states and the District of Columbia. *Morbidity and Mortality Weekly Report,* 65, 40, 1121.

Ip, S., Chung, M., Raman, G., Chew, P., Magula, N., DeVine, D., Trikalinos, T., & Lau, J. (2007). Breastfeeding and maternal and infant health outcomes in developed countries. *Evidence report/technology assessment,* (153), 1–186.

Bianchi, D., Zickwolf, G., Weil, G., Sylvester, S., & DeMaria, M. (1996). Male fetal progenitor cells persist in maternal blood for as long as 27 years postpartum. *Proceedings of the National Academy of Sciences, 93*(2), 705–708.

Gadi, V., & Nelson, J. (2007). Fetal Microchimerism in Women with Breast Cancer. *Cancer Research, 67*(19), 9035–9038.

Chan, W., Gurnot, C., Montine, T., Sonnen, J., Guthrie, K., & Nelson, J. (2012). Male Microchimerism in the Human Female Brain. *PLOS ONE, 7*(9), e45592.

Rijnink, E., Penning, M., Wolterbeek, R., Wilhelmus, S., Zandbergen, M., & van Duinen, S. et al. (2015). Tissue microchimerism is increased during pregnancy: a human autopsy study. *Molecular Human Reproduction, 21*(11), 857–864.

Broestl, L., Rubin, J. B., & Dahiya, S. (2018). Fetal microchimerism in human brain tumors. *Brain Pathology, 28*(4), 484–494.

Boddy, A. M., Fortunato, A., Wilson Sayres, M., & Aktipis, A. (2015). Fetal microchimerism and maternal health: a review and evolutionary analysis of cooperation and conflict beyond the womb. *BioEssays, 37*(10), 1106–1118.

CHAPTER 4

Peter Irons, 1998, *The Courage of Their Convictions: 16 Americans Who Fought Their Way to the Supreme Court*, New York: Penguin Books, pp. 307, 309–10.

Thomas, T. R. (2014). The Struggle for Gender Equality in the Northern District, in Justice on the Shores of Lake Erie: A History of the U.S. District Court for the Northern District of Ohio edited by Paul Finkelman and Roberta Sue Alexander. *Ohio History, 121*(1), 148–149.

Perales, M., Artal, R., & Lucia, A. (2017). Exercise During Pregnancy. *JAMA, 317*(11), 1113.

Wynn, M. (1999). Pregnancy Discrimination: Equality, Protection or Reconciliation? *Modern Law Review, 62*(3), 435–447.

Stories. Pregnant Then Screwed. (2021). Retrieved 15 January 2021, from https://pregnantthenscrewed.com/stories

Franceschi-Bicchierai, L., & Koebler, J. (2019). Google Employee Alleges Discrimination Against Pregnant Women in Viral Memo. Retrieved 22 December 2020, from https://www.vice.com/en/article/59nmkx/google-employee-alleges-discrimination-against-pregnant-women-in-viral-memo

Kitroeff, N., & Silver-Greenberg, J. (2019). Pregnancy Discrimination Is Rampant Inside America's Biggest Companies. Retrieved 22 December 2020, from https://www.nytimes.com/interactive/2018/06/15/business/pregnancy-discrimination.html

Hennekam, S. (2016). Identity transition during pregnancy: The importance of role models. *Human Relations, 69*(9), 1765–1790.

Gatrell, C. (2011). Policy and the Pregnant Body at Work: Strategies of Secrecy, Silence and Supra-performance. *Gender, Work & Organization, 18*(2), 158–181.

Kitzinger, S. (2005). *The Politics of Birth*. Edinburgh: Elsevier Butterworth Heinemann.

PL+US. (2021). Retrieved 9 February 2021, from https://paidleave.us

Unicef. (2019). Are the world's richest countries family friendly? Retrieved from https://www.unicef-irc.org/family-friendly

Collins, J., & Mayer, V. (2010). *Both Hands Tied*. Chicago, Illinois: University of Chicago Press.

Usborne, S. (2021). 'It was seen as weird': why are so few men taking shared parental leave? Retrieved 9 February 2021, from https://www.theguardian.com/lifeandstyle/2019/oct/05/shared-parental-leave-seen-as-weird-paternity-leave-in-decline

Kaufman, G. (2018). Barriers to equality: why British fathers do not use parental leave. *Community, Work & Family, 21*(3), 310– 325.

O'Brien, M., Aldrich, M., Connolly, S. et al. (2017), Inequalities in access to paid maternity and paternity leave and flexible work. London: UCL Grand Challenges Report.

America is the only rich country without a law on paid leave for new parents. (2020). Retrieved 21

December 2020, from https://www.economist.com/
united-states/2019/07/18/america-is-the-only-rich-
country-without-a-law-on-paid-leave-for-new-parents

'The greatest mother in the world' / A.E. Foringer. (1917).
Retrieved 30 January 2021, from https://www.loc.gov/
item/94513568/

Nepomnyaschy, L., & Waldfogel, J. (2007). Paternity leave
and fathers' involvement with their young children.
Community, Work & Family, 10(4), 427–453.

Farré, L., & González, L. (2019). Does paternity leave reduce
fertility? *Journal of Public Economics, 172,* 52–66.

Margolis, R., Choi, Y., Holm, A., & Mehta, N. (2020).
The Effect of Expanded Parental Benefits on Union
Dissolution. *Journal of Marriage and Family, 83*(1),
191–208.

Johansson, E. (2010). The effect of own and spousal
parental leave on earnings. Retrieved 16
January 2021, from https://www.econstor.eu/
bitstream/10419/45782/1/623752174.pdf

The Nordic Glass Ceiling, The Cato Institute, cato.org/
sites/cato.org/files/pubs/pdf/pa-835.pdf

World Values Survey, Wave 3 (1995–1999), World Value
Survey Association, http://www.worldvaluessurvey.
org/WVSDocumentationWV3.jsp; World Values
Survey, Wave 6 (2010–2014), World Value Survey
Association, http://www.worldvaluessurvey.org/
WVSDocumentationWV6.jsp

Morton, M., Klugman, J., Hanmer, L., & Singer, D.
(2014). Gender at Work: A Companion to the World
Development Report on Jobs. Retrieved 9 February
2021, from https://www.worldbank.org/en/topic/
gender/publication/gender-at-work-companion-repor
t-to-world-development-report-2013-jobs

Nakazato, H., Nishimura, J. and Takezawa, J. (2018). 'Japan country note', in Blum, S., Koslowski, A., Macht, A. and Moss, P. (eds) *International Review of Leave Policies and Research 2018*. Available at: http://www.leavenetwork. org/lp_and_r_reports/

McCurry, J. (2020). Culture shock: can trailblazing Japanese minister change minds on paternity leave? Retrieved 16 January 2021, from https://www.theguardian.com/ world/2020/jan/17/japanese-paternity-leave-shinjiro-koizumi.

Rich, M. (2019). Two Men in Japan Dared to Take Paternity Leave. It Cost Them Dearly, They Say. Retrieved 16 January 2021, from https:// www.nytimes.com/2019/09/12/world/asia/ japan-paternity-leave.html

Miyajima, T., & Yamaguchi, H. (2017). I Want to but I Won't: Pluralistic Ignorance Inhibits Intentions to Take Paternity Leave in Japan. *Frontiers in Psychology*, *8*.

Timsit, A. (2019). Japan is trying really hard to persuade women to start having babies again. Retrieved 16 January 2021, from https://qz.com/1646740/japan-wants-to-raise-its-fertility-rate-with-new-perks/

Budig, M. (2014). The Fatherhood Bonus and the Motherhood Penalty: Parenthood and the Gender Gap in Pay. Third Way. Retrieved from https://www. thirdway.org/report/the-fatherhood-bonus-and-the-motherhood-penalty-parenthood-and-the-gender-gap-in-pay

Budig, M. J., Misra, J., & Boeckmann, I. (2016). Work–Family Policy Trade-Offs for Mothers? Unpacking the Cross-National Variation in Motherhood Earnings Penalties. *Work and Occupations*, *43*(2), 119–177.

DeMeis, D. K., Hock, E. and McBride, S. L. (1986). The balance of employment and motherhood: Longitudinal study of mothers' feelings about separation from their first-born infants, *Developmental Psychology*, 22(5), 627–632.

Kleven, H., Landais, C., Posch, J., Steinhauer, A., & Zweimüller, J. (2019). Child Penalties across Countries: Evidence and Explanations. *AEA Papers and Proceedings*, *109*, 122–126.

Women in work: how East Germany's socialist past has influenced West German mothers. (2020). Retrieved 17 October 2020, from https://theconversation.com/women-in-work-how-east-germanys-socialist-past-has-influenced-west-german-mothers-147588

Hyde, J. S., Klein, M. H., Essex, M. J., & Clark, R. (1995). Maternity Leave and Women's Mental Health. *Psychology of Women Quarterly, 19*(2), 257–285.

Avendano, M., Berkman, L., Brugiavini, A., & Pasini, G. (2014). The Long-Run Effect of Maternity Leave Benefits on Mental Health: Evidence from European Countries. *SSRN Electronic Journal.*

Albiston, C., Tucker, T., Correll, S., & Stevens, C. (2012). Law, Norms, and the Motherhood/Caretaker Penalty. *SSRN Electronic Journal.*

Long, V. (2012): Statutory Parental Leave and Pay in the UK: Stereotypes and Discrimination, *Equal Rights Review 9.*

Gnewski, M. (2019). Sweden's parental leave may be generous, but it's tying women to the home. Retrieved 21 December 2020, from https://www.theguardian.com/commentisfree/2019/jul/10/sweden-parental-leave-corporate-pressure-men-work

Lindahl, B. (2018). Paternal leave extremely important

to reach gender equality Retrieved 21 December 2020, from http://www.nordiclabourjournal. org/i-fokus/in-focus-2018/nordic-working-life/ article.2018-06-14.5410895249

CHAPTER 5

Hall, P., & Wittkowski, A. (2006). An Exploration of Negative Thoughts as a Normal Phenomenon After Childbirth. *Journal of Midwifery & Women's Health*, 51(5), 321–330.

Nolan, M. L., Mason, V., Snow, S., Messenger, W., Catling, J., & Upton, P. (2012). Making friends at antenatal classes: a qualitative exploration of friendship across the transition to motherhood. *Journal of Perinatal Education*, 21(3), 178–185.

Harwood, K., McLean, N., & Durkin, K. (2007). First-time mothers' expectations of parenthood: What happens when optimistic expectations are not matched by later experiences? *Developmental Psychology*, 43(1), 1–12.

Millward, L. (2006). The transition to motherhood in an organizational context: An interpretative phenomenological analysis. *Journal of Occupational and Organizational Psychology*, 79(3), 315–333.

Ladge, J. J., Clair, J. A. and Greenberg, D. (2012). Cross-domain identity transition during liminal periods: Constructing multiple selves as professional and mother during pregnancy, *Academy of Management Journal*, 55(6), 1449–1471.

Lee, K., Vasileiou, K., & Barnett, J. (2017). 'Lonely within the mother': An exploratory study of first-time mothers' experiences of loneliness. *Journal of Health Psychology,* 24(10), 1334–1344.

Mac Carron, P., Kaski, K., & Dunbar, R. (2016). Calling Dunbar's numbers. *Social Networks, 47,* 151–155.

CHAPTER 6

Chesley, N. (2017). What Does It Mean to Be a "Breadwinner" Mother? *Journal of Family Issues, 38*(18), 2594–2619.

McKay, J. (2011). 'Having it All?' Women MPs and Motherhood in Germany and the UK. *Parliamentary Affairs, 64*(4), 714–736.

Horowitz, J. (2019). Despite challenges at home and work, most working moms and dads say being employed is what's best for them. Retrieved 21 December 2020, from https://www.pewresearch.org/fact-tank/2019/09/12/despite-challenges-at-home-and-work-most-working-moms-and-dads-say-being-employed-is-whats-best-for-them/

Hewlett, S. A., & Luce, C. B. (2005). Off-ramps and on-ramps: keeping talented women on the road to success. *Harvard Business Review, 83*(3).

Goldstein, K. (2018). 'I was a Sheryl Sandberg superfan. Then her "Lean In" advice failed me.' Retrieved 21 December 2020, from https://www.vox.com/first-person/2018/12/6/18128838/michelle-obama-lean-in-sheryl-sandberg

McKinsey & Company, LeanIn.org. Women in the Workplace 2020. Retrieved 21 December 2020, from https://www.mckinsey.com/featured-insights/diversity-and-inclusion/

women-in-the-workplacehttps://www.mckinsey.
com/featured-insights/diversity-and-inclusion/
women-in-the-workplace

Miller, D., Nolla, K., Eagly, A., & Uttal, D. (2018). The
Development of Children's Gender-Science Stereotypes:
A Meta-analysis of 5 Decades of U.S. Draw-A-Scientist
Studies. *Child Development, 89*(6), 1943–1955.

Jacobs, J. A., & Gerson, K. (2016). Unpacking Americans'
Views of the Employment of Mothers and Fathers
Using National Vignette Survey Data: SWS Presidential
Address. *Gender & Society, 30*(3), 413–441.

The Harried Life of the Working Mother. (2009). Retrieved
21 December 2020, from https://www.pewsocialtrends.
org/2009/10/01/the-harried-life-of-the-working-mother

Gardiner, S. (2019). I dismissed warnings about being
a working mother as antiquated. Then I became
one. Retrieved 17 January 2021, from https://www.
theguardian.com/commentisfree/2019/dec/19/
i-dismissed-warnings-about-being-a-
working-mother-as-antiquated-then-i-became-one

Glass, C., & Fodor, É. (2011). Public maternalism goes
to market: Recruitment, hiring, and promotion in
postsocialist Hungary, *Gender & Society, 25*(1), 5–26.

Pas, B., Peters, P., Eisinga, R., Doorewaard, H., &
Lagro-Janssen, T. (2011). Explaining career motivation
among female doctors in the Netherlands: the effects
of children, views on motherhood and work-home
cultures. *Work, Employment and Society, 25*(3), 487–505.

Kmec, J. A., Huffman, M. L., & Penner, A. M. (2014).
Being a Parent or Having a Parent? The Perceived
Employability of Men and Women Who Take
Employment Leave. *American Behavioral Scientist,
58*(3), 453–472.

Heilman, M. E., & Okimoto, T. G. (2008). Motherhood: A potential source of bias in employment decisions. *Journal of Applied Psychology, 93*(1), 189–198.

Okimoto, T. G., & Heilman, M. E. (2012). The 'badparent' assumption: How gender stereotypes affect reactions to working mothers. *Journal of Social Issues, 68*(4), 704–724.

Padgett, M., Harland, L., & Moser, S. B. (2009). The bad news and the good news: The long-term consequences of having used an alternative work schedule. *Journal of Leadership & Organizational Studies, 16*(1), 73–84.

King, E. (2008). The effect of bias on the advancement of working mothers: Disentangling legitimate concerns from inaccurate stereotypes as predictors of advancement in academe. *Human Relations, 61*(12), 1677–1711.

Liu, M. and Buzzanell, P. M. (2004), Negotiating maternity leave expectations. *Journal of Business Communication, 41*(4), 323–349.

Gatrell, C. (2007). A fractional commitment? Part-time work and the maternal body, *International Journal of Human Resource Management. 18*(3), 462–475.

Williams, J. C., Blair-Loy, M., & Berdahl, J. L. (2013). Cultural Schemas, Social Class, and the Flexibility Stigma. *Journal of Social Issues, 69*(2), 209–234.

Amis, J., Mair, J., & Munir, K. (2020). The Organizational Reproduction of Inequality. *Academy of Management Annals, 14*(1), 195–230.

Gatrell, C. J. (2007). Secrets and lies: Breastfeeding and professional paid work. *Social Science & Medicine, 65*(2), 393–404.

van Amsterdam, N. (2014). Othering the 'leaky body'. An autoethnographic story about expressing breast milk in the workplace. *Culture and Organization, 21*(3), 269–287.

Wakabayashi, D., & Frenkel, S. (2020). Parents Got More Time Off. Then the Backlash Started. Retrieved 17 January 2021, from https://www.nytimes.com/2020/09/05/technology/parents-time-off-backlash.html

Vinkenburg, C., van Engen, M., Coffeng, J., & Dikkers, J. (2012). Bias in Employment Decisions about Mothers and Fathers: The (Dis)Advantages of Sharing Care Responsibilities. *Journal of Social Issues*, 68(4), 725–741.

#EqualPayDay: Netherlands just slightly above European avg. for gender pay gap. (2020). Retrieved 9 December 2020, from https://nltimes.nl/2019/11/04/equalpayday-netherlands-just-slightly-european-avg-gender-pay-gap

Netherlands Policy Brief, Gender Equality (2020). Retrieved 9 December 2020, from https://www.oecd.org/policy-briefs/Netherlands-Gender-equality-EN.pdf

Bureau of Labor Statistic. (2019). American Time Use Survey. 2019 Results. Retrieved from https://www.bls.gov/news.release/pdf/atus.pdf

Catalyst. (2020). Women in the Workforce – United States: Quick Take. Retrieved 17 January 2021, from https://www.catalyst.org/research/women-in-the-workforce-united-states/

Baxter, J., Hewitt, B., & Haynes, M. (2008). Life Course Transitions and Housework: Marriage, Parenthood, and Time on Housework. *Journal of Marriage and Family*, 70(2), 259–272.

Who was the 'typical' Australian in 2016? (2016). Retrieved 17 January 2021, from https://www.abs.gov.au/websitedbs/D3310114.nsf/home/2016+Census+National

OECD. (2014). Unpaid Care Work: The missing link in the analysis of gender gaps in labour outcomes. Retrieved from https://www.oecd.org/dev/development-gender/Unpaid_care_work.pdf

Neumann, A. (2020). Why I don't have a child: I cherish my freedom. Retrieved 17 January 2021, from https://www.theguardian.com/lifeandstyle/2020/jul/08/childfree-why-i-dont-have-children-freedom

Kitroeff, N., & Rodkin, J. (2015). Bloomberg – Are you a robot? Retrieved 22 December 2020, from https://www.bloomberg.com/news/articles/2015-10-20/the-real-cost-of-an-mba-is-different-for-men-and-women

Parents at Work. (2019). National Working Families Report 2019. Retrieved from http://parentsandcarersatwork.com/wp-content/uploads/2019/10/NWFSurvey-Executive-Summary.pdf

Median usual weekly earnings ... (2020). Retrieved 17 January 2021, from https://www.bls.gov/news.release/wkyeng.t03.html

Gender pay gap in the UK: 2019 – Office for National Statistics. (2020). Retrieved 17 January 2021, from https://www.ons.gov.uk/employmentandlabourmarket/peopleinwork/earningsandworkinghours/bulletins/genderpaygapintheuk/2019

Kleven, H., Landais, C., & Søgaard, J. (2018). Children and Gender Inequality: Evidence from Denmark. *SSRN Electronic Journal*.

Correll, S., Benard, S., & Paik, I. (2007). Getting a Job: Is There a Motherhood Penalty? *American Journal of Sociology, 112*(5), 1297–1339.

Carnes, M., Bartels, C. M., Kaatz, A., & Kolehmainen, C. (2015). Why is John More Likely to Become Department Chair Than Jennifer? *Transactions of the American Clinical and Climatological Association, 126*, 197–214.

Collins, C., Landivar, L., Ruppanner, L., & Scarborough, W. (2020). COVID-19 and the Gender Gap in Work Hours. *Gender, Work & Organization*.

Bureau of Labor Statistics, U.S. Department of Labor, The Economics Daily, Access to paid and unpaid family leave in 2018. Retrieved March 28, 2020, from https://www.bls.gov/opub/ted/2019/access-to-paid-and-unpaid-family-leave-in-2018.html

Noya Rimalt, (2018) The Maternal Dilemma, Cornell Law Review, 103, 977.

McGinn, K. L., Ruiz Castro, M., & Lingo, E. L. (2019). Learning from Mum: Cross-National Evidence Linking Maternal Employment and Adult Children's Outcomes. *Work, Employment and Society, 33*(3), 374–400.

Fernandez, R., Fogli, A., & Olivetti, C. (2004). Mothers and Sons: Preference Formation and Female Labor Force Dynamics. *Quarterly Journal of Economics, 119*(4), 1249-1299.

Mind the 100 Year Gap. Global Gender Gap Report 2020. (2019). Retrieved 17 January 2021, from https://www.weforum.org/reports/gender-gap-2020-report-100-years-pay-equality

Stanton, J. (2020). How the Child Care Crisis Will Distort the Economy for a Generation. Retrieved 17 January 2021, from https://www.politico.com/news/magazine/2020/07/23/child-care-crisis-pandemic-economy-impact-women-380412

Collins, C. (2019). *Making Motherhood Work*, Princeton University Press, pp. 35–36.

Schank, H. (2016). What Happens to Women's Ambitions in the Years After College. Retrieved 17 January 2021, from https://www.theatlantic.com/business/archive/2016/12/ambition-interview/486479/

Weisshaar, K. (2018). From Opt Out to Blocked Out: The Challenges for Labor Market Re-entry after Family-Related Employment Lapses. *American Sociological Review, 83*(1), 34–60.

Weisshaar, K., & Cabello-Hutt, T. (2020). Labor Force Participation Over the Life Course: The Long-Term Effects of Employment Trajectories on Wages and the Gendered Payoff to Employment. *Demography, 57*(1), 33–60.

Robin J. Ely, Pamela Stone & Colleen Ammerman. (2014) Rethink What You 'Know' About High-Achieving Women, *Harvard Business Review, 100,* 103.

Women still missing from top ranks of law firms. (2020). Retrieved 28 September 2020, from https://www.ft.com/content/aa517372-14fa-11ea-8d73-6303645ac406

Müller, B. (2019). The Careless Society—Dependency and Care Work in Capitalist Societies. *Frontiers in Sociology, 3.*

Dotti Sani, G. (2020). Is it 'Good' to Have a Stay-at-Home Mom? Parental Childcare Time and Work–Family Arrangements in Italy, 1988–2014. *Social Politics: International Studies In Gender, State & Society.*

Livingston, G. (2018). About one-third of U.S. children are living with an unmarried parent. Retrieved 11 February 2021, from https://www.pewresearch.org/fact-tank/2018/04/27/about-one-third-of-u-s-children-are-living-with-an-unmarried-parent

CHAPTER 7

Menkedick, S. (2017). Why don't people take writing about motherhood seriously? Because women do it. Retrieved

11 February 2021, from https://www.latimes.com/opinion/op-ed/la-oe-menkedick-literary-value-of-motherhood-20170416-story.html

Wiseman, E. (2020). Will maternity leave make me invisible? Retrieved 17 January 2021, from https://www.theguardian.com/lifeandstyle/2020/mar/22/will-my-second-maternity-leave-make-me-invisible-eva-wiseman

McKinney, C., & Renk, K. (2008). Differential parenting between mothers and fathers: Implications for late adolescents. *Journal of Family Issues, 29,* 806–827.

van Holland de Graaf, J., Hoogenboom, M., De Roos, S., & Bucx, F. (2018). Socio-demographic Correlates of Fathers' and Mothers' Parenting Behaviors. *Journal of Child and Family Studies, 27*(7), 2315–2327.

Lam, C. B., McHale, S. M., & Crouter, A. C. (2013). Parent-child shared time from middle childhood to late adolescence: Developmental course and adjustment outcomes. *Child Development, 83,* 2089–2103.

Endendijk, J., Derks, B., & Mesman, J. (2017). Does Parenthood Change Implicit Gender-Role Stereotypes and Behaviors? *Journal of Marriage and Family, 80*(1), 61–79.

van der Pol, L.D., Groeneveld, M.G., Van Berkel, S.R., Endendijk, J.J., Hallers-Haalboom, E.T., Bakermans-Kranenburg, M.J., & Mesman, J. (2015). Fathers' and mothers' emotion talk with their girls and boys from toddlerhood to preschool age, *Emotion 15*(6), 854–864.

Mondschein, E., Adolph, K., & Tamis-LeMonda, C. (2000). Gender Bias in Mothers' Expectations about Infant Crawling. *Journal of Experimental Child Psychology, 77*(4), 304–316.

Fagot, B.I., Hagan, R. (1985). Aggression in toddlers: Responses to the assertive acts of boys and girls. *Sex Roles 12*, 341–351.

Zosuls, K., Ruble, D., Tamis-LeMonda, C., Shrout, P., Bornstein, M., & Greulich, F. (2009). The acquisition of gender labels in infancy: Implications for gender-typed play. *Developmental Psychology*, *45*(3), 688–701.

Brescoll, V., & Uhlmann, E. (2008). Can an Angry Woman Get Ahead? *Psychological Science*, *19*(3), 268–275.

Mesman, J., & Groeneveld, M. (2017). Gendered Parenting in Early Childhood: Subtle But Unmistakable if You Know Where to Look. *Child Development Perspectives*, *12*(1), 22–27.

Acosta, R.M., & Hutchison, M. (2017). *The Happiest Kids in the World*, Doubleday, p. 197.

Noya, R. (2018). The Maternal Dilemma, *Cornell Law Review*, *103*, 977.

Hideg, I., & Ferris, D. L. (2016). The compassionate sexist? How benevolent sexism promotes and undermines gender equality in the workplace. *Journal of Personality and Social Psychology*, *111*(5), 706–727.

Mom shaming or constructive criticism? Perspectives of mothers. (2020). Retrieved 7 October 2020, from https://mottpoll.org/reports-surveys/mom-shaming-or-constructive-criticism-perspectives-mothers

Francis-Devine, B., & Foley, N. (2020). Women and the economy. Retrieved 18 January 2021, from https://commonslibrary.parliament.uk/research-briefings/sn06838/

Percentage of employed women working full time little changed over past 5 decades. (2017). Retrieved 18 January 2021, from https://www.bls.gov/opub/

ted/2017/percentage-of-employed-women-working-
full-time-little-changed-past-5-decades.html

Dotti Sani, G., & Treas, J. (2016). Educational Gradients
in Parents' Child-Care Time Across Countries, 1965–
2012. *Journal of Marriage and Family, 78*(4), 1083–1096.

Kentish, B. (2017). Jacob Rees-Mogg, father of six, declares
he has never changed a nappy. Retrieved 18 January
2021, from https://www.independent.co.uk/news/uk/
politics/jacob-rees-mogg-never-changed-a-nappy-lbc-
nigel-farage-nanny-conservatives-a7854791.html

Moore, S. (2021). If Russell Brand wants to change the
world, he could try changing a nappy. Retrieved 18
January 2021, from https://www.theguardian.com/
commentisfree/2019/jan/21/russell-brand-change-
the-world-try-changing-nappies

Daminger, A. (2019). The Cognitive Dimension of
Household Labor. *American Sociological Review,
84*(4), 609–633.

Walzer, S. (1996). *Thinking About the Baby*. Philadelphia:
Temple University Press, p. 122.

Ehrensaft, D. (1987). *Parenting Together. Men & Women
Sharing the Care of Their Children*. New York:
Free Press.

Schoppe-Sullivan, S. J., Altenburger, L. E., Lee, M. A.,
Bower, D. J., & Kamp Dush, C. M. (2015). Who are the
Gatekeepers? Predictors of Maternal Gatekeeping.
Parenting, Science and Practice, 15(3),
166–186.

Allen, S., & Hawkins, A. (1999). Maternal Gatekeeping:
Mothers' Beliefs and Behaviors That Inhibit Greater
Father Involvement in Family Work. *Journal of
Marriage and the Family, 61*(1), 199.

Carlson, D., Hanson, S., & Fitzroy, A. (2016). The Division

of Child Care, Sexual Intimacy, and Relationship Quality in Couples. *Gender & Society*, *30*(3), 442–466.

Berridge, C. W., & Romich, J. L. (2011). 'Raising Him … to Pull His Own Weight': Boys' Household Work in Single-Mother Households. *Journal of Family issues*, *32*(2), 157–180.

Letherby, G. (1999). Other than mother and mothers as others. *Women's Studies International Forum*, *22*(3), 359–372.

Chesley, N., & Flood, S. (2017). Signs of Change? At-Home and Breadwinner Parents' Housework and Child-Care Time. *Journal of Marriage and Family*, *79*, 511–534

Chesley, N. (2011). Stay-at-home fathers and breadwinning mothers: Gender, Couple Dynamics, and Social Change. *Gender and Society*, *25*(5), 642–664.

CHAPTER 8

Hubert, S., & Aujoulat, I. (2018). Parental Burnout: When Exhausted Mothers Open Up. *Frontiers in Psychology*, *9*, 1021.

Tubb, A. (2019). Maternal suicide still a leading cause of death in first postnatal year | Maternal Mental Health Alliance. Retrieved 3 January 2021, from https://maternalmentalhealthalliance.org/news/maternal-suicide-still-the-leading-cause-of-death-in-first-postnatal-year/

Brianda, M., Roskam, I., & Mikolajczak, M. (2020). Hair cortisol concentration as a biomarker of parental burnout. *Psychoneuroendocrinology*, *117*, 104681.

IPPB Consortium. (2020). Parental burnout around the globe: A 42-country study.

Mikolajczak, M., Raes, M., Avalosse, H., & Roskam, I. (2017). Exhausted Parents: Sociodemographic, Child-Related, Parent-Related, Parenting and Family-Functioning Correlates of Parental Burnout. *Journal of Child and Family Studies, 27*(2), 602–614.

Damaske, S., Smyth, J. M., & Zawadzki, M, J. (2014). Has Work Replaced Home as a Haven? Examining Arlie Hochschild's Time Bind Proposition. *Social Science and Medicine 115*, 130–138.

Oster, E. (2019). *Cribsheet*. New York: Penguin Press.

Milkie, M., Nomaguchi, K., & Denny, K. (2015). Does the Amount of Time Mothers Spend With Children or Adolescents Matter? *Journal of Marriage and Family, 77*(2), 355–372.

Lucas-Thompson, R., Goldberg, W., & Prause, J. (2010). Maternal work early in the lives of children and its distal associations with achievement and behavior problems: A meta-analysis. *Psychological Bulletin, 136*(6), 915–942.

Vandell, D. L., Belsky, J., Burchinal, M., Steinberg, L., & Vandergrift, N. (2010). Do Effects of Early Child Care Extend to Age 15 Years? Results From the NICHD Study of Early Child Care and Youth Development. *Child Development, 81*(3), 737–756.

Milkie, M., Wray, D., & Boeckmann, I. (2020). Creating Versus Negating Togetherness: Perceptual and Emotional Differences in Parent-Teenager Reported Time.

Rizzo, K., Schiffrin, H., & Liss, M. (2012). Insight into the Parenthood Paradox: Mental Health Outcomes of Intensive Mothering. *Journal of Child and Family Studies, 22*(5), 614–620.

National Academies Press. (2009). *Depression in Parents, Parenting, and Children*. Washington, DC.

Dotti Sani, G., & Treas, J. (2016). Educational Gradients in Parents' Child-Care Time Across Countries, 1965–2012. *Journal of Marriage and Family*, 78(4), 1083–1096.

Mathy, E. (2019) Prévalence 'vie entière' du burnout parental via une étude rétrospective et quantitative sur des personnes âgées entre 60 et 100 ans [Lifetime prevalence of parental burnout via a retrospective and quantitative study of people aged between 60 and 100 years old]. Unpublished master's thesis. UCLouvain, Belgium

World Happiness Report 2020. (2020). Retrieved 11 February 2021, from https://worldhappiness.report/

CHAPTER 9

Perry, P. (2019). *The Book You Wish Your Parents Had Read*, London: Penguin.

Collins, C. (2020). Is Maternal Guilt a Cross-National Experience? *Qualitative Sociology*, (44)2

Doyle, G. (2020). *Untamed*. London: Vermilion.

Borelli, J., Katherine, N.C., & Laura, R., et al. (2017). Bringing Work Home: Gender and Parenting Correlates of Work-Family Guilt among Parents of Toddlers. *Journal of Child and Family Studies* 26(6):1734–45.

Henderson, A., Harmon, S., & Newman, H. (2015). The Price Mothers Pay, Even When They Are Not Buying It: Mental Health Consequences of Idealized Motherhood. *Sex Roles*, 74(11–12), 512526.

CHAPTER 10

Stevens, G., van Dorsselaer, S., Boer, M., de Roos, S., Duinhof, E., & ter Bogt, T. et al. (2017). *Gezondheid en welzijn van jongeren in Nederland*. HBSC. Retrieved from https://hbsc-nederland.nl/wp-content/uploads/2018/09/Rapport-HBSC-2017.pdf

Sung, J., Beijers, R., Gartstein, M., de Weerth, C., & Putnam, S. (2014). Exploring temperamental differences in infants from the USA and the Netherlands. *European Journal of Developmental Psychology*, 12(1), 15–28.

Harkness, S., Super, C. M., Rios Bermudez, M., Moscardino, U., Blom, M. J. M., Rha, J.- H., Mavridis, C. J., Bonichini, S., Huitrón, B., Welles-Nyström, B., Palacios, J., Hyun, O.-K., Soriano, G., Zylicz, P. O. (2010). Parental Ethnotheories of Children's Learning. In D. F. Lancy, J. Bock, and S. Gaskins (eds), *The Anthropology of Learning in Childhood* (pp. 65–81). Lanham, Maryland: Alta-Mira Press.

Walch, O., Cochran, A., & Forger, D. (2016). A global quantification of 'normal' sleep schedules using smartphone data. *Science Advances*, 2(5), e1501705.

Harkness, S., Zylicz, P. O., Super, C. M., Welles-Nyström, B., Bermúdez, M. R., Bonichini, S., Moscardino, U., & Mavridis, C. J. (2011). Children's activities and their meanings for parents: A mixed-methods study in six Western cultures. *Journal of Family Psychology*, 25(6), 799–813.

Hays, S. (1996). *The Cultural Contradictions of Motherhood*. New Haven, CT, Yale University Press.

Yogman, M., Garner, A., Hutchinson, J., Hirsh-Pasek, K., & Golinkoff, R. (2018). The Power of Play: A Pediatric

Role in Enhancing Development in Young Children. *Pediatrics, 142*(3), e20182058.

Interview with Harkness – unpublished research.

Lancy, D. (2012). *The Anthropology of Learning in Childhood*. Walnut Creek, USA: AltaMira Press.

Brulé, G., & Veenhoven, R. (2014). Participatory Teaching and Happiness in Developed Nations. *Advances in Applied Sociology, 04*(11), 235–245.

Margolis, R., & Myrskylä, M. (2011). A Global Perspective on Happiness and Fertility. *Population and Development Review, 37*(1), 29–56.

Margolis, R., & Myrskylä, M. (2015). Parental Well-being Surrounding First Birth as a Determinant of Further Parity Progression. *Demography, 52*(4), 1147–1166.

Mitnick, D., Heyman, R., & Smith Slep, A. (2009). Changes in relationship satisfaction across the transition to parenthood: A meta-analysis. *Journal of Family Psychology, 23*(6), 848–852.

Glass, J., Simon, R., & Andersson, M. (2016). Parenthood and Happiness: Effects of Work-Family Reconciliation Policies in 22 OECD Countries. *American Journal of Sociology, 122*(3), 886–929.

Twenge, J., Campbell, W., & Foster, C. (2003). Parenthood and Marital Satisfaction: A Meta-Analytic Review. *Journal of Marriage and Family, 65*(3), 574–583.

Zelizer, V. (1994). *Pricing the Priceless Child*. Princeton: Princeton University Press.

Have children? Here's how kids ruin your romantic relationship. (2020). Retrieved 14 December 2020, from https://theconversation.com/have-children-heres-how-kids-ruin-your-romantic-relationship-57944

Volling, B., Oh, W., Gonzalez, R., Kuo, P., & Yu, T. (2015).

Patterns of marital relationship change across the transition from one child to two. *Couple and Family Psychology: Research and Practice*, 4(3), 177–197.

Wolfinger, N. (2018). Does Having Children Make People Happier in the Long Run? Retrieved 11 February 2021, from https://ifstudies.org/blog/does-having-children-make-people-happier-in-the-long-run

Becker, C., Kirchmaier, I., & Trautmann, S. (2019). Marriage, parenthood and social network: Subjective well-being and mental health in old age. *PLOS ONE*, 14(7), e0218704.

Audette, A., Lam, S., O'Connor, H., & Radcliff, B. (2018). (E)Quality of Life: A Cross-National Analysis of the Effect of Gender Equality on Life Satisfaction. *Journal of Happiness Studies*, 20(7), 2173–2188.

Young, K., Parsons, C., Jegindoe Elmholdt, E., Woolrich, M., van Hartevelt, T., & Stevner, A. et al. (2015). Evidence for a Caregiving Instinct: Rapid Differentiation of Infant from Adult Vocalizations Using Magnetoencephalography. *Cerebral Cortex*, 26(3), 1309–1321.

Jeffries, S., & Konnert, C. (2002). Regret and Psychological Well-Being among Voluntarily and Involuntarily Childless Women and Mothers. *International Journal of Aging and Human Development*, 54(2), 89–106.

Koert, E., & Daniluk, J. (2017). When time runs out: reconciling permanent childlessness after delayed childbearing. *Journal of Reproductive and Infant Psychology*, 35(4), 342–352.

CHAPTER 11

Garg, Z., Gomez, E., & Yael Petrzela, L. (2019). If You Didn't 'Sharent,' Did You Even Parent?. Retrieved 11 February 2021, from https://www.nytimes.com/2019/08/07/opinion/parents-social-media.html

Hughes, B. (2015). Would you be beautiful in the ancient world? Retrieved 28 January 2021, from https://www.bbc.co.uk/news/magazine-30746985

Liu, H.. (2018). The Behavioral Economics of Multilevel Marketing, *Hastings Business Law Journal*. 14, 109

Tiffany Lamoreaux. (2013). Home is where the Work is: Women, Direct Sales, and Technologies of Gender (unpublished PhD dissertation, Arizona State University).

Schoppe-Sullivan, S. J., Yavorsky, J. E., Bartholomew, M. K., Sullivan, J. M., Lee, M. A., Kamp Dush, C. M., & Glassman, M. (2017). Doing Gender Online: New Mothers' Psychological Characteristics, Facebook Use, and Depressive Symptoms. *Sex Roles*, 76(5), 276–289.

West, C., & Zimmerman, D. H. (1987). Doing gender. *Gender and Society*, 1(2), 125–15.

Lin, L. Y., Sidani, J. E., Shensa, A., Radovic, A., Miller, E., Colditz, J. B., Hoffman, B. L., Giles, L. M., & Primack, B. A. (2016). Association between Social Media Use and Depression among U.S. Young Adults. *Depression and Anxiety*, 33(4), 323–331.

Primack, B., Shensa, A., Sidani, J., Whaite, E., Lin, L., & Rosen, D. et al. (2017). Social Media Use and Perceived Social Isolation Among Young Adults in the U.S. *American Journal of Preventive Medicine*, 53(1), 1–8.

Patel, S., Subbiah, S., Jones, R., Muigai, F., Rothschild, C., & Omwodo, L. et al. (2018). Providing support to pregnant women and new mothers through moderated WhatsApp groups: a feasibility study. *Mhealth*, 4, 14–14.

McDaniel, B., Coyne, S., & Holmes, E. (2011). New Mothers and Media Use: Associations Between Blogging, Social Networking, and Maternal Well-Being. *Maternal and Child Health Journal*, 16(7), 1509–1517.

van de Ven, N., & Zeelenberg, M., & Pieters, R. (2009). Leveling Up and Down: The Experiences of Benign and Malicious Envy. *Emotion*, 9, 419–29.

Hirsh-Pasek, K., Alper, R., & Golinkoff, R. (2018). Living in Pasteur's Quadrant: How Conversational Duets Spark Language at Home and in the Community. *Discourse Processes*, 55(4), 338–345.

Piazza, E. A., Hasenfratz, L., Hasson, U., & Lew-Williams, C. (2020). Infant and Adult Brains Are Coupled to the Dynamics of Natural Communication. *Psychological Science*, 31(1), 6–17.

Tronick, E., Als, H., Adamson, L., Wise, S., & Brazelton, T. (1978). The Infant's Response to Entrapment between Contradictory Messages in Face-to-Face Interaction. *Journal of the American Academy of Child Psychiatry*, 17(1), 1–13.

Bigelow, A. E., & Power, M. (2014). Effects of maternal responsiveness on infant responsiveness and behavior in the Still-Face Task. *Infancy*, 19, 558–584.

Reed, J., Hirsh-Pasek, K., & Golinkoff, R. M. (2017). Learning on hold: Cell phones sidetrack parent-child interactions. *Developmental Psychology*, 53(8), 1428–1436.

Roseberry, S., Hirsh-Pasek, K., & Golinkoff, R. M. (2014). Skype me! Socially contingent interactions help toddlers learn language. *Child Development*, 85, 956–970.

Roseberry, S., Hirsh-Pasek, K., Parish-Morris, J., &

Golinkoff, R. (2009). Live Action: Can Young Children Learn Verbs From Video? *Child Development, 80*(5), 1360–1375.

Wooldridge, M., & Shapka, J. (2012). Playing with technology: Mother–toddler interaction scores lower during play with electronic toys. *Journal of Applied Developmental Psychology, 33*(5), 211–218.

McDaniel, B. T., & Coyne, S. M. (2016). 'Technoference': The interference of technology in couple relationships and implications for women's personal and relational well-being. *Psychology of Popular Media Culture, 5*(1), 85–98.

CHAPTER 12

Radesky, J. S., Kistin, C. J., Zuckerman, B., Nitzberg, K., Gross, J., Kaplan-Sanoff, M., Silverstein, M. (2014). Patterns of mobile device use by caregivers and children during meals in fast food restaurants. *Pediatrics, 133*, e843–e849.

Sadler, W., & Sadler, L. (1906). The Project Gutenberg eBook of the Mother and her Child. Retrieved 25 January 2021, from http://www.gutenberg.org/files/20817/20817-h/20817-h.htm

Jefferis, B., & Nichols, J. (1920). Searchlights on Health, the Science of Eugenics. Retrieved 25 January 2021, from http://www.gutenberg.org/files/13444/13444-h/13444-h.htm#

Watson, J., & Watson, R. (1928). *Psychological Care of Infant and Child*. London: G. Allen & Unwin.

Raphael-Leff, J. (1986), Facilitators and Regulators: Conscious and unconscious processes in pregnancy and early motherhood. *British Journal of Medical Psychology, 59*, 43–55.

Sears, William, & Sears, Martha (1993). *The Baby Book: Everything You Need To Know About Your Baby From Birth To Age Two*, Boston: Little, Brown.

Ainsworth, Mary (1967). *Infancy in Uganda: Infant Care and the Growth of Love.* Johns Hopkins Press.

Karasik, L., Tamis-LeMonda, C., Ossmy, O., & Adolph, K. (2018). The ties that bind: Cradling in Tajikistan. *PLOS ONE, 13*(10), e0204428.

Cristia, A., Dupoux, E., Gurven, M., & Stieglitz, J. (2017). Child-Directed Speech Is Infrequent in a Forager-Farmer Population: A Time Allocation Study. *Child Development, 90*(3), 759–773.

LeVine, R., & LeVine, S. (2016) Do Parents Matter?: Why Japanese Babies Sleep Soundly, Mexican Siblings Don't Fight, and American Families Should Just Relax. New York: *PublicAffairs.*

Mindell, J. A., Kuhn, B., Lewin, D. S., Meltzer, L. J., Sadeh, A., & American Academy of Sleep Medicine (2006). Behavioral treatment of bedtime problems and night wakings in infants and young children. *Sleep, 29*(10), 1263–1276.

Price, A. M., Wake, M., Ukoumunne, O. C., & Hiscock, H. (2012). Five-year follow-up of harms and benefits of behavioral infant sleep intervention: randomized trial. *Pediatrics, 130*(4), 643–651.

Keller, H. (2017). Cultural and historical diversity in early relationship formation. *European Journal of Developmental Psychology, 14*(6), 700–713.

Meehan, C. L., & Hawks, S. (2013). Cooperative breeding and attachment among the Aka foragers. In N. Quinn & J. Mageo (eds), *Attachment Reconsidered: Cultural*

Perspectives on a Western Theory (pp. 85–113). New York: Palgrave.

Gervai, J. (2009). Environmental and genetic influences on early attachment. *Child and Adolescent Psychiatry and Mental Health*, 3(1).

Crowell, J., Treboux, D., & Brockmeyer, S. (2009). Parental divorce and adult children's attachment representations and marital status. *Attachment & Human Development*, 11(1), 87–101.

Ainsworth, Mary (1967). *Infancy in Uganda: Infant Care and the Growth of Love*. Johns Hopkins Press.

NICHD. (1997), The Effects of Infant Child Care on Infant-Mother Attachment Security: Results of the NICHD Study of Early Child Care NICHD Early Child Care Research Network. *Child Development*, 68, 860–879.

Iacovou, M. , & Sevilla, A. (2013). Infant feeding: The effects of scheduled vs on-demand feeding on mothers' wellbeing and children's cognitive development. *European Journal of Public Health*, 23(1), 13–19.

Harries, V., & Brown, A. (2017). The association between use of infant parenting books that promote strict routines, and maternal depression, self-efficacy, and parenting confidence. *Early Child Development and Care*, 189(8), 1339–1350.

Raboteg-Saric, Z., & Sakic, M. (2013). Relations of Parenting Styles and Friendship Quality to Self-Esteem, Life Satisfaction and Happiness in Adolescents. *Applied Research in Quality of Life*, 9(3), 749–765.

Milevsky, A., Schlechter, M., Netter, S., & Keehn, D. (2007). Maternal and paternal parenting styles in adolescents: Associations with self-esteem, depression and life satisfaction. *Journal of Child and Family Studies*, 16(1), 39–47.

LeMoyne, T., & Buchanan, T. (2011). Does 'hovering' matter? Helicopter parenting and its effect on well-being. *Sociological Spectrum, 31*(4), 399–418.

Luebbe, A. M., Mancini, K. J., Kiel, E. J., Spangler, B. R., Semlak, J. L., & Fussner, L. M. (2018). Dimensionality of Helicopter Parenting and Relations to Emotional, Decision-Making, and Academic Functioning in Emerging Adults. *Assessment, 25*(7), 841–857.

Liu, Z., Riggio, R. E., Day, D. V., Zheng, C., Dai, S., & Bian, Y. (2019). Leader development begins at home: Overparenting harms adolescent leader emergence. *Journal of Applied Psychology, 104*(10), 1226–1242.

Nomaguchi, K., & Milkie, M. (2020). Parenthood and Well-Being: A Decade in Review. *Journal of Marriage and Family, 82*(1), 198–223.

Rifkin-Graboi, A., Kong, L., Sim, L., Sanmugam, S., Broekman, B., & Chen, H. et al. (2015). Maternal sensitivity, infant limbic structure volume and functional connectivity: a preliminary study. *Translational Psychiatry, 5*(10), e668–e668.

Rifkin-Graboi, A., Khng, K., Cheung, P., Tsotsi, S., Sun, H., & Kwok, F. et al. (2019). Will the future BE POSITIVE? Early life experience as a signal to the developing brain pre school entry. *Learning: Research and Practice, 5*(2), 99–125.

Tsotsi, S., Borelli, J., Abdulla, N., Tan, H., Sim, L., & Sanmugam, S. et al. (2018). Maternal sensitivity during infancy and the regulation of startle in preschoolers. *Attachment & Human Development, 22*(2), 207–224.

Zeegers, M., Colonnesi, C., Stams, G., & Meins, E. (2017). Mind matters: A meta-analysis on parental mentalization and sensitivity as predictors of infant–parent attachment. *Psychological Bulletin*, *143*(12), 1245–1272.

Metz, A., Imwalle, M., Dauch, C., & Wheeler, B. (2017). The Influence of the Number of Toys in the Environment on Play in Toddlers. *American Journal of Occupational Therapy*, *71*(4_Supplement_1), 7111505079p1.

Briggs, J. (1978). *Never in Anger*. Cambridge: Harvard University Press, pp. 128–129.

Alcalá, L., Rogoff, B., Mejía-Arauz, R., Coppens, A., & Dexter, A. (2014). Children's Initiative in Contributions to Family Work in Indigenous-Heritage and Cosmopolitan Communities in Mexico. *Human Development*, *57*(2–3), 96–115.

Lancy, D. (2017). *Raising Children: Surprising Insights From Other Cultures*. Cambridge University Press.

Suggate, S. P., Schaughency, E. A., & Reese, E. (2013). Children learning to read later catch up to children reading earlier. *Early Childhood Research Quarterly*, *28*, 33–48.

Yogman, M., Garner, A., Hutchinson, J., Hirsh-Pasek, K., & Golinkoff, R. (2018). The Power of Play: A Pediatric Role in Enhancing Development in Young Children. *Pediatrics*, *142*(3), e20182058.

Warneken, F., & Tomasello, M. (2008). Extrinsic rewards undermine altruistic tendencies in 20-month-olds. *Developmental Psychology*, *44*(6), 1785–1788.

Coppens, A, D. (2015). Parental Guidance and Children's Development of Collaborative Initiative: Cultural Contexts of Children's Prosocial Development. *(Peer reviewed thesis)*.

Wolfenstein, M. (1951). The Emergence of Fun Morality. *Journal of Social Issues*, *7*(4), 15–25.

Bitsko, R., Holbrook, J., Ghandour, R., Blumberg, S.,

Visser, S., Perou, R., & Walkup, J. (2018). Epidemiology and Impact of Health Care Provider–Diagnosed Anxiety and Depression Among US Children. *Journal of Developmental & Behavioral Pediatrics, 39*(5), 395–403.

Hewlett, B. (1994). *Intimate Fathers*. Ann Arbor, Mich.: University of Michigan Press.

Hewlett, B. (2008). Fathers and infants among Aka pygmies. In: LeVine, R., & New, R. (2008). *Anthropology and Child Development*. Malden, MA: Blackwell Pub.